OXFORD WORLD'S CLASSICS

THE EPIC OF CHRIST

MARCO GIROLAMO VIDA was one of the foremost poets of the sixteenth century. Born in Cremona in northern Italy in the 1480s, he spent much of his early career at the papal court in Rome under the patronage of the Medici popes Leo X and Clement VII, before being appointed bishop of Alba in 1533. Vida is most celebrated for his six-book Latin epic on the life of Christ (the *Christias*, or *Epic of Christ*, first published in 1535) and his influential verse treatise on the art of poetry (*De arte poetica*), but also achieved success with poems on the game of chess (*De ludo scaccorum*) and the cultivation of the silkworm (*De bombyce*, dedicated to the Renaissance patron of the arts Isabella d'Este). He was also the author of a number of substantial prose works. Vida's epic represents the pinnacle of a long and varied tradition of neo-Latin epic poetry on biblical subjects, which includes well-known works such as Jacopo Sannazaro's *De partu Virginis* (1526) as well as countless less familiar items. His work achieved enormous popularity among his contemporaries and in subsequent generations, and inspired many later writers, including Torquato Tasso, John Milton, and Abraham Cowley. Vida died at Alba in the territory of the Duchy of Mantua in 1566.

L. B. T. HOUGHTON is Lecturer in Latin at the University of Edinburgh. His publications include *Virgil's Fourth Eclogue in the Italian Renaissance* (2019), *Virgil and Renaissance Culture* (edited with Marco Sgarbi, 2018), *Neo-Latin Poetry in the British Isles* (edited with Gesine Manuwald, 2012), and *Perceptions of Horace* (edited with Maria Wyke, 2009).

OXFORD WORLD'S CLASSICS

For over 100 years Oxford World's Classics have brought readers closer to the world's great literature. Now with over 700 titles—from the 4,000-year-old myths of Mesopotamia to the twentieth century's greatest novels—the series makes available lesser-known as well as celebrated writing.

The pocket-sized hardbacks of the early years contained introductions by Virginia Woolf, T. S. Eliot, Graham Greene, and other literary figures which enriched the experience of reading. Today the series is recognized for its fine scholarship and reliability in texts that span world literature, drama and poetry, religion, philosophy, and politics. Each edition includes perceptive commentary and essential background information to meet the changing needs of readers.

OXFORD WORLD'S CLASSICS

MARCO GIROLAMO VIDA

The Epic of Christ

Translated with an Introduction and Notes by

L. B. T. HOUGHTON

OXFORD
UNIVERSITY PRESS

OXFORD
UNIVERSITY PRESS

Great Clarendon Street, Oxford, OX2 6DP,
United Kingdom

Oxford University Press is a department of the University of Oxford.
It furthers the University's objective of excellence in research, scholarship,
and education by publishing worldwide. Oxford is a registered trade mark of
Oxford University Press in the UK and in certain other countries.

Published in the United States of America by Oxford University Press
198 Madison Avenue, New York, NY 10016, United States of America

British Library Cataloguing in Publication Data
Data available

Library of Congress Control Number: 2025946889

ISBN 9780198948780

Printed and bound in the UK by
Clays Ltd, Elcograf S.p.A.

The manufacturer's authorized representative in the EU for product safety is
Oxford University Press España S.A. of Parque Empresarial San Fernando de Henares,
Avenida de Castilla, 2 – 28830 Madrid (www.oup.es/en or product.safety@oup.com).
OUP España S.A. also acts as importer into Spain of products made by the manufacturer.

CONTENTS

INTRODUCTION

The Poet and His Work

THE first half of the sixteenth century is the era traditionally identified as the High Renaissance in Rome. In the early years of the century Bramante erected a *tempietto* (little temple) in neoclassical style on the supposed site of the martyrdom of St Peter, and in 1506 construction began on the new basilica of St Peter's under his direction. Two or three years later Raphael and his assistants embarked on their redecoration of the papal apartments in the Vatican, and at the same time Michelangelo was at work on the ceiling frescoes of the Sistine Chapel.[1]

It was an era when admiration for the cultural achievements of classical antiquity—and for the works of the Roman poet Virgil in particular—ran high, and nowhere higher than in Marco Girolamo Vida.[2] The third and final book of Vida's *De arte poetica* (*On the Art of Poetry*), a treatise in Latin verse on the art of poetry written around 1515 and first published in 1527, concludes with a rapturous hymn to Virgil, hailed as model and inspiration for his would-be literary successors: 'You we worship, to you we bring garlands, to you we offer incense and altars, and for you we shall always declare the sacred honour that is your due, recalling you in our songs. Hail, most holy bard! Your glory cannot be increased further by praises, and has no need of our utterance; look upon us in person, by your arrival infuse the heat of your inspiration into pure hearts, father, and plant yourself within our souls'.[3] The author of this extraordinary tribute to a pagan poet would go on to hold high office in the Roman Church, becoming bishop of Alba in northern Italy in 1533.

Vida's success as a Latin poet in the Virgilian mould was recognized by his contemporary Lilio Gregorio Giraldi, who wrote in his first dialogue on the poets of his time that 'in no one, to be sure, is the

[1] For general background, see C. L. Stinger, *The Renaissance in Rome* (Bloomington, IN, 1998).

[2] For a fuller survey of Vida's life and works, see M. A. Di Cesare, *Vida's* Christiad *and Vergilian Epic* (New York, 1964), 1–39.

[3] *De arte poetica* 3.586–92, with echoes from Virgil's own poetry.

character of Virgil more clearly to be detected. This is the anvil he hammers at day and night, on this alone he plugs away'.[4] Although Giraldi demonstrates awareness of Vida's forthcoming epic, the *Christias* (often anglicized as *Christiad*, the epic of Christ), his dialogue was composed while the finishing touches were still being put to the latter's magnum opus, which first appeared in print in 1535 after years of eager anticipation. This judgement is thus largely based on the works Vida had completed before the appearance of his Christian epic. Following a number of early pieces, including an epic on the achievements of Pope Julius II and a long classicizing pastoral poem lamenting Julius' death, Vida had risen to fame through his Latin poems on the game of chess (*De ludo scaccorum*), the silkworm and the production of silk (*De bombyce*, dedicated to Isabella d'Este), and the art of poetry (*De arte poetica*).[5] The first of these, an elegant, light-hearted account of the popular board game with a mythological setting and much mock-heroic language and imagery, was widely printed in the sixteenth century and was translated into several modern languages.

The poet was born Marcantonio Vida in the early to mid-1480s in the northern Italian city of Cremona—hence John Milton's celebration of Vida's Christian epic with the line 'Loud o're the rest Cremona's Trump doth sound' (*The Passion*, line 26). He was educated in Cremona, in Mantua (famed as the birthplace of Virgil) and elsewhere, and later moved to Rome, where he became attached to the court of Pope Leo X. It was for Leo, apparently inspired to offer the commission after reading Vida's poem on chess, that he began work on the *Christiad* around 1518. Leo X died in December 1521, but work on the poem continued under Leo's nephew Clement VII, pope from 1523 to 1534. By the time the epic was finally printed in 1535, Clement had been succeeded by Pope Paul III, but the poet had already been rewarded with promotion to the bishopric of Alba, which he held conscientiously and energetically until his death in 1566, two and a half years after the death of his slightly older contemporary Michelangelo.

[4] *De poetis nostrorum temporum* (*On the Poets of Our Times*) 1.111.

[5] For editions in English, see M. A. Di Cesare (ed. and trans.), *The Game of Chess: Marco Girolamo Vida's* Scacchia Ludus (Nieuwkoop, 1975); S. Pullein (trans.), *The Silkworm: A Poem in Two Books written by Marcus Hieronymus Vida* (Dublin, 1750); R. G. Williams (ed. and trans.), *The* De arte poetica *of Marco Girolamo Vida* (New York, 1976).

In addition to his enormously successful poetical works, Vida was a prolific prose writer, producing a weighty treatise *Dialogi de rei publicae dignitate* (*Dialogues on the Worthiness of the State*, published in 1556), a collection of three Ciceronian speeches (*Orationes tres pro Cremonensibus*, composed in 1549) asserting the interests of his native Cremona against a challenge from nearby Pavia, and a disquisition on the affairs of the diocese of Alba (*Constitutiones synodales*, 1562). Over the following centuries, however, it was for his Latin verse that Vida would be celebrated, and for the *Christiad* in particular, which was printed in numerous editions across Europe, translated into Spanish within the poet's lifetime and later (repeatedly) into Italian, Croatian, English, German, and French, followed in the nineteenth century by translations into Armenian and Portuguese.[6] The literary significance of the *Christiad* extends well beyond its impressive publication history: Vida's epic served as an important model and source of inspiration for such central works of European literature as Torquato Tasso's *Gerusalemme liberata* (*Jerusalem Delivered*, 1591) and John Milton's *Paradise Lost* (1667) and *Paradise Regained* (1671).[7] If Cremona's trump was a little more muted following the waning of Vida's critical reputation in the late nineteenth and twentieth centuries, the first quarter of the twenty-first century has seen a revival of scholarly interest in the *Christiad*, with new translations, a German commentary, and renewed attention in studies of Renaissance literature and culture.

A Classical Epic for Renaissance Christianity

The Renaissance predilection for classical antiquity owed much to an appreciation of the literary style of ancient authors. At the pinnacle of prose stood Cicero, while the summit of poetry was occupied by Virgil, poet of the *Eclogues*, *Georgics*, and *Aeneid*. Yet intellectuals of the early modern period were acutely aware that their favourite works of literature had been created in and for a society not only remote from them in time, but which also did not share their fundamental

[6] For bibliography, see M. A. Di Cesare, *Bibliotheca Vidiana: A Bibliography of Marco Girolamo Vida* (Florence, 1974), and catalogue of texts and translations in J. Gardner (trans.), *Marco Girolamo Vida: Christiad* (I Tatti Renaissance Library; Cambridge, MA, 2009), 441–5.

[7] See the studies by Haan, Currell, Butler, and Di Cesare listed in the Select Bibliography.

religious assumptions. The Christian gospels, on the other hand, though revered for their theological and moral content, could not satisfy the aesthetic requirements of generations raised to exalt and to emulate the stylistic refinement of the luminaries of classical literature. Already in the late fourth century St Augustine, looking back on his youth, recalled his feeling that the Christian scriptures could not stand comparison with 'Ciceronian dignity' (*Confessions* 3.5.9), while the only thing lacking in the works of the Roman orator was the name of Christ (3.4.8). The fusion of spiritual truth with classical style could thus be seen not only as a path to the creation of a Renaissance bestseller but also as a sacred duty.

Vida was by no means the first poet to attempt to enshrine the teachings of Christianity and the narrative of the gospels in classicizing Latin verse. Even before the time of Augustine, in the first half of the fourth century, the Spanish poet Juvencus had produced an account of the life of Christ (*Evangeliorum libri quattuor*) in the poetic metre of Virgil, closely modelled on the gospels and in conscious opposition to the 'lies' of Homer and Virgil—though he acknowledges the latter's 'sweetness' (*dulcedo*). Shortly afterwards the aristocratic Roman lady Faltonia Betitia Proba assembled a poetic patchwork (cento) of lines from Virgil to recount biblical stories, including the history of Christ; other poets of the same period similarly extracted and reordered material from Virgil to form poems on Christian subjects. In the following century Sedulius composed a *Carmen Paschale* (*Paschal Song*) likewise imitating the form and style of Virgil, and in the mid-sixth century Arator produced a poem in two books on the acts of the Apostles.[8] Juvencus and Sedulius were read in the Middle Ages and Renaissance and their texts were known to Vida, as was the other important early Christian Latin poet Prudentius; but their attempts to unite classical literary form with Christian doctrine were evidently viewed as valuable preliminary models rather than as a definitive solution to the need for doctrinally acceptable poetry conforming to the stylistic canons of the Virgilian tradition.

[8] See especially M. Roberts, *Biblical Epic and Rhetorical Paraphrase in Late Antiquity* (Liverpool, 1985); R. P. H. Green, *Latin Epics of the New Testament: Juvencus, Sedulius, Arator* (Oxford, 2006); P. Hardie, *Classicism and Christianity in Late Antique Latin Poetry* (Oakland, CA, 2023).

By the early sixteenth century the reclamation of Virgil's epic legacy for the central narrative of the Christian faith had still not been decisively accomplished. Petrarch (1304–74), often considered a pioneer of Renaissance attitudes and scholarship, raised the idea of the life of Christ as a subject for epic (*Invective contra medicum* 3.126) but proceeded no further, working instead on an epic treatment of the exploits of the Roman general Scipio Africanus (the *Africa*). The leading Renaissance intellectual Erasmus called Battista Spagnoli (1447–1516), the Carmelite friar known as Mantuan, the 'Christian Virgil' for his vast body of Latin verse on religious topics, which extends well beyond the celebrated collection of pastoral poems known as *Adulescentia*. Maffeo Vegio (1407–58), author of a hugely successful thirteenth book supplementing the original twelve of Virgil's *Aeneid*, also wrote a short *Antoniad* in four books on an episode from the life of St Anthony the Abbot, while the Croatian Marko Marulić (1450–1524) composed an epic *Davidias*, in which King David is presented as a forerunner of Christ. Nor had attempts to handle the theme of the life of Christ in Latin verse been lacking: in the mid-fifteenth century Girolamo dalle Valli from Padua produced a short *Jesuida*, and Macario Muzio achieved some success with his *De triumpho Christi* (*On the triumph of Christ*), first printed in 1499. Ventures into this territory in the early decades of the sixteenth century include Jakov Bunić's *De vita et gestis Christi* (*On the Life and Deeds of Christ*, in more than 10,000 Latin hexameters, published in 1526) and Battista Fiera's *Evangelicae historiae, sive de deo homine libri quatuor* (*Four Books of Gospel History, or On God made Man*, first published in 1522).[9]

It is against the backdrop of this growing body of Christian Latin verse, of which he was surely well aware, that Vida's composition of his epic must be viewed. A significant quantity of Latin pastoral poetry on Christian themes had also begun to appear, taking its cue from the prominent part played by shepherds in the Christmas story, from the more general preponderance of pastoral imagery in Judaeo-Christian discourse, and from the long-standing interpretation of Virgil's fourth Eclogue (the so-called 'messianic eclogue') as

[9] For an introductory review of neo-Latin biblical epic, see Di Cesare, *Vida's* Christiad, 72–84.

a conscious or unconscious prophecy of the birth of Christ.[10] The last of these threads is strongly apparent throughout Vida's poem, in which language from the fourth Eclogue is extensively and repeatedly deployed and which concludes with an unmistakable echo of Virgil's proclamation of a new Golden Age (*Christiad* 6.985–6).[11]

This tendency had perhaps already reached its apogee in a work composed at the same time as Vida's epic, Jacopo Sannazaro's *De partu Virginis* (*On the Virgin Birth*), which appeared in print in 1526. In the third book of Sannazaro's poem the shepherds greet the newborn Christ with a song consisting of lines taken directly or lightly adapted from the messianic eclogue, and phrasing and imagery from the Virgilian model permeate much of the rest of the work. Sannazaro's *De partu Virginis* focuses on one episode in the Christian story, but uses prophecy to touch on other events in the life of Christ. It is a different kind of poem from Vida's epic, but its articulation of concepts from Christian doctrine in Virgilian terms is in some respects comparable. Together, these two works represent the high point of Christian Virgilianism, clothing the sacred narratives of the gospels in the classical literary attire (some would say straitjacket) so much admired by Renaissance readers.

Virgil and Beyond

Vida's poem announces its epic credentials on the levels of form, structure, and verbal texture. The metre of Vida's lines is the hexameter, the heroic measure of Homer and Virgil; the total of six books continues the decreasing sequence from twenty-four books in each of the *Iliad* and *Odyssey* to the twelve books of Virgil's *Aeneid* (and also perhaps challenges Lucretius' six-book philosophical epic, which vigorously denied the existence of the afterlife and divine interest in human affairs). The story begins, like the *Aeneid* and the Homeric epics, in the midst of the action, rather than setting out events in a rigidly chronological sequence—indeed the opening of Vida's

[10] See L. B. T. Houghton, *Virgil's Fourth Eclogue in the Italian Renaissance* (Cambridge, 2019), 252–85.

[11] Di Cesare, *Vida's* Christiad, 160–1; C. Kallendorf, 'From Virgil to Vida: The *Poeta Theologus* in Italian Renaissance Commentary', *Journal of the History of Ideas* 56 (1995), 41–62; Houghton, *Virgil's Fourth Eclogue*, 226–39; J. A. Glodzik, *The Reception of Vergil in Renaissance Rome* (Leiden, 2023), 74–81.

narrative after the initial invocation makes it clear that we are anywhere but at the beginning of the story: 'Now the goal of Christ's death and the end of his labours was at hand' (1.15). Events prior to this point in the action are recounted in extensive flashback narratives (by Joseph in Book 3, and by John in Book 4), just as Aeneas describes the fall of Troy and his subsequent wanderings in Books 2 and 3 of the *Aeneid*, and Odysseus tells of his adventures in Books 9–12 of the *Odyssey*.

Vida's diction is generally elevated (including the archaisms, compound adjectives, and patronymics so characteristic of the epic tradition) and for the most part impeccably Virgilian. The reader encounters such epic devices as formulaic expressions opening and closing speeches ('So he spoke') or indicating times of day, recurring epithets, a catalogue of peoples (here occupying a significant part of Book 2, as Homer's catalogue of the Greek forces at Troy is to be found in the second book of the *Iliad*), invocations, and similes comparing the action or situation in the poem to different aspects of human behaviour or the natural world. Many of these similes can easily be imagined in the pages of Virgil, but there are some telling exceptions.[12] Most striking is the famous simile at 2.205–13 comparing the reaction of Nicodemus' speech before the Sanhedrin to the firing of a cannon, which demonstrates Vida's knowledge of the workings of this item of post-classical military equipment. The simile likening Christ's appearance to his disciples after the Resurrection to the passage of sunlight through a glazed window at 6.568–72 similarly displays a scientific interest, this time in natural phenomena. These vivid flashes of contemporary reality remind the reader that the story of the *Christiad* holds a direct and urgent relevance for the poet's own time: it is not simply a literary and historical curiosity remote from the reader's everyday existence.

The story of the gospels offers relatively little scope for the narration of martial activity, but the epic stature of Vida's protagonist is

[12] On Vida's similes, see Di Cesare, *Vida's* Christiad, 132–41, 264–6; J. P. Holoka, 'A Neoplatonic Simile in Vida's *Christiad* (4.10–15)', *Romance Notes* 18 (1977), 243–6; W. J. O'Neal, 'The Simile in Vida's *Christiad*', in R. J. Schoeck (ed.), *Acta Conventus Neo-Latini Bononiensis* (Binghamton, NY, 1985), 558–63; T. Gregory, *From Many Gods to One: Divine Action in Renaissance Epic* (Chicago, 2006), 74–6, 86–7; F. Schaffenrath, 'Narrative Structures in Neo-Latin Epic: 16th–19th Century', in C. Reitz and S. Finkmann (eds.), *Structures of Epic Poetry*, 3 vols. (Berlin, 2019), iii.301–29 at 318–20.

emphasized by the repeated description of Christ as 'the hero' (*heros*),[13] and an opportunity for the staging of military manoeuvres is created by the insertion of the abortive muster of the angelic forces into the narrative of the Crucifixion in Book 5. Other themes of ancient—and especially Virgilian—epic can be seen in the presence of a divine audience reacting to events on earth, the visitation of a heavenly messenger and dream visions, the untimely deaths of the young and beautiful (accompanied by similes comparing the dead youth to cut or trampled flowers: 4.318–28), the sacrifice of one individual for all,[14] the prophecies of a future destiny beyond the time frame of the narrative, and the use of ekphrasis.[15] This last category refers to the description of a work of art, as seen in Virgil's depiction of the scenes on the temple of Juno at Carthage in the first book of the *Aeneid*, of Daedalus' carvings on the temple of Apollo at Cumae in Book 6, and of the divinely fashioned shield of Aeneas with its prophetic scenes from Roman history in Book 8.

The main examples of ekphrasis in Vida's epic are the mysterious non-pictorial representations of the Creation and other Old Testament stories in the temple at Jerusalem in the first book, the images of the war in heaven on the celestial gates in Book 5, and the scene of Jonah and the whale (interpreted as an anticipation of Christ's release from the jaws of death) depicted on the tomb of Christ in Book 6.[16] As in Virgil, these inset descriptions extend the range of the narrative, setting the events narrated within a broader context and interpreting their larger significance. And like Virgil, Vida stresses the incapacity of verbal description to convey the character of the artwork before giving an extended verbal description of precisely that subject.[17]

[13] On Christ as epic hero in the *Christiad*, see Gregory, *From Many Gods to One*, 80–9.

[14] On 'the dialectic of *unus/omnes*' in Latin epic, see P. Hardie, *The Epic Successors of Virgil: A Study in the Dynamics of a Tradition* (Cambridge, 1993), 3–10, 27–32. See also P. Hardie, 'After Rome: Renaissance Epic', in A. J. Boyle (ed.), *Roman Epic* (London, 1993), 294–313 at 308 on the *Christiad*: 'There is much play on *unus* [one] and *omnes* [all], or *multi* [many], in this poem'.

[15] On prophecies in Vida, see especially Di Cesare, *Vida's* Christiad, 103–9, and on ekphrasis 109–13.

[16] See 1.582–724, 5.589–615, 6.351–68.

[17] Compare Virgil's 'indescribable fabric' (*non enarrabile textum*, *Aeneid* 8.625) of the shield of Aeneas with Vida's 'work impossible to describe in human words' (*haud humanis opus enarrabile verbis*, 1.586).

At a number of points in the poem we find coordinated clusters of echoes from a particular episode in the *Aeneid*, which prompt reflection on the parallels between the situation in Vida's epic and the original Virgilian setting evoked by these reminiscences. At moments of destiny, for example, including the Transfiguration, the Annunciation, the Baptism of Christ, and Pentecost,[18] Vida displays a tendency to engage with the Virgilian passage describing the portents—harmless tongues of flame and crashing thunder—which mark out the child Ascanius as the future of Troy at *Aeneid* 2.679–98 (also echoed in these contexts is the thunder reassuring Aeneas of divine favour at *Aeneid* 8.520–9). Such allusions confer upon Vida's characters in these passages a sense of divine election, whether of Christ, the Virgin Mary, or the Apostles. When Vida refers to Christ's Harrowing of Hell, his rescue of human souls from confinement in the underworld,[19] there are numerous verbal recollections not only of Virgil's underworld in *Aeneid* Book 6, but also of the struggle between Hercules and Cacus narrated by Evander at *Aeneid* 8.184–275. By implication, Christ is cast as the avenging hero, the benefactor of humanity and victor over monstrous infernal powers. Readers of the *Aeneid* have long recognized the infernal character of Virgil's Cacus, and Vida will certainly have been familiar with the long-standing typological association between Hercules and Christ, both conquerors of death received into heaven after their exploits on earth.

There is nothing casual, covert, unimaginative, or mechanical about these parallels: Vida expects his educated readers to recognize his verbal cues, to be aware of the original literary context of this material, and to import the connotations bestowed on these cues by their original context into the reader's response to Vida's own poem.[20] It is not simply a question of the author's trying to write as much like Virgil as possible; rather, we are invited to read Vida's text *with* Virgil (and with other sources) in order to fathom the richness and resonance of his poetic compound. Having said that, it is entirely plausible that Vida believed that this was precisely what Virgil himself was doing in his engagement with his own ancient sources.

[18] See 1.932–46, 3.273–6, 4.212–22, 6.914–32.

[19] See 1.121–5, 6.121–39, 6.198–235.

[20] Di Cesare, *Vida's* Christiad, 149–50 calls this 'evocative allusion'; see generally 149–62.

Nor is Virgil the only model marshalled by Vida to construct his classicizing Latin epic. The attentive reader will detect phrasing from Catullus, Claudian (who had already begun the tradition of infernal councils which Vida would transmit to Tasso, Milton, and others), Horace, Lucan, Lucretius,[21] Ovid, Propertius, and Statius, among others, in addition to elements taken from the late antique Christian poets mentioned above and from still more recent Latin and vernacular authors, such as Dante.

The hunt for sources, however, should not obscure the poetical power, brilliance, and even humour of Vida's own contribution (for humour, see the social comedy of Pilate's efforts to shed responsibility for dealing with the allegations against Christ, and his impotent disgruntlement when the case keeps coming back to him: 'although innocent he was returned once more to the keeping of the Roman, who was far from happy about it', 5.199). Here it must suffice to give just one (literally) heart-stopping example of the poet's verbal artistry. In the very last line of Book 5 Christ's agony on the cross finally comes to an end; after commending his soul to God, he breathes his last—*supremamque auram ponens caput exspiravit* ('and laying down his head, he breathed out his final breath', 5.995). The line begins with seven consecutive long syllables as the saviour slowly sinks in death (the first half of the verse is a single breath on its own, with no break between *supremamque* and *auram*), and it ends in an audible sigh as his last breath escapes in the four further long, heavy syllables of *exspiravit*, discarding the usual pattern of the hexameter line-ending for a long-drawn-out closural exhalation. Nothing could be more final than this: surely this is the end? But then Book 6 begins with *iamque* (6.1)—what a weight of theology is implicit in that resumptive 'And now. . .'!

To dismiss Vida's epic of Christ (as influential critics in the nineteenth and twentieth centuries did)[22] as a derivative, anachronistic pastiche of the classical epic genre fundamentally misrepresents the nature and ambition of this ingenious, moving, and multifaceted poem. This is a highly sophisticated, intensely allusive text; but its

[21] See especially S. Cianciosi, 'The Presence of Lucretius' *De Rerum Natura* in Girolamo Vida's *Christiad*', *Classical World* 116 (2022), 23–49.

[22] C. S. Lewis, for example, talked of 'the bad tradition (seen at its worst in Vida's *Christiad* and at its best in the *Gierusalemme Liberata*) of trying to make Heaven too like Olympus': *A Preface to Paradise Lost* (Oxford, 1942), 127.

literary strategies are much more than an intellectual game designed merely to engage the wits of the reader and to elicit admiration for the author's cleverness in transforming his ancient source material to fit a new, Christian context. Rather, Vida invites his readers to experience the events of the New Testament through a Virgilian lens, to bring to their response to the biblical story the feelings of horror, excitement, pathos, delicacy, and grandeur evoked by their reading of the ancient classic. It is a form of spiritual meditation conducted through the medium of Latin literature, intensifying the devout reader's feeling for the momentous significance of the narrative of human salvation. The drama and entertainment of Vida's storytelling are there for all to enjoy, but ultimately they exist to serve a higher purpose—for a sixteenth-century Christian audience, the highest purpose of all.

The Vision of Rome

Vida sought in his epic to give expression to the fundamental truths of Christianity; yet by 1535 much had changed in the Christian world since work on the poem had begun around 1518. In 1517 Martin Luther had promulgated his *Ninety-Five Theses*, and in the ensuing years reformist thought, which had already made an appearance in many parts of the continent, gained an ever-stronger foothold in northern Europe and beyond. Ten years later, in 1527, the disaffected troops of the emperor Charles V inflicted a brutal sack on Rome, slaughtering the pope's bodyguard and forcing Clement himself to seek refuge in Castel Sant'Angelo. As composition of his epic proceeded, the world in which Vida had grown up and embarked on his literary and ecclesiastical career must have seemed increasingly under threat from forces of disorder and destruction.

On purely literary grounds, there can never have been any doubt that the primary model for Vida's epic would be Virgil's *Aeneid*. But it is important also for the form the *Christiad* would take that Virgil's poem was above all the poem of Rome.[23] In its opening lines and over its whole course it maps out a trajectory from Homeric Troy to the poet's own Rome,[24] articulating an origin myth, a sense of destiny,

[23] On Vida's treatment of the 'Roman theme', see Di Cesare, *Vida's* Christiad, 155–61, 223, 253–73, 282–3; also Glodzik, *The Reception of Vergil*, 124–5.

[24] See Virgil, *Aeneid* 1.1–7, trans. F. Ahl (Oxford World's Classics, 2007).

a scheme of values, and (at least ostensibly) an imperial mission. Although the foundation of the city lies far in the future at the point where the narrative ends, the teleological point of the *Aeneid* is Rome, and in particular the Rome of Augustus. This is conveyed in the poem in a number of ways. One is through prophetic utterances and images spelling out what lies ahead for Aeneas' descendants once his own immediate mission is complete: Jupiter's prophecy of Roman 'empire without end' (*imperium sine fine*, 1.279) in Book 1, the parade of figures from future Roman history in the underworld in Book 6, the scenes on Aeneas' divine shield in Book 8. Another is through the poet's interest in aetiology—that is, the tracing of current customs, institutions, and practices back to their origins in the distant past.[25]

The *Aeneid* in its entirety is a profoundly aetiological poem, accounting for the origins of Rome and the claims of the Julian imperial family; but this is reflected on a smaller scale by its attention to the origins of Roman place names and family names, of religious practices such as the worship at the Ara Maxima, and of distinctive Roman practices such as the cavalry display known as the Troy Game.[26] Juno's final grudging acceptance of Rome's destiny and the compromise she exacts from Jupiter account for the fact that the Romans speak Latin and wear the toga, rather than preserving Trojan customs.[27]

Following Virgil's lead, Vida's epic is also a thoroughly aetiological poem, charting the origins not of ancient Rome but of contemporary Christian, papal Rome (as Augustan Rome had been contemporary for Virgil). Why are Christians so called? Because they are named after Christ. Why do they pray using the words of the Lord's Prayer? Because Christ originally told them to.[28] Why is the Mass celebrated with bread and wine? Because that is what happened at the Last Supper.[29] Why is the symbol of the cross set upon altars? Because this

[25] See e.g. N. Horsfall, 'Virgil and the Poetry of Explanations', *Greece & Rome* 38 (1991), 203–11.

[26] See *Aeneid* 6.378–81, 7.1–4, 8.357–8 (place names); 1.286–8, 5.121–3, 7.706–9 (family names); 8.268–72 (Ara Maxima: see especially 8.268–9, 'from that time on the honour has been celebrated, and later generations have joyfully preserved the day'); 5.596–602 (Troy Game).

[27] *Aeneid* 12.821–8.

[28] See 6.984–5 (Christians), 4.971–80 (Lord's Prayer).

[29] See 2.651–70, especially 2.663–5, 670: 'Ever since then, later generations have preserved this ritual in commemoration, and on the altars we consecrate unspoiled bread and sweet juice from the vine [. . .] This rite has come to be held in the highest honour' (compare *Aeneid* 8.268–9, quoted in n. 26 above).

was the means of Christ's execution. And why is Rome the rightful capital of the Christian world? Because God decreed that it should be.[30]

As in the Virgilian conception, there is a pervasive sense of historical mission, of a divinely ordained destiny with eternal consequences; but the empire in question is not the martial sway of imperial Rome,[31] but the spreading authority of the Roman Church, now being carried beyond the seas to new continents and thereby achieving global dimensions of which the Romans, with all their boasts of empire without end, could never have dreamed. The true Golden Age is not the consulship of Gaius Asinius Pollio, as celebrated in the fourth Eclogue, but the Golden Age of the gospel, initiated by the divinely inspired activities of the Apostles.[32] Rome may be facing threats in the early decades of the sixteenth century, but as the vessel of divine purpose it will emerge from its tribulations in triumph. Such is the will of God:

> Often you will see that city which I just referred to practically uprooted from the ground and cut down by the onslaughts of invading peoples. But the more she is chastened by sufferings, the higher she will forever rise and raise her head aloft among the stars. She will forever be renewing her walls, making them better and better, and will not stop until the earth is subject to her throughout its length and breadth. So it has been decided. Let this be the seat of my divine power. (1.924–30)

Such ideological implications suggest a further explanation for Vida's choice of Virgilian verse for his reclothing of the gospels, rather than (say) the stylistic elegance of Ciceronian prose. In antiquity, epic was recognized as the universal genre: it comprised the whole world within a single literary form.[33] Virgil's act of appropriating epic for the expression of Roman imperial ideals was thus in itself an act of imperialism, a way of Romanizing the cosmos equivalent to the limitless territorial conquests of Augustus, whose progress he imagined extending 'beyond the stars, beyond the paths of the year and the

[30] See 5.411–19, again echoing *Aeneid* 8.268–9 (cross); 1.579–81, 1.911–30, 6.662–76 (Rome).

[31] See 1.911, 'haughty Rome, pregnant with empire'; also 2.300–2.

[32] See 6.863–7, 6.973–86.

[33] See P. R. Hardie, *Virgil's* Aeneid*: Cosmos and Imperium* (Oxford, 1986); also Hardie, *Classicism and Christianity in Late Antique Latin Poetry*, 75–102; Di Cesare, *Vida's* Christiad, 212–14, 244–54.

sun'.[34] This universal aspect of Virgilian epic may well have formed part of its appeal for a poet asserting transcendent spiritual claims: from this perspective, the ideology of the *Christiad* is Catholic in every respect, both capitalized and lower-case.

And yet Rome, even Christian Rome, is not after all the ultimate teleological point of Vida's poem: the final word of his seven-line opening sentence is not 'Rome', as in Virgil, but 'heaven' (or rather 'Olympus').[35] In the minds of sixteenth-century believers, Vida's subject possessed genuinely cosmic dimensions: its destination is not so much empire without end as a kingdom not of this world.[36] As John says in Book 4 (echoing several passages of the *Aeneid*), the Jews 'know—and they admit they know—that a prophet will come forth into the light of day, the only one who can unbar for us the impassable gates of heaven and bring the spirits of the righteous out of the darkness to the stars on high' (4.798–801). For the cleric Vida, ancient aspirations to universal empire paled into empty hyperbole in comparison with the comprehensive reach of the Christian story, which moved literally between heaven and hell and back again.[37] Earthly empires rise and fall, but the narrative of salvation offered by Vida's poem represents epic from the viewpoint of eternity.

'Immortal Vida'

The impact of Vida's Christian epic on the work of such literary celebrities as Tasso (1544–95), Milton (1608–74), and English poet Abraham Cowley (1618–67) is well known, as is the importance of *De arte poetica* for literary criticism of the later sixteenth century and beyond. But it is clear that these notable traces are only the most visible peak of a far more extensive afterlife enjoyed by Vida's refashioning of the gospels in the medium of Virgil. Here it is possible to mention only a few examples of later authors who followed the lead of the poet from Cremona, in order to give some impression of the widespread attention paid to the *Christiad* by Vida's literary successors in Europe and beyond.

[34] *Aeneid* 6.795–6. [35] See Hardie, 'After Rome: Renaissance Epic', 309.
[36] John 18:36; see 1.54–9, 6.889–94.
[37] Di Cesare, *Vida's* Christiad, 244–50. On heaven and hell as a thematic strand in Latin epic, see Hardie, *The Epic Successors of Virgil*, 57–87, and Hardie, *Classicism and Christianity in Late Antique Latin Poetry*, 46–8, 81–2.

Before the end of the sixteenth century, the Jesuit Francesco Benci had made significant use of Vida's poem as a model for his epic *Quinque martyres e Societate Iesu in India* (*Five Martyrs of the Society of Jesus in India*, 1591),[38] and in the following centuries the Society of Jesus continued to produce prolific versifiers whose Latin works drew on the precedent set by Vida. In 1644 François Vavasseur's *Theurgicon sive de miraculis Christi libri IV* (*Four Books of Divine Works, or On Christ's Miracles*) appeared in Paris, and in 1690 the Latin text of Tommaso Ceva's *Jesus puer* (*Jesus' Boyhood*) in nine books was published in Milan; like Vida's epic, Ceva's poem would be translated into several different languages. The first Christian epic to be composed in the Americas was the work of a Dominican, Diego de Hojeda's *La Christiada* (1611), in Spanish but drawing inspiration from Vida's *Christiad*; it would much later be followed by the Mexican Jesuit Diego José Abad's forty-three-book Latin work *De Deo Deoque homine heroica* (*Heroic Poetry on God, and God as Man*, 1780). In 1805 the Jesuit Nicodemus Musnicki, author of a Polish epic *Pultawa*, produced a three-book Latin hexameter poem *De Christi ab inferis reditu* (*On Christ's Return from Hell*). Even in works where the subject is not primarily religious, signs of Vida's influence can be detected: the scholar Florian Schaffenrath has pointed to the appearance of a simile involving a cannon ball in the didactic poem *Nautica* (1685) by another Jesuit Latinist, Niccolò Partenio Giannettasio.[39]

Hojeda was not the only later author to borrow Vida's title. The Scotsman Alexander Ross adopted the cento technique to create his *Virgilii evangelisantis Christiados libri XIII* (*Thirteen Books of* Christias *of evangelizing Virgil*, 1634); and in the seventeenth century alone further Latin or vernacular poems featuring the word *Christias* or *Christiade* in the title were produced by Johannes Klockus (1601), Antoine de La Pujade (1604), Jean d'Escorbiac (1613), Marcantonio Laporelli (1618), and the English Carthusian Robert Clarke (1670).[40]

[38] See P. Gwynne (ed.), *Francesco Benci's* Quinque martyres (Leiden, 2018), 59–61 and *passim*.

[39] Schaffenrath, 'Narrative Structures', 319–20, on *Nautica* 8.299–303; he also mentions Musnicki's *De Christi ab inferis reditu*.

[40] For these and other post-Vidan ventures, see C. P. E. Springer, *The Gospel as Epic in Late Antiquity: The* Paschale Carmen *of Sedulius* (Leiden, 1988), 141–2, and Gardner (trans.), *Marco Girolamo Vida: Christiad*, pp. xxvi–xxvii, citing B. K. Lewalski, *Milton's Brief Epic: The Genre, Meaning, and Art of* Paradise Regained (Providence, 1966), 87–93, and W. Kirkconnell, *Awake the Courteous Echo* (Toronto, 1973), 315–22. The German history of the genre is traced by R. G. Czapla, *Das Bibelepos in der frühen Neuzeit* (Berlin, 2013).

These would later be joined by Henry Kirke White's *The Christiad, A Divine Poem*, first printed posthumously in 1807, and by William Alexander's *Christiad*, published in Philadelphia in 1847.[41] Meanwhile epic poetry on the subject of the life of Christ continued to proliferate under other titles, such as Friedrich Gottlieb Klopstock's *Der Messias* (*The Messiah*, 1748–73).

Such general enthusiasm would not outlast the nineteenth century. It may be that the towering literary stature attained by Vida's work during his lifetime and in the centuries immediately following played some part in fuelling the adverse reaction that ensued. Yet at the height of his critical fortunes, in Alexander Pope's *An Essay on Criticism* (1711), Vida could be paired with Raphael as representative of the Renaissance revival of classical antiquity:[42]

> But see! each Muse, in Leo's golden days,
> Starts from her trance, and trims her withered bays,
> Rome's ancient genius, o'er its ruins spread,
> Shakes off the dust, and rears his rev'rend head.
> Then Sculpture and her sister-arts revive;
> Stones leaped to form, and rocks began to live;
> With sweeter notes each rising temple rung;
> A Raphael painted, and a Vida sung.
> Immortal Vida: on whose honoured brow
> The poet's bays and critic's ivy grow:
> Cremona now shall ever boast thy name,
> As next in place to Mantua, next in fame!

More than three centuries after Pope's verdict, and nearly five hundred years since the first publication of Vida's poem, the power, drama, imagination, and humanity of *The Epic of Christ* can still enthral and move its readers. It fully deserves its place alongside the works of classical literature from which its author drew so much of his inspiration, and the great vernacular epics which would build on Vida's achievement. If any product of the early modern enthusiasm for classicizing Latin verse merits the status of a classic in its own right, it is the biblical epic of Marco Girolamo Vida.

41 See Gardner (trans.), *Marco Girolamo Vida: Christiad*, p. xxvi.
42 Pope, *An Essay on Criticism*, lines 697–708.

NOTE ON THE TEXT AND TRANSLATION

EVERY translator is obliged, in some degree, to make a case for the work he or she has chosen to translate. This is perhaps especially the case when the work in question is cast in a literary medium (neo-Latin verse) which for a long time laboured under widespread scholarly disparagement, as lacking in feeling, imagination, and originality. To my mind, Vida's *Christiad* is unquestionably a masterpiece—even if one previous translator of the poem into English took the view that it 'does not attain to the highest ranks of poetry'. Read in the original Latin, it more than makes the case for itself: its language is vivid, powerful, and densely allusive. What I have tried to do above all is to convey something of the richness, exuberance, and drama of Vida's verse, qualities abundantly present in the Latin—and not just in highlights such as the infernal gathering of the clans and the wonderfully lubricious description of the seductress in Book 1, or the mighty simile in Book 2 comparing the reaction to Nicodemus' words in the Sanhedrin to the firing of a cannon (see Introduction).

In preparing the translation I have used primarily the Latin text edited by James Hankins for James Gardner's edition in the I Tatti Renaissance Library. Like Gardner, I have not aimed at consistency in translating classical terms such as Olympus and Tartarus, appropriated by Vida from the Roman literary tradition for his epic biblical narrative: sometimes these appear in their classical forms, at other times as 'heaven' and 'hell'. The forms used for Hebrew names in the catalogue of Book 2 (and elsewhere) have come from Gardner, who in turn took them over from Drake and Forbes. Whether or not the reader accepts Gardner's verdict that Vida's style results in 'cloying redundancy' when rendered in English prose, any excision of material on those grounds is false to the historical character of the work. When the translation appears alongside a Latin text, as in the I Tatti series, readers can verify any omissions for themselves, but in a free-standing translation it is even more incumbent on the translator to attempt to offer a faithful reflection of what Vida wrote.

References to the text in the Introduction and the Explanatory Notes refer to book and line numbers within Vida's Latin poem; line numbers are given in the running heads at the top of each page of the translation.

Alice Lambrecht has followed the progress of the translation for much of its course with enthusiastic interest and encouragement, and has been a sensitive and sympathetic first reader of both translation and introduction. My more general debt, both conscious and unconscious, to Philip Hardie and his work will be apparent from the Introduction. I am grateful also to Luciana O'Flaherty and Henry Clarke at Oxford University Press and to my copy-editor Rowena Anketell for their help in seeing this volume into print.

L.B.T.H.

SELECT BIBLIOGRAPHY

Editions, Translations, and Commentaries (in chronological order)

Cranwell, J. (trans.), *The Christiad, A Poem in Six Books* (Cambridge, 1768).

Granan, E. (trans.), *The Christiad: An Heroic Poem, in Six Books* (London, 1771).

Drake, G. C., and Forbes, C. A. (eds. and trans.), *Marco Girolamo Vida's The Christiad: A Latin-English Edition* (Carbondale, IL, 1978).

Gardner, J. (trans.), *Marco Girolamo Vida: Christiad* (I Tatti Renaissance Library; Cambridge, MA, 2009) (Latin text edited by James Hankins).

von Contzen, E., Glei, R. F., Polleichtner, W., and Schulze Roberg, M. (eds. and trans.), *Marcus Hieronymus Vida, Christias*, 2 vols. (Trier, 2013).

Critical Works

Bruère, R. T., 'Review Article: Virgil and Vida', *Classical Philology* 61 (1966), 21–43.

Butler, G. F., 'Satan and Briareos in Vida's *Christiad* and Milton's *Paradise Lost*', *ANQ: A Journal of Short Articles, Notes and Reviews* 20 (2007), 11–16.

Cianciosi, S., 'Ancient Latin Epics in Girolamo Vida's *Christiad*' (DPhil thesis, University of Oxford, 2022).

Cianciosi, S., 'The Presence of Lucretius' *De Rerum Natura* in Girolamo Vida's *Christiad*', *Classical World* 116 (2022), 23–49.

Currell, D., 'How Changed? Milton, Vida, Vergil, and a Network of Allusion', *Translation and Literature* 30 (2021), 277–306.

Di Cesare, M. A., *Vida's* Christiad *and Vergilian Epic* (New York, 1964).

Di Cesare, M. A., *Bibliotheca Vidiana: A Bibliography of Marco Girolamo Vida* (Florence, 1974).

Di Cesare, M. A., 'From Virgil to Vida to Milton', in J.-C. Margolin (ed.), *Acta Conventus Neo-Latini Turonensis* (Paris, 1980), 153–61.

Drake, G. C., 'Satan's Councils in the *Christiad*, *Paradise Lost* and *Paradise Regained*', in J.-C. Margolin (ed.), *Acta Conventus Neo-Latini Turonensis* (Paris, 1980), 979–89.

Glodzik, J. A., *The Reception of Vergil in Renaissance Rome* (Leiden, 2023).

Gregory, T., *From Many Gods to One: Divine Action in Renaissance Epic* (Chicago, 2006).

Gwynne, P., 'Epic', in V. Moul (ed.), *A Guide to Neo-Latin Literature* (Cambridge, 2017), 200–20.

Haan, E., 'Milton's *Paradise Regained* and Vida's *Christiad*', in E. Haan (ed.), *From Erudition to Inspiration: Essays in Honour of M. J. McGann* (Belfast, 1992), 53–77.

Haan, E., 'From Helicon to Heaven: Milton's Urania and Vida', *Renaissance Studies* 7 (1993), 86–107.

Haan, E., 'Heaven's Purest Light: *Paradise Lost* 3 and Vida', *Comparative Literature Studies* 30 (1993), 115–36.

Haan, E., 'Milton's Latin Poetry and Vida', *Humanistica Lovaniensia* 44 (1995), 282–304.

Haan, E., 'From Neo-Latin to Vernacular: Celestial Warfare in Vida and Milton', in P. Defosse (ed.), *Hommages à Carl Deroux*, v: *Christianisme et Moyen Âge—Néo-Latin et survivance de la latinité* (Brussels, 2003), 408–19.

Hardie, P., 'After Rome: Renaissance Epic', in A. J. Boyle (ed.), *Roman Epic* (London, 1993), 294–313.

Hardie, P., *Rumour and Renown: Representations of* Fama *in Western Literature* (Cambridge, 2012).

Holoka, J. P., 'A Neoplatonic Simile in Vida's *Christiad* (4.10–15)', *Romance Notes* 18 (1977), 243–6.

Houghton, L. B. T., *Virgil's Fourth Eclogue in the Italian Renaissance* (Cambridge, 2019).

Kallendorf, C., 'From Virgil to Vida: The *Poeta Theologus* in Italian Renaissance Commentary', *Journal of the History of Ideas* 56 (1995), 41–62.

Kallendorf, C., 'The Neo-Latin Epic', in P. Ford, J. Bloemendal, and C. Fantazzi (eds.), *Brill's Encyclopaedia of the Neo-Latin World*, 2 vols. (Leiden, 2014), i.449–60.

O'Neal, W. J., 'The Simile in Vida's *Christiad*', in R. J. Schoeck (ed.), *Acta Conventus Neo-Latini Bononiensis* (Binghamton, NY, 1985), 558–63.

Reddemann, L., 'Epic Salvation: Christ's Descent into Hell and the Landscape of the Underworld in Neo-Latin Christian Epic', in K. A. E. Enenkel and W. S. Melion (eds.), *Landscape and the Visual Hermeneutics of Place, 1500–1700* (Leiden, 2021), 479–506.

Schaffenrath, F., 'Narrative Poetry', in S. Knight and S. Tilg (eds.), *The Oxford Handbook of Neo-Latin* (New York, 2015), 57–71.

Schaffenrath, F., 'Narrative Structures in Neo-Latin Epic: 16th–19th Century', in C. Reitz and S. Finkmann (eds.), *Structures of Epic Poetry*, 3 vols. (Berlin, 2019), iii.301–29.

Schulze Roberg, M., 'The Poet Prophesied: Marco Girolamo Vida's Self-Portrayal and Virgilian Epigonism in the *Christiad*', *Neulateinisches Jahrbuch* 17 (2015), 295–306.

Springer, C. P. E., 'The Biblical Epic in Late Antiquity and the Early Modern Period: The Poetics of Tradition', in Z. von Martels and V. M. Schmidt (eds.), *Antiquity Renewed: Late Classical and Early Modern Themes* (Leuven, 2003), 103–26.

Szendrényi, M., 'Epic and Creation: Vida and Milton in the Development of Vergilian Epic Tradition', in R. Schnur et al. (eds.), *Acta Conventus Neo-Latini Budapestinensis* (Tempe, AZ, 2010), 747–54.
Warner, J. C., *The Augustinian Epic, Petrarch to Milton* (Ann Arbor, MI, 2005).

Further Reading in Oxford World's Classics

The Bible: Authorized King James Version with Apocrypha, ed. R. Carroll and S. Prickett.
The Gospels: Authorized King James Version, ed. W. R. Owens.
Dante, *The Divine Comedy*, trans. C. H. Sisson, ed. D. Higgins.
Homer, *The Iliad*, trans. A. Verity, ed. B. Graziosi.
Homer, *The Odyssey*, trans. A. Verity, ed. W. Allan.
Lucretius, *On the Nature of the Universe*, trans. R. Melville, ed. D. and P. Fowler.
Milton, John, *Paradise Lost*, ed. S. Orgel and J. Goldberg.
Tasso, Torquato, *The Liberation of Jerusalem*, trans. M. Wickert.
Virgil, *The Eclogues and The Georgics*, trans. C. Day Lewis, ed. R. O. A. M. Lyne.
Virgil, *Aeneid*, trans. F. Ahl, ed. E. Fantham.

A CHRONOLOGY OF MARCO GIROLAMO VIDA

*c.*1480–5 Born in Cremona as Marcantonio Vida.

1492 First voyage of Christopher Columbus.

*c.*1505 Vida enters the Order of Canons Regular of St John Lateran, adopting the name Marco Girolamo.

1513 Death of Pope Julius II, lamented by Vida in a pastoral poem, *Quercens*; Giovanni de' Medici elected to the papacy as Leo X.

*c.*1518 Leo X commissions Vida to write an epic poem in Latin on the life of Christ; Vida made prior of San Silvestro in Monte Corno, near Frascati.

1519 Death of Emperor Maximilian I; Charles V elected Holy Roman Emperor.

1520 Leo X condemns Martin Luther's *Ninety-Five Theses* in papal bull *Exsurge Domine*.

1521 Martin Luther condemned as a heretic at the Diet of Worms; capture of Belgrade by the Ottoman Turks under Suleiman the Magnificent; death of Pope Leo X.

1522 Adriaan Boeyens elected to the papacy as Adrian VI.

1523 Death of Pope Adrian VI; Giulio de' Medici elected to the papacy as Clement VII.

1525 Charles V defeats French forces of François I at the Battle of Pavia.

1526 Suleiman the Magnificent defeats Hungarian army at the Battle of Mohács; Jacopo Sannazaro's *De partu Virginis* published in Naples and later in Rome.

1527 Vida's *De arte poetica*, *De bombyce*, *De ludo scaccorum*, *Hymni*, and *Bucolica* published in Rome; Sack of Rome by troops of Charles V.

1532 Complete version of Ludovico Ariosto's *Orlando Furioso* published in Ferrara.

1533 Vida appointed bishop of Alba by Pope Clement VII.

1534 Death of Pope Clement VII; Alessandro Farnese elected to the papacy as Paul III.

1535 Vida's *Christiados libri sex* published in Cremona.

1542 Vida leads the defence of Alba against French forces.

1545–63 Council of Trent reinforces traditional Catholic teachings.
1550 Vida's *Poemata omnia* published in two volumes in Cremona.
1556 Vida's *Dialogi de rei publicae dignitate* published in Cremona.
1562 Vida's *Constitutiones synodales* published in Cremona.
1566 Vida dies in Alba, and is buried in the cathedral.
1569 Bartolomeo Botta's commentary on Vida's epic published in Pavia.
1764 Vida's *Orationes tres pro Cremonensibus* published in Venice.
2010 Rediscovery of Vida's lost early epic *Felsinais*.

SUMMARY AND BIBLICAL CORRESPONDENCES

BOOK ONE

1–14	Invocation to the Holy Spirit
15–31	Christ arrives in Jerusalem [Matthew 21:1; Mark 11:1; Luke 19:28]
32–89	Christ prophesies his death to the disciples, and rebukes Peter [Matthew 16:21–3, 17:22–3, 20:17–19, 26:2; Mark 8:31–3, 10:32–4; Luke 9:22, 18:31–4]
90–120	Dinner at the house of Zacchaeus [Luke 19:2–10]; the death of Lazarus is announced
121–235	Satan calls an infernal council, instructing his agents to inflame the priests with hatred
236–99	Christ restores Lazarus to life [John 11:1–46]
300–67	Visit to the house of Simon; conversion of Mary, the unchaste woman [Matthew 26:7–13; Mark 6:55–6, 14:3–9; Luke 7:36–50; John 11:2, 12:3–8]
368–74	Healing of the sick, blind, deaf, mute, paralysed, and possessed [Matthew 4:23–4, 8:16, 9:35, 11:5, 15:50–1; Mark 1:32–4, 3.10–11, 7:32–7, 8:22–5, 9:17–29; Luke 4:33–41, 6:17–19, 7:21–2, 9:42, 11:14, 17:12–19, 18:35–43; John 9:1–7]
375–435	Rapturous reception of Christ in Jerusalem [Matthew 21:8–11; Mark 11:8–10; Luke 19:37–8; John 12:12–18]
436–510	Healing water of the Sheep Pool (Pool of Bethesda); healing of Jethro [John 5:2–15]
511–50	Expulsion of vendors from the temple [Matthew 21:12–13; Mark 11:15–17; Luke 19:45–6; John 2:13–16]
551–81	Christ prophesies the destruction of the temple [Matthew 24:1–2, 26:61; Mark 13:1–2, 15:29; Luke 21:5–6]
582–643	Ekphrasis: the story of Creation [Genesis 1:1–25]
644–673	Ekphrasis (continued): the creation of Adam and Eve, and their temptation [Genesis 1:27–8, 2:7, 2:8–25, 3:1–24]
674–92	Ekphrasis (continued): the souls of the righteous awaiting salvation
693–710	Ekphrasis (continued): the Flood [Genesis 6–9], Abraham and Isaac [Genesis 22:1–13], Joseph sold into slavery [Genesis 37:3–36]

711–24	Ekphrasis (continued): Moses and the bronze serpent [Numbers 21:4–9; John 3:14]; the self-wounding pelican
725–92	Christ spares the woman taken in adultery [John 8:3–11]
793–829	Christ complains of his enemies among the Jews; teachings on food, ritual purity, and sacrifice [Matthew 5:17–18, 15:1–20; Mark 7:1–23; Luke 11:37–40]
830–89	Dialogue between Christ and God the Father on Mount Tabor; the betrayal of Judas prophesied
890–930	Prophecy of the spread of God's kingdom on earth and the conversion of Rome
931–63	The Transfiguration [Matthew 17:1–9; Mark 9:2–9; Luke 9:28–36]

BOOK TWO

1–21	Jesus' enemies among the leaders and priests pass an anxious night
22–72	Satan's devils inspire Jesus' enemies with hatred and attempt to subvert the disciples
73–118	Judas Iscariot is persuaded by the Devil (disguised as his kinsman Jora) to betray Christ [Luke 22:3; John 13:2, 13:27]
119–32	The narrator addresses Judas, urging him to abandon his betrayal
133–215	Meeting of the Sanhedrin [Matthew 26:3–4; Mark 14:1–2; John 11:47–8]; testimony of Nicodemus
216–52	Speech of Caiaphas urging the destruction of Jesus as sacrifice of one for all [John 11:49–52, 18:14]
253–72	Judas offers to betray Christ for thirty pieces of silver [Matthew 26:14–15; Mark 14:10–11; Luke 22:4–6]
273–84	Feast of Passover [Mark 14:1; Luke 22:1, 22:7; John 11:55]
285–315	Arrival of the twelve tribes of Israel in Jerusalem
316–31	Invocation to angels to assist with recital of catalogue
332–529	Catalogue of territories from which the Jews flocked to Jerusalem for Passover, ending with prophecy of the future career of St Paul
530–606	Preparations for the Last Supper [Matthew 26:17–19; Mark 14:12–16; Luke 22:8–13]
607–41	Simon the singer tells of Moses' parting of the Red Sea [Exodus 14:15–31], the manna in the wilderness [Exodus

16:1–35; John 6:30–5, 6:48–51, 6:58], the striking of water from the rock [Exodus 17:1–7; Numbers 20:1–13], and the offering of Melchizedek [Genesis 14:18–20]

642–70 The Last Supper; consecration of bread and wine [Matthew 26:26–8; Mark 14:22–4; Luke 22:14–20]

671–9 Christ washes the feet of the disciples [John 13:2–15]

680–730 Christ prophesies his betrayal by Judas [Matthew 26:21–4; Mark 14:18–21; Luke 22:21–2; John 6:70–1, 13:18–27]; Peter swears vengeance and loyalty [Matthew 26:33–5; Mark 14:29–31; Luke 22:33–4; John 13:36–8]

731–64 Christ's agony in the Garden of Gethsemane [Matthew 26:36–45; Mark 14:32–41; Luke 22:39–46]

765–851 Judas betrays Christ [Matthew 26:47–50; Mark 14:43–6; Luke 22:47–8; John 18:3–5]; Peter cuts off the ear of Malchus [Matthew 26:51–3; Mark 14:47; Luke 22:50–1; John 18:10–11]

852–65 Indignant address by the narrator to God on Jesus' arrest

866–74 The disciples flee [Matthew 26:56; Mark 14:50]

875–917 Jesus is led before Caiaphas and declares his divine nature [Matthew 26:57–66; Mark 14:53–65; Luke 22:54, 22:66–71]

918–63 Peter denies Christ three times [Matthew 26:69–75; Mark 14:66–72; Luke 22:54–62; John 18:15–18, 18:25–7]

964–1001 Christ is brought to Pontius Pilate [Matthew 27:2; Mark 15:1; Luke 23:1; John 18:28]

BOOK THREE

1–8 News of Christ's arrest spreads; ominous feelings of Mary

9–52 Joseph sets out for Jerusalem and meets John; they decide to seek an audience with Pilate

53–72 Joseph introduces himself to Pilate and pleads Christ's innocence

73–96 Pilate receives Joseph graciously and wonders at Jesus' appearance; he instructs Joseph to speak

97–104 Joseph hesitates, but is encouraged by John

105–39 Joseph recounts his own ancestry and that of Christ

140–58 Prophecy of the future greatness of the offspring of Mary; divine instructions for her marriage

159–204 Mary's suitors gather; Joseph attends as an elderly kinsman but is chosen as husband

205–53 Mary proclaims her commitment to virginity; Joseph receives a divine command and agrees to live with Mary like a father and daughter

254–90 Joseph finds Mary illuminated by supernatural light and in a trance; he asks her what has happened

291–396 Mary tells the story of the Annunciation [Luke 1:26–38]

397–464 Mary's story is confirmed to Joseph by the appearance of an angel; Joseph understands the fulfilment of ancient prophecies [Matthew 1:19–24]

465–504 Mary and Joseph visit her kinswoman Elizabeth, who hails Mary as the Mother of God [Luke 1:39–55]

505–15 Portents foretelling the birth and destiny of Christ

516–40 Mary is tended by an angel; Joseph looks forward to the birth of Christ and prophesies a new Golden Age

541–70 Mary and Joseph travel to Bethlehem for the census [Luke 2:1–5]; they find shelter among animals in a humble building [Luke 2:7]

571–94 The birth of Christ [Luke 2:7]

595–633 Shepherds arrive to pay homage to the child; one recounts how the news was brought to them [Luke 2:8–16]

634–46 The child is cared for by his parents and given the name Jesus [Luke 2:21]

647–83 Purification in the temple [Luke 2:22–4]; portents of the divinity of Christ

684–738 Christ acknowledged by Simeon (*Nunc Dimittis*) [Luke 2:25–35]

739–99 Arrival and adoration of the Magi (three kings from the East) [Matthew 2:1–12]

800–5 Herod orders the massacre of the Innocents [Matthew 2:16]

806–70 Joseph is warned in a dream to flee; flight into Egypt [Matthew 2:13–15]

871–91 Massacre of the Innocents [Matthew 2:16–18]

892–918 Joseph, Mary, and Jesus return from Egypt [Matthew 2:19–21]; unusual childhood of Christ

919–79 The child Jesus teaches the elders in the temple [Luke 2:42–7]

980–1002 Christ turns water into wine at the wedding at Cana [John 2:1–10]

1003–20 Joseph concludes his speech; Pilate asks John to continue the story

BOOK FOUR

1–19	John is hesitant at first; simile of the eagle; finally he begins to speak
20–58	John expounds the mystery of the Word [John 1:1–14]
59–79	Narrative of the fall of the rebel angels [Revelation 12:7–9]
80–122	The Creation of Man; the Fall and consequences of Original Sin [Genesis 1:27–8, 2:7, 2:8–25, 3:1–24]
123–45	Prayer of the souls of the righteous under the earth
146–54	God resolves to sacrifice his Son to atone for human sins
155–203	John the Baptist foretells the coming of Christ and a new Golden Age [Matthew 3:1–12; Mark 1:4–8; Luke 3:3–17; John 1:15–27]
204–38	Christ is baptized in the River Jordan by John the Baptist [Matthew 3:13–17; Mark 1:9–11; Luke 3:21–2]
239–74	Christ chooses his twelve disciples [Matthew 4:18–22; Mark 1:16–20, 3.14–19; Luke 6:13–16]
275–314	Miracles and healings performed by Christ
315–42	Christ raises from the dead the son of the widow of Nain [Luke 7:11–15]
343–8	Christ raises Jairus' daughter from the dead [Matthew 9:18–19, 9:23–5; Mark 5:22–4, 5:35–43; Luke 8:41–2, 8:49–56]
349–88	Feeding of the Five Thousand [Matthew 14:14–21; Mark 6:33–44; Luke 9:12–17; John 6:5–14]
389–98	Christ curses the fig tree [Matthew 21:19–21; Mark 11:12–14, 11:20–1]
399–438	Christ walks on water and stills a storm [Matthew 8:23–7, 14:22–33; Mark 4:36–41, 6:45–51; Luke 8:22–5; John 6:16–21]
439–531	Healing of a demoniac and destruction of the Gadarene swine [Matthew 8:28–33; Mark 5:1–19; Luke 8:26–36]
532–64	Christ instructs the disciples to heal the sick and raise the dead [Matthew 10:1, 10:8; Mark 4:15, 6:7, 6:13; Luke 9:1–6, 10:9]
565–71	Christ reads the minds of friends and enemies [Matthew 9:4; Luke 5:22, 6:8, 11:17; John 6:61, 16:19]
572–97	A woman is healed by touching the hem of Christ's cloak [Matthew 9:20–2; Mark 5:25–34; Luke 8:43–8]
598–655	Death of John the Baptist [Matthew 14:1–12; Mark 6:21–9]; Jesus is tempted in the wilderness by the Devil [Matthew 4:1–11; Mark 1:13; Luke 4:1–13]

656–73 Jesus refuses to take revenge on the people of Sidon [Luke 9:52–6]
674–89 Christ associates with sinners [Matthew 9:10–13; Mark 2:15–17; Luke 5:29–32, 7:34, 15:1–10, 19:7]
690–703 Parable of the Good Shepherd [Matthew 18:12–13; Luke 15:3–7]
704–15 Christ and the woman at the well [John 4:5–30]
716–23 Christ blesses the young [Matthew 18:1–6, 18:10, 19:14–15; Mark 9:36–7, 10:13–16; Luke 9:47–8, 18:15–17]
724–58 The disciples dispute vainly about their own precedence [Mark 9:33–5; Luke 9:46–8, 22:24–6]; the mother of James and John asks Christ for special treatment for her sons [Matthew 20:20–8; Mark 10:35–44]
759–79 Christ conceals his powers and refuses offers of earthly kingdoms [John 6:15]
780–816 John asserts that Christ is being wrongly persecuted by the Jews; he is not sacrilegious but is fulfilling ancient prophecies
817–43 Christ foretells the exile and sufferings of the disciples [Matthew 24:9; Mark 13:9; John 16:2–4]; he insists on poverty [Matthew 6:25–32, 10:9–10; Mark 6:8–9, 10:21–5; Luke 10:4, 12:33]
844–78 More disciples flock to Jesus; he preaches from a boat [Matthew 13:1–3; Mark 3:9–10, 4:1; Luke 5:1–3]
879–967 Teachings of Christ [Matthew 5–7; Luke 6:20–49, 12:1–34]
968–80 The Lord's Prayer [Matthew 6:9–13; Luke 11:2–4]
981–1024 Christ foretells the Last Judgement [Matthew 13:41–3, 13:49–50, 24:29–31; Mark 13:24–7; Luke 21:20–33; John 5:25–9]; simile of the sheep and the goats [Matthew 25:32–3]
1025–41 John recalls Jesus' teaching and declares the present age to be fortunate in having heard the voice of God directly [Matthew 13:16–17; Luke 10:23–4]
1042–7 John's speech is cut short by the interruption of an unruly crowd

BOOK FIVE

1–12 Pilate is inclined to spare Jesus and dismisses the crowd [John 18:38]
13–29 Judas regrets his betrayal and returns the thirty pieces of silver; the priests laugh at him [Matthew 27:3–5]

30–54 Monologue of Judas, who resolves to commit suicide
55–81 Judas initially hesitates, before hanging himself from a tree [Matthew 27:5]
82–100 Pilate invites the Jews to acknowledge Jesus as their king [John 19:14–15]
101–52 Speech of Annas [John 18:13–24], condemning Christ's claim to divine authority and the behaviour of Christ and his disciples
153–82 Pilate is unmoved, but the temper of the crowd rises [Luke 23:4, 23:13–22; John 19:12]
183–99 Pilate passes Christ over to Herod, but Christ says nothing and is returned to Pilate [Luke 23:7–9]
200–24 The narrator invokes the Holy Spirit for support in telling of Christ's sufferings; he addresses Christ, decrying human unworthiness
225–54 Pilate offers to free Christ, but the crowd insists that Barabbas be freed instead [Matthew 27:15–18, 27:20–1; Mark 15:6–15; Luke 23:16–19; John 18:38–40]
255–81 Pilate hands over Christ to be flogged, hoping to spare him from death [Matthew 27:26; Mark 15:15; John 19:1]
282–99 Pilate's wife recounts a dream in which nature mourns for a lamb and a voice gives orders to spare Christ [Matthew 27:19]
300–25 Pilate threatens the Jews, but Satan sends the monster Fear from hell to attack Pilate
326–47 The crowd warns that Christ is a threat to Roman authority, and Pilate capitulates [Luke 23:2, 23:5, 23:24–5; John 19:12, 19:15–16]
348–68 Pilate washes his hands and denies responsibility; the Jews accept responsibility for Christ's death [Matthew 27:24–5]
369–400 Christ is mocked and abused by his captors [Matthew 8:20, 27:27–30; Mark 15:17–20; Luke 9:58, 22:64, 23:11; John 19:2–3]
401–19 The cross, a means of executing criminals, is prepared for Christ; it is now held in honour as a symbol of Christ's sacrifice
420–47 Christ carries the cross [John 19:17]
448–80 God and the angels watch from heaven
481–93 Christ's disciples have abandoned him; simile of the scattered sheep [Matthew 26:31; Mark 14:27; John 16:32]

494–503 Christ calls upon his Father [Matthew 27:46; Mark 15:34]
504–88 Muster of the angels, intending to save Christ
589–615 Ekphrasis of the gates of heaven, depicting the defeat of the rebel angels
616–47 God despatches Clemency to halt the advance of the angels
648–702 God rebukes the angels and explains his purpose
703–20 Christ is nailed to the cross, and placed between two criminals [Matthew 27:38; Mark 15:27; Luke 23:32–3; John 19:18]
721–42 The narrator addresses the Jews, contrasting their treatment of Christ with God's historic kindnesses towards them [Luke 13:34–5]
743–57 Christ hangs on the cross; simile of the morning star
758–814 Mary arrives, learns of Christ's capture, and sees the cross
815–45 Mary is petrified by the sight of Christ on the cross; she is comforted by Christ, who entrusts her to John [John 19:25–7]
846–93 Lament of Mary at the cross
894–912 The soldiers mock Christ, saying that he cannot save himself [Matthew 27:42; Mark 15:31; Luke 23:35]; he asks for forgiveness for them [Luke 23:34]
913–39 The criminals being crucified on either side of Christ quarrel [Matthew 27:44; Mark 15:32; Luke 23:39–41]; the one who proclaims Christ's innocence is promised a place in heaven [Luke 23:43]
940–51 The dying Christ requests a drink, and is given tainted wine [Matthew 27:34, 27:48; Mark 15:23, 15:36; Luke 23:36; John 19:28–30]
952–8 The attendants play dice for Christ's clothing [Matthew 27:35; Mark 15:24; Luke 23:34; John 19:23–4]
959–79 The sky grows dark [Matthew 27:45; Mark 15:33: Luke 23:44–5], heaven thunders, and the earth shakes [Matthew 27:51]
980–95 Fear strikes the Jews [Luke 23:48]; the veil of the temple is rent in two [Matthew 27:51; Mark 15:38; Luke 23:45], and the pillars break; Christ utters his last words and dies [Matthew 27:50; Mark 15:37; Luke 23:46; John 19:30]

BOOK SIX

1–30 Joseph of Arimathea asks Pilate for Christ's body for burial [Matthew 27:57–8; Mark 15:43–5; Luke 23:50–2; John 19:38]

31–67 The soldiers hasten the deaths of the two men crucified with Jesus; Longinus pierces Christ's side with a lance [John 19:31–7]

68–76 Deposition from the cross [Luke 23:53]

77–98 Mourning over the dead Christ; Mary holds her son (*Pietà*)

99–109 Guards posted at the tomb to prevent theft of the body [Matthew 27:62–6]

110–20 Invocation by the narrator to the Holy Spirit; anticipation of the Resurrection

121–235 The Harrowing of Hell

236–66 The souls of the righteous rejoice at Christ's appearance [Psalms 16:8–11; Acts 2:25–8]

267–93 The souls of the wicked are consigned to hell, those of the righteous transported to heaven

294–312 The Resurrection; simile of the phoenix

313–48 The women go to the tomb, and find it empty; an angel announces the Resurrection [Matthew 28:1–7; Mark 16:2–7; Luke 24:1–7; John 20:1, 20:11–13]

349–68 Mary Magdalene views the carvings on the tomb, which depict the story of Jonah and the whale [Jonah 1:17–2:10; Matthew 12:40]

369–91 The resurrected Christ appears to Mary Magdalene [Matthew 28:9; Mark 16:9; John 20:14–17]

392–404 The report of the Resurrection spreads, despite attempts to suppress it [Matthew 28:11–15]

405–24 Mourning of the disciples [Mark 16:10]

425–40 The women bring news of the Resurrection to the disciples [Matthew 28:8; Mark 16:10; Luke 24:9–10; John 20:18]; some are uncertain until Christ himself appears among them [Matthew 28:17–18; Mark 16:11–14, Luke 24:11, 24:36–48; John 20:19–20]

441–86 Thomas doubts the report of the Resurrection, despite Peter's assurances [John 20:24–5]

487–559 Cleophas tells of his encounter with Christ on the road to Emmaus [Mark 16:12; Luke 24:13–35]; parable of the wicked husbandmen [Matthew 21:33–41; Mark 12:1–9; Luke 20:9–16]

560–95 Thomas remains doubtful until Christ appears in person and reveals his wounds [John 20:26–9]

596–628 Christ appears to the disciples while they are fishing; Peter recognizes him and jumps from the boat [John 21:1–8]

629–83 Christ gives instructions to his disciples, and entrusts authority to Peter [Matthew 16:18–19, 28:19–20; Mark 16:15–18; Luke 24:49; John 21:15–17]

684–707 Christ is received into heaven [Mark 16:19; Luke 24:51; Acts 1:9–11]; simile of Roman triumph

708–31 The Instruments of the Passion are carried to heaven with Christ

732–800 Hymn of the disciples

801–12 The disciples remain afraid and await further divine support

813–97 Christ asks his Father for aid for the disciples [John 17:9–26]; the Father agrees and prophesies the spread of the gospel [Matthew 24:14] and the coming of a Golden Age (and Vida's own poem)

898–972 Pentecost: tongues of flame stand over the disciples, and they speak in different languages [Acts 2:1–18]

973–86 The disciples spread news of the gospel and establish Christian rites throughout the world [Mark 16:20]; the Golden Age begins

THE EPIC OF CHRIST

BOOK ONE

YOU who fill with your power the sea, the earth, and the sky, nurturing Spirit,* allow me by your aid to tell of the king twice-born,* who, from the seat of his Father above, came down into the swollen womb of an untouched virgin and drew mortal breath as a boy, so that by his death he might avenge the human race and rescue it from the darkness of the cruel prison, and bring the spirits of the righteous to heaven.* In wretchedness the earth bore him as he died willingly for human transgressions, and from the height of heaven the sun felt shame to look upon it and terrified the world with unaccustomed darkness. With you as my leader, let me speak in worthy strains, mortal as I am, of things immortal; and at times let me raise my eyes to heaven and receive the celestial light, and unroll the plans of the supreme Father and the causes of so terrible a death.

Now the goal of Christ's death and the end of his labours was at hand. For this reason, he was making his way in full knowledge to the city of Jerusalem, returning from the furthest borders of Phoenicia. A vast number of companions, both young and old, followed him freely, lured by the report of his deeds to gather from all sides. Whether he made his journey through sprawling cities or was passing among deserted mountains, they attached themselves to him in countless numbers, ready to follow his commands wherever he might lead them. New arrivals could constantly be seen thronging to him, just like the River Po at first goes forth from the summit of pine-clad Monte Viso,* furrowing the fertile fields with its tiny stream; after that it rises more and more, gaining in strength as it flows, and roaring in broad spate it spreads itself out, victorious over all around. Different currents add their power from this side and that with auxiliary waves, and the river no longer confines itself within its own course, until in a whirl it bursts into the sea through multiple mouths.

It was at this time that Christ drew aside out of the total number of his followers twelve companions whom he had previously selected to preserve the memory of his great works and be witnesses to his labours. When he had called them apart into a secluded grove, leaning against a towering cedar he spoke to them with an expression of great sadness, sending forth a sigh from the very depth of his heart:

'We have come to the end,* my friends; I have completed the lifetime allotted to me on earth. Now the awful day is approaching and the spirits of the righteous are waiting for me. Therefore I have come up willingly, see, to the hostile city of Jerusalem. There the terrible torments of a disfiguring death are being devised for me; now against me alone the bloodthirsty band of priests is conspiring, though I have done nothing to deserve it, as I myself have so often foretold in full knowledge, revealing the whole story to you. But I shall go, and by my death I shall expiate our ancestors' every sin.

'You, first father Adam, are piling these sufferings upon me; for it was you yourself who took the sweet fruit,* but now *I* must atone for your dark deeds. Yet when the light of the third day has driven the darkness from the world, I shall be called back to the sky above, with the bloodstains washed away.

'For you too, who have never grown weary of our association, bitter deaths await you. Be brave, and together with me put before your love of the light of mortal existence, all of you, the everlasting honour of immortal life. This is not the home that is given to you, this is not your true abode.* The gleaming temples of heaven on high are calling you, the realms dotted with stars, where there is untroubled peace and longed-for rest from your labours.* There is your home, there your country:* hurry there joyfully along the narrow pathway, and there make your dwelling place.'

So he spoke. But his companions, their eyes downcast, stood rooted to the spot with sorrowful hearts and pondered many sad things. Then Peter, the eldest, did not hold his tongue or refrain from speech, and with such words as these he addressed the deity imploringly:

'Son of God, what overwhelming force of heaven is making you, god as you are, willing to settle for a cruel death on behalf of someone else, or give yourself up freely to certain danger? Come (since you can do everything, and it is not for nothing that you have a Father who moves the stars),* accomplish instead without harm to yourself what now remains for you to do, without hating the light and disregarding your safety. I pray you, discard at once these thoughts and this intention.* Take pity on yourself, take pity on your people, and do not willingly cast us aside, for we shall follow you wherever you go.'

Thus he spoke; but the hero rebuked him with such words as these:

'Are you not ashamed, in your perpetual lack of wisdom, to be always considering mortal things, your eyes fogged with cloud and with no place in you for the things of heaven? Can't you ever leave the realm of pointless worries? Are *these* the resolutions my toils have taught you? This is not the time for such counsels, nor for such guidance:* my Father is pressing on me with no gentle commands. But you, despising mortal matters, bear and endure in your heart like men your harsh toils,* all of you. Forgetting humankind, raise your minds on high to heaven, and when mortals loose their tongues in abuse against you, burdening your names with false charges, rejoice and bear it with a steadfast heart, and joyfully despise the unearned humiliation. From this call yourselves fortunate, since assured rewards await you* and from this your boundless glory springs.'

Saying this, he gloomily made his way into the high mountains. With him went his companions, ready to face all sufferings with their king and feeling resentment at the young man's unjust lot. And now he proceeded to the city of palm-bearing Jericho. He was received in the house of Zacchaeus, where dinner was waiting ready. Zacchaeus had once had a keen love of amassing boundless wealth by any means, fair or foul; but after receiving illumination on the arrival of his guest, he began to give back in atonement the things he had unlawfully acquired, restoring to each their own and sharing the rest with the poor: so many heaped-up talents of worked and unworked gold!

Here suddenly grim news struck their ears,* bringing unhappy tidings, and pierced their spirits with a bitter report. Not far away, Lazarus ruled over Bethany, a man rich in resources and distinguished for his descent from a long line of kings. His father had once tamed the vast shores of Syria and had brought the captured cities under his control by force. No one was a more genial host to visitors than Lazarus; his home was freely open to all, night and day.* Very often Christ himself felt no qualms at going there too, and frequently he took pleasure in the hospitality of that welcoming home, casting aside the concealing cloud and revealing his divinity. So when he heard that Lazarus was dying and, stricken with a harsh illness, was at his last gasp and was already struggling, as it were, before the gates of death, he shed tears and spoke to his companions as follows: 'Let's go there. Our friend must be called back at once from death to the light, should the supreme Father himself only hear me and be willing to show his power in this case, as he often has done.' He spoke, and directed his steps towards the city of Bethany. A huge band of companions went with him, and straightaway countless multitudes attached themselves to the company, in their eagerness to see.

Meanwhile, far away, the ruler of the world of gloom,* the monster of ill omen, was all too well aware that the day was now close at hand when the mightiest avenger,* on the orders of his Father on high, would penetrate the regions of hell to bring aid to the spirits of the dead and lay waste to the hidden halls. In his anxiety he turned his thoughts in every direction* to try to find some means of averting this disaster from his kingdom, and he schemed to engineer the death of God. This one concern settled deep in his mind, and this single fixation frequently resurfaced. In his folly he had not seen that the young man had been sent down from heaven for this very purpose: to atone willingly, by going to meet death, for the fault of the people of old and our ancestors' every transgression.

Immediately he gave orders that his fearsome brethren and the whole race of his people be summoned to the entrance of the palace in frightful council. And behold, a trumpet gave the mighty signal,* at which the yawning abode, gloomy and gaping on all sides, suddenly resounded in its sightless caverns. The unfathomable caves resounded, and far off the earth was made to tremble in its gravid body. Straightaway the whole race rushed to the gates, and there they were, the assorted twin-bodied freaks of the horde that shuns the light. As far as the groin their appearance is human,* but it ends squalidly in the form of a snake, with a tail coiling in vast spirals.* Some fashion with their horrid bodies Gorgons and Sphinxes; others Centaurs and Hydras and fire-spewing Chimaeras; a hundred others Scyllas and polluting Harpies, and all the many hideous forms conjured up by the human imagination.*

Overtopping them all with his flaming head stood the hundred-handed master of Erebus himself, his hundred arms flailing, and belching streams of fire from his hundredfold throats. All of them exhaled noisome smoke and dark fire from their lewd lips, their eyes, and their enormous nostrils; from the heads of all, in place of hair, hung twisting snakes,* writhing and wrapping themselves around their necks in knots. In their hands were torches glowing red and barbed tridents, with which they thrust down the souls of the wicked and force them into the flames. Equally there were gathered there, racing from the different corners of the earth, those who wander over every land to rouse people to crime, who deceive mortal hearts with a whole variety of illusions and cajole them into forgetting what is right. Present too were those with power over the winds and storms, the cloud-wandering race, set in no fixed location but accustomed to wander in the storm clouds' midnight.

And so they assembled, with eager spirits and equipped with resources,* all of them together as one. With a babel of bellowing the palace of gloom resounded within, until the king, his black hand armed with three-pronged fire, began to speak as follows in the midst of the throng:

'Princes of Hell, you race who rose in cloudless heaven, whom once, together with me, the pitiless king above cast down from the sky and thrust here with his blazing bolt, while he was taking care of his kingdom and in his envy was thoroughly stricken with fear for his sceptre, shunning a rival. What battles we fought throughout heaven, and with what hatred the struggle was waged then on both sides—this is well known and must be held in memory.

'He has power over the stars, and occupies more than a fair share of heaven, and exacts cruel punishments from the race that hates him. In place of the stars, in place of the unclouded light, he has given us wastelands rough with decay* and dwellings deprived of the sun, and he has ordered us in the depths of darkness to torment the ungentle souls of humanity. It is a rule in which there can be no pleasure: no more is it granted us to aspire to the court of heaven above. With a vast barrier the vast earth shuts us in; our share of the palace of heaven has been allotted to mankind. And that's not enough: once again he is setting arms in motion, and he is stirring up further wars against us and is even driving us from the realms of the deep.

'This is why he has sent down a young man from the fortress of heaven, either his Son or one of the winged brotherhood. And now he will be here:* relying on celestial arms, he will bring destruction to this seat and will open up the realms below and will take away from our world the souls conceded to us. Perhaps, if we don't mount a vigorous resistance, he will put us too in tight chains and will lead us in bonds to heaven in victory as he celebrates his triumph—and throughout the sky the heavenly beings will mock us in our captivity.

'Yet he, although he has put on mortal limbs as a being subject to death, is nonetheless invulnerable to our weapons. To be sure, I have often gone up to him, and pressing him fearlessly face to face I have made trial of him with my snares—in vain (this fact did not escape me, nor do I perceive such things now for the first time). What appearances, what faces, did I not change myself into to approach him, to no effect? Always he himself drove me off, not relying on any weapons, nor using his strength, but simply by repeating the incantations of the ancient prophets he escaped my trials, bringing them to nothing, along with my trickery and all my force.

'Therefore I shall reveal to you the resolution which is now rising within me.* He is embarking on a journey to the ancient stronghold of Jerusalem, despite the fact that he is hated by the leaders of that mighty city. Indeed, the priests, who loathe him with immeasurable hatred, are setting traps for him, so far as the resources of each of them allow. They are concerned for the religion of their ancient forefathers, and their aim is to overpower him with the sword when he least expects it and to punish him with death, since he has instituted new rituals and new sacraments throughout the cities and is daring to revoke the old laws. This is where your help is needed—see, the time has now come for the matter to be accomplished! Go, all of you, and inflame those men against him with greater hatred; sound notes both true and false, and secretly breathe corrupting poison into their minds. Let them not be prevailed upon and forget their anger and lay aside their harsh feelings, but with ever greater savagery, driven on by your bitter goads, may they never let go until the slaughter has been achieved. And yet, if someone could ensnare and lead astray by deception one of his own twelve companions, the matter would be accomplished and all fear completely removed. Cast off delay! Bring help to our unstable fortunes! Now there is need for hidden snares, now is the time to use your strength.'*

Scarcely were the words out of his mouth, and already the devisers of wickedness were rushing around on all sides carrying out his orders. From every gate they burst in all directions, while the hidden depths of the earth trembled at the uproar. They straddled the winds, they beat their snake-haired wings through the dark void, and they pressed on to the lands. Not in so thick a cloud do the flower-gathering bees swarm through the air aloft in the cloudless summer when the cloud-scattering North Wind and dripping South Wind cease, whenever strife arises among the bee-kings and they advance into savage battle with opposing standards. Woe to the lands, to the regions of the earth, on which the terrible cohort alights! How great a ruin will it bring to the nations!

And now the hero, the true offspring of God,* was reaching the end of his journey, with a great throng accompanying him, and was in close range of the walls of Bethany. There he spotted sorrowful sisters tearing their hair as they bore the final offerings to their brother's tomb: these were the spinster Martha, and Magdalene, so called from the name of her ancestral city Magdala. He advanced and made his way towards the tomb. As soon as Martha, in the depths of her sorrow, saw him, she left her companions and her brother's tomb and went to meet him with great reverence as he approached. Then her sister followed her, and the eyes of both were damp with tears, immersed as they were in their womanly mourning: 'How glad we are to receive you at last, after the death of our beloved brother! How often he called upon you, august guest, as the chill of icy death crept over him! I do believe that if some chance had brought you to us then, he would even now be drawing the breath of life. And even now—since the ruler of shining Olympus* refuses you nothing—all hope has not been completely taken from us.'

These were their prayers. As they spoke, their companions filled the whole place with their grieving and every corner resounded with their sorrowful lamentations. But the hero, consoling them with friendly words in their sadness,* promised his help, reassuring them that their brother would return in a moment, safe and sound, to the light of the world above, though the sun had not looked upon him for four days now, since he had been swallowed up in the jaws of the earth.

The rumour of this spread rapidly through the whole city; the report seemed to everyone unbelievable and amazing. From all sides everybody came running from the nearby mountains in their eagerness to see, and crowded tightly into every space. They came to the tomb, where the young men stood round in a huddle. The hero himself, in the middle, stretching out his hands and raising his eyes to heaven, was motionless in prayer and called silently upon his Father to hear his supplication. They watched him in silence as he prayed, and gazed intently to see what commands he would give, what signs he would make, and how the matter would turn out. Twice the colour drained from his whole face; twice with panting heart he groaned and shook his noble head with a nod. And look! The doors of the tomb suddenly seemed to tremble. Immediately everyone's blood froze solid in sudden terror, and a chill ran through the innermost depths of their hearts. Then at last the god poured out these words to heaven:

'Supreme Father, you have never refused any prayers of mine, whatever I ask for; yet for this favour I shall forever give you thanks. The assembled company has seen how great is your power, the thronging crowds have seen it. But you servants, make haste and uncover the marble tomb: take away the enormous stone and loosen the man's wrappings.'

His instructions met with no delay. The fastenings of the tomb were opened. In a great press the spectators pushed forward, struck dumb with fear, and peered in and saw the misshapen corpse, and could scarcely bring themselves to believe that it was moving without any compulsion. There was no delay: called upon three times by the voice of his friend who cried out to him, Lazarus got up, and spoke, and drew in the air of heaven.* The people were stunned, all of them: it was not enough to see him or hear him speaking just once, as he recounted everything in order in the midst of the throng—what he had experienced at the very point of death; with what intensity of pain his soul had left his earthly limbs after a long struggle, thrust out by the force of impending death; what faces he had seen as he died, the dire features of Furies terrifying him close at hand, and their angry threats, so that the winged attendants sent from the starry citadel of heaven could scarcely keep these ravening creatures from their depredations by their aid. He told too of the punishments for sins and the joyful rewards of the righteous,* the judgement that wretched souls must undergo, and the everlasting fires in the black furnaces.

When all this had been accomplished, the god entered the nearby house of Simon, whom he had once rescued from illness and restored to his former health when his limbs were scarred all over with ulcers. While he graciously reclined at the table of his grateful friend, in the midst of the leading men of the city, all at once—look!—there entered a figure of remarkable beauty, and sumptuously adorned: a girl, in exotic embroidered garments, the folds of her clothing lavishly replete with sounding silver and interwoven gold. Her head was circled with gems, and a vast band of gold wound around her neck, a necklace heavy with the pearls set into it. Her hair, combed straight, shone with the softness of amber; she had gathered it into knots using intertwining pins. A golden brooch secured the robe that fell from her shoulder, laden with eastern riches and the treasure of the

Ganges.* In the centre of her forehead there flickered a fiery ruby, and numerous strings hung down, threaded with gems—like when the earth joyously opens its bosom to reveal the glory of spring, and in its bounty lets loose its favours from its budding lap.

This woman had once been left an orphan following the loss of both her parents, and as the only child she had come into the inheritance of the ancestral wealth which her father, an exceedingly affluent man, had possessed in limitless quantities. In her childhood, her one passion above all else had been religion and the concern for preserving her chastity. But later on, little by little, as her youth began to heat up with the passing of the years, the lust of sexual attraction, with all its evil promptings, slipped stealthily into her senses and reduced her to a state of subjection to wicked infatuations, altering her mind. Poor girl! No care stood in the way of the loss of her chastity, tossed aside, and appearances and reputation made no difference to her.* All her inhibitions disappeared, her religion was forgotten, and having now reached marriageable age she left her home. She spent her time in the delights of parties and entertainments, and scorning her guardians she burst every restraint, like a ship without oars on the deep of the Aegean: as soon as the breath of the wind has whipped up the waves, it tosses now this way, now that, on the swaying surge, deprived of a pilot and carried wherever the winds and the waves drive it. And now, relying on her wealth, she went round in pursuit of the exquisite pleasure of love affairs with young men in the bloom of life, whenever anyone outdid all others in the attractions of matchless face and figure.

And so, when to her delight she heard that a man of incomparable physique had arrived, whom rumour reported to be a god, she suffered no delay: gripped by eagerness to see him, she was there in a trice. But when her besotted gaze had got a full dose of his glorious face, of the divine splendour of his matchless brow, and of his divine eyes, food fit for the nourishment of burning love, she stiffened and the resolution in her spirit was completely altered: a very different kind of flame took hold in her breast. And look—suddenly, as the breath left her mouth, seven torches were seen to emerge, in the gloomy haze of a black cloud, just as when the final flame of a finished firebrand flees upward, leaving behind only smoke. 'This thing,' said the god, 'this vile Fury with seven heads, had taken possession of the poor woman's mind and was tormenting it.'

Then Mary (for that was her name) was a changed person, no longer that woman who had just come in, the golden folds of her clothing tricked out with silver. She now removed the golden hairband from her head and the necklace from her neck, and stripped off the garments stiff with gold. And now she was filled with self-loathing and was stung by anxieties—decent ones, now. Then she started to beg the god to pardon her, grovelling on her knees like a dog habituated to lying prostrate at its master's table, and she began to kiss his bare feet* and dampen them with her tears, wiping them with the clothing which not so long ago she had worn for very different ends. Then from a marble jewel-box she took out a variety of scents: wild cinnamon and stalks of delicate spikenard, drops of incense and the aroma of fragrant balsam. And leaning forward she caressed his bare soles with the liquid ointment, while a sweet fragrance dispersed into the air. The god received all these things with untroubled composure, saw fit to pardon her, and filled her with friendly advice.

Meanwhile, from the cities situated round about, a horde of invalids could be seen approaching in a great throng. Many of those who came were blind, many were born incurably deaf or unable to speak, and those who could only drag their ailing limbs were carried. Those whom a Fury drove out of their mind,* forgetful of their true selves, the god relieved in person by his aid, and all returned in full health and joyful.

Eventually, departing from this place, he made his way to the stronghold of Jerusalem. Father Noah, sower of the vine,* your offspring Shem is said to have founded this city, once the rains were over and the wide earth ceased to stagnate in vast swamps, and the ample freedom of the boundless ocean had been checked.* Then came those who crushed the native race in war, and called the city after their own name: the Jebusites.* Immediately after this the kings, the bloodline from ancient Judah, subjugated the neighbouring territories far and wide and established their city as the dominant power. Here Solomon as king once founded the temple with barbarian wealth,* when he had overthrown all the altars throughout the lands—a temple sumptuous, huge, its bulk rising up to heaven. Here he transferred tables and sacred altars and bronze basins, and the vestments and apparatus of the old temple, robes steeped in purple dye and stiff with gold.* Then he brought in lamps and platters and hollow incense-holders, and cups and tripods and cauldrons of tawny bronze, and, enclosed within the sacred wooden chest,* the laws and covenants that the Father himself had inscribed on the twin tablets of stone. Here the king and priest of the race, together with all the people, carried the sacred objects and in the prescribed manner poured out the lifeblood of sheep: no other place did the sacrificial victim stain with its blood. It was the custom for the people to come here from all parts three times a year, and the race of Isaac's descendants* performed their special offerings. The hero himself too was in the habit of making his way here frequently.

And now he was proceeding along the packed roads together with many thousands of people, and from here the towers and lofty rooftops of the city could be seen. Joyfully everyone broke off boughs of verdant olive and palm branches from the stem to carry in their hands. In front came the whole band of people on foot, far and wide; behind came a huge mass of people on horseback. In the middle the hero, though not riding on a high-spirited horse with majestic trappings, stood out for his exceptional beauty. In order to teach his companions that his preference was for blessed poverty, the king rode on the back of a four-legged donkey, as the prophets had once foretold.* His head was bare; from his shoulders to his ankles a flowing robe hung down, which once his mother herself had hastily made and given him to wear as a boy, though it had not been worn away by any use or consumed by age. His bare feet were bound in leather sandals. Like this he made his journey, heading towards the city walls.

In front of the city boys and girls all together ran to meet him, their heads adorned with flowers and garlands of different shades. In all their hands were palm branches, and all sang joyful songs in their jubilation and shaded their faces with close-clipped wreaths. Exultantly they vied with each other to get a glimpse of the tranquil features of the god. Then at last they entered the city through the open gates and hailed their king and saviour at close quarters, holding out the rods* in their hands and waving their leafy olive branches. A mighty clamour rose into the sky above them. At this point word suddenly spread and made its way through the whole city. The leaders of the people got up, and far off—look!—they saw, rising to heaven through the air, a cloud of dust. Completely unaware of what was going on, they sought out the causes of so sudden a commotion: who was it that so many thousands were following as their leader, and what was this almighty clamour of people rejoicing? But those who were familiar with the fame of his divinity ran up eagerly to the king, and joined his train and redoubled the acclamation. Wherever he went, see—on all sides they strewed the ground with red-dyed cloth and exotic rugs, and spread out garlands over the streets, adding flowers to them.

Scarcely had he made his way in, when behold, he saw, at the point where two roads met, a densely packed crowd, and a mighty clamour filled his ears; in private astonishment, he checked his footsteps. There was a valley, enclosed on all sides by leafy hills all around, in the midst of which forever stood a pool formed by streams and rain, a source of water all year round. Here the unmarried girls of the prosperous city were in the habit of coming to collect water; likewise the shepherds of old used to drive their animals here to drink, and would refresh their flock with the wholesome waters. For this reason it's said that later generations called it the Sheep Pool.

Here, on certain days, it was customary for there to be a gathering: a crowd would turn up, helpless and afflicted with a whole range of illnesses. For sometimes, in the middle of the pool, a wave seemed to be set in motion with a loud noise, and all at once the sky would be flecked with spray as it was struck by the surge rearing up to heaven. The cause of this motion, however, was generally unknown. Youthful boys and unmarried girls* had previously given distinct portents of it, declaring that they could see a winged boy shining through the air with a billowing cloak and wings gleaming with gold, who descended from heaven and disturbed the calm surface of the pool with both hands, marking his path far and wide as he came down.* He was like the star which the Father of the heavenly beings sends from heaven as a sign to sailors or to warring nations massed in their camps, which hurtles down, flickering with flashing flames far and wide, and the hearts of ignorant mortals shudder.

Therefore the poor invalids, in a close-packed crowd, were gathered around waiting intently for a sign from heaven. They were watching the still waters with their eyes, and kept their ears pricked for every breath of wind, so that immediately upon hearing the sound each one might be the first to rush into the waves and immerse his limbs in the splashing pool. For it was invariably the case that healing from that source was granted not to many, but to the one who had leapt in first as soon as the surface of the water had been disturbed. Just as when young men strive to compete in strength and in swift running in the centre of the flat expanse of an empty plain: they all rouse their spirits* and, having prepared themselves, await the signal. Breathless nerves buffet the hearts within them all, and every one vows he will take first place.

Among these people was one stricken by a long illness in his arms, unable to make use of his arms and feet and indeed all his limbs: this was Jethro.* Once he had had both wealth and splendid ancestral estates, but in order to banish illness from his youthful body he had, alas, trusted too much in false expertise. In investigating every possible course and trying out the efficacy of medical aid, the poor man added unfair poverty to the illness which had now settled permanently in the inmost part of his bones, right down to the quick. And now he had spent almost forty years in grief, assailed by countless ailments and by hunger. When the son of the king of starry Olympus saw him at close quarters, he spoke like this, with a gentle countenance: 'Unhappy man, what lingering delay keeps you here alone, haunting these banks in vain beside the water so effective against grim diseases, when all the others depart from here straightaway rejoicing, and forgetting their toils recover their accustomed strength in their restored body?'

On hearing these words, Jethro replied, dampening his cheeks with a plentiful shower of tears: 'This isn't the fault of the water; the power of the spring is not unfair to me. But while I am waiting for the movement of the jumping water, others hurl themselves before me headlong into the pool with a leap at the sound, and because I need assistance from other people, no one sees fit to dip me in the curative pool* before the others.' As he told his tale, the god looked at him with a gentle expression and said: 'Stand up by yourself on your own feet, and go on your way in full health. You don't have to owe everything to the waves.' Scarcely had he said this, when suddenly, before the eyes of all—look!—the man got up, and (amazing to see) carrying his bedding by himself on his own shoulders, he walked as well as anyone else. His strength, fully renewed, matched his own natural vigour. Just as when in the woods a shepherd, while gathering branches, has bound up in his bundle of leaves a snake, put to sleep by the cold and stiff with frost, and puts it close to the fire unawares—instantly, scarcely able to endure the heat of the flames nearby, it raises its head and rolls its fiery eyes, and crawling through the house it rears up and flickers with its forked tongue.*

Elsewhere, in front of the doors of the temple, in the middle of the porch, attendants were sitting selling offerings for the common people to place on the bronze altar, making a tremendous din as they did so. They were selling woolly sheep, bulls, and pairs of doves, in accordance with the sacrifice prescribed for each person's atonement and according to each one's means. As soon as the hero saw them on his way in, and observed the whole place in tumult with all the rushing about and the ungodly racket, he could not endure it. Profoundly shaken, he laid into them with bitter words, lashing their backs with a twisted scourge, and with resounding blows he drove them from the holy threshold, just as when the North Wind bursts forth from the caves of the far north: sweeping through the plains of the air with a whirring whirlwind,* it goes wildly through the heavens, pursuing the pitch-black clouds across the whole expanse of the sky, and the hollow clouds give way in defeat and make their retreat.

'This house is sacred to God,' he said. 'This is the Lord's house. But you have turned it to criminal ends, converting it to unworthy uses. Up till now there has been shedding of blood at the altars, and live sacrifice, in keeping with the ritual tradition granted to our ancestors. But you have indulged enough and more than enough in the slaughter of sheep; now the almighty Father bids you henceforth spare the blood of livestock and of birds, and the smoking entrails.* A very different kind of worship awaits you, for the rites will be altered. Only learn justice,* offer your devotions with a pure mind, and appease a willing god with pious prayers. Let these be your rituals, and these your atonements,* I tell you.' So he spoke, and in supplication on bended knee at the altar he worshipped his Father's divinity with a secret prayer, his head bowed.

And now in the peevish hearts of the chief priests there blazed up an overwhelming resentment,* and the flames of anger scorched them within.* Nor was this a new fury or bitter hatred welling up in them for the first time. The age-old motives for their anger and the inveterate resentment had by no means disappeared from their minds, but remained firmly lodged there.* At this point, however, they did not dare to rise up against him directly, but fearing the vengeance of the common people and the crowd of his followers they left the shrine, vainly threatening unspeakable retaliation, just like wolves at night, when the fold has been left open by chance and they advance towards the flock, but the vigilant watch blocks their way and forces them back, with loud barking from the dogs. Despite the terrible hunger goading them on from within, they are driven off and retreat, filling the mountains in vain with their howling.

While the divinity was speaking to his Father at the altar, his companions wandered through the temple, marvelling at each individual feature,* the bulk of the building with its towering height and the workmanship of the craftsmen: a hundred columns hewn from stone, a hundred of bronze, all of them solid and all as tall as high mountains; beams and coffers made from everlasting cedar, and bronze doors creaking on brazen hinges;* and pavements smoothly levelled off with an intricate tessellation of stone mosaics. Then their eyes take in the doorposts of pure gold and the tables of a similar metal, and chariots affixed to the high altars, decorated with ebony and gleaming ivory.*

As they were examining everything, there he was among them, appearing unexpectedly and coming upon them silently, his prayers duly completed: the hero. He said, 'This vast mass, this colossal temple, like a pine tree torn up from its very roots in an instant by the wind, will be overturned all of a sudden and will come crashing down, wreaking immense ruin. A reward worthy of your deeds hangs over you, Jerusalem, you who dared to slay with the sword or hurl from hard rocks so many prophets divinely sent to you. How often have I myself tried in vain to bring together your citizens as one, so that I might teach them the truth in person, like the crested hen that summons the scattered ranks of her young with clucking and with beating wings! You shall fall, cut down by the sword; your realms, even now on the very point of collapse, and your weapons shall instantly fall in ruin, and avenging fire will gut them; and in every part this land shall sweat a great gout of blood. Don't you already see* how your fortunes have given way and now lie prostrate, and it no longer does you any good to string together prayer on prayer? The almighty Father has transferred his sacraments to far different shores; in a far different city* it is his will that he be worshipped and appeased. So let the boundary stone be fixed here, driven deep into the earth.'

Speaking thus, he showed them the marvellous forms fashioned from marble, depicting a mighty subject*—a memorial of the six days in which the massive structure of the vast universe* was put together, and the events of ancient times, and the earliest deeds of their ancestors, all represented in order. It was a work impossible to describe in human words.* There were no likenesses of people or images of gods, but the craftsman's hand had set down everything using esoteric notation and cryptic characters, up till then undeciphered by anyone; nor had the prophets themselves been able to grasp them.

Here the creator of the heavenly beings, looking down on the shapeless heap, the everlasting night, and the unordered deep,* was seen fashioning the first beginnings of things,* himself beaming with radiance and brilliant with intense luminosity. And now he was seen creating from a tawny cloud the vault of starry heaven and the earth and the strait of ocean, and with them the light wandering over the waters, from which he could then ignite the beaming rays of the sun and the fires of heaven. Now, murmuring in a thick swarm around their creator and leader, and sounding with acclamation, were seen the winged brotherhood in the bastion of heaven, the airborne throng, the work of the first day. But not yet had he separated the flaming sky from the deepest earth, or the earth from the waters: the constituents of creation* were simply lying about in confusion. Without delay, he had barely hammered out the globe of sevenfold heaven,* in order to fix to it in varying sequence the glittering fires; and already, little by little, all things were starting to take on their new form, and the heaven was beginning to be held together by its own framework.

Now that the mass of dry land had been left behind in the middle, it was possible to see* the watery seas being poured out all around with their curving shores, and the waves foaming up towards the stars, dashed against the shallows. Not yet were ocean-faring ships bending their broad sails, nor was there any flexing of oars in the watery plane of the sea,* but the North-Westerly Winds harmlessly swept the spreading expanse of the ocean. But look—beech-bearing mountains are now lifting up their towering heads, and below lie sunken valleys. At once the resourceful earth put forth buds and grew bright with flowers,* while the trees unfurled their leaves. And now you could see the fields clothed in green grass, and the hilltops bursting into leaf with dense woods—oaks and olive trees and cone-bearing cypresses. Without delay the two lights* began to shine with flames in the blue heaven for the first time upon the newborn earth, and like watchmen of the universe succeeded each other at their post in turns, giving their light according to a fixed arrangement. For the sun, the fount of light, passes through the measured course of heaven by day, bringing colour to the earth with its new splendour, while by night the moon follows its phases in the shadows with a pale countenance, pouring its fire from gilded horns, and the shining stars adorn the sky with their nocturnal jewels, gliding round in ceaseless motion. Then the speechless droves of scaly fish were sweeping the surface of the ocean everywhere with their two-pronged tails* and were swimming in the sea, while the colourful birds held their bodies steady in the air with their wings and fought among themselves with their curved beaks. Not far from here,* herds of cattle wandered through the wide fields and woolly flocks bounded over the luxuriant pastures.* Now you could see the terrible offspring of wild beasts seeking out their lairs, and long serpents crawling along the ground. You would think the king of the heaven-dwellers was exhorting them from above from a shining cloud, uttering joyful words: 'Grow, my offspring, and propagate your race, and join generation to unending generation, each after your own kind.'*

Finally a man appeared, naked, fashioned from the earth. The creator of the heavenly beings seemed to address him and lay down laws face to face, and to place him in charge of the kingdoms, so that he might hold the earth in his sway,* being immortal. If only he had abided by those words, and had kept the terms that had been agreed! But you could see a field nearby,* resplendent with trees and green grass, a meadow dotted with flowers, where there were apples closely guarded by a dark-hued serpent. In the middle was a fountain, silvery with its translucent waters,* rolling forth four streams* to opposite regions, which served to water the fields far and wide in the lap of the earth as they poured into it. And here you could see the young man, tricked by the deceit of the evil-counselling serpent, tasting the forbidden fruit from the tree, forgetful of the commandment and the strict law; and now—scarcely had he brought the ill-fated apple to his mouth—you would think he regretted it, as he wrapped himself in leaves and could no longer endure the stern face of the king of heaven. For among the fleecy wisps of a tawny cloud God was seen looming over the mortals with a terrifying countenance, severely censuring them and pronouncing a harsh penalty in keeping with their deserts, which thereafter Adam himself would pay, as would all those descended from him who would come into the light of day.* Meanwhile his wife, who, seized by an awful desire, had been the first to break the laws, the rules which had been set, and the terms of the agreement, was unhappily hiding herself in vain in the thickets of the bushes. But the victorious serpent, having now proved triumphant in his deception, shone out with his bronze scales and slippery folds, encircling the trunk of the tree three times and twisting round it in gigantic spirals,* and he flapped his wings and gloated from on high, shamelessly taunting those he had deceived with his innocent demeanour.

Not far from here you could see the infernal realms stretching far around, the gloomy regions with their grudging sunlight,* where the chaste spirits and souls of the pious, shut out on account of one man's sin from the seat of the heaven they had earned, were waiting in a long line. Here were standing white-haired chieftains and ranks of prophets sporting their sacred headbands, and they were raising their outstretched hands to the stars. Father Abraham, his shoulders protruding far above the crowd, was sheltering all of them with the aid of his right hand and his left, opening his ample cloak and stretching forth his arms far and wide. You would believe that they were praying, and addressing the Father of the heavenly beings with words of entreaty, imploring him to spare his anger and refrain from destroying all the nations because of one man's wrongdoing. Here the divinity stopped, sighing from the depth of his heart, and said: 'See, those things there demand my labour. On my side there is no delay;* I am the forfeit owed to so great an anger, and by my death I shall rescue these people from darkness and break their bars. Indeed, you must understand the scenes immediately following, grasped by few, which foreshadow my unspeakable death.'

Here, following the extermination of all other mortals, a few were proceeding unscathed over the tops of the waves, shut in the wooden ark. The enormous vessel was floating on the sprawling ocean, and the very mountains with their mighty bulk scarcely protruded above the water; the fire that crashed down as the storm clouds collided was striking these, its assault repeatedly redoubled, as the sky glowed red. Here the elderly Abraham was poised over his son Isaac with his blade bared, an unhappy father carrying out his cheerless orders.* You could see him straining now with his whole body as he raised his right hand to strike; he had not yet looked back, but already a messenger—see!—was at hand, sent down from the stronghold of heaven, bringing instructions contrary to the first ones. A sacrificial victim was grazing nearby, provided in place of the sacrifice of the unsuspecting boy: a shining ram silvery with its shaggy fleece of white. After this, Joseph's brothers were selling the brother they hated because of the dreams he told them, lying to their poor father about his awful death, torn apart by wild beasts. The father himself was turning over the bloodied tunic of his son and watering it with his tears.

Here too, while the lawgiver Moses was leading the citizens out of the territory of the Pharaohs after their long exile into their homeland and the promised kingdom, the hero relying on celestial aid, a lamentable plague had arisen suddenly and was consigning the wandering populace to death, caused by the breath of serpents, and bodies were lying everywhere, dying from the wasting bite. In the middle of the plain the leader hung a bronze serpent from a huge pole and was commanding those who were stretched out on the ground to direct their gaze intently towards this and look upon the wood, which was the only way of sure salvation for those poor people. Elsewhere, piercing her own vitals with her sharp beak, a mother bird was feeding her unfledged offspring from her wound.* They stood around her, rejoicing in their mother's blood and all jostling each other as they rummaged for food in her opened breast.*

After examining these scenes, the hero went out by the double doors, pondering many things; and he had not yet descended the whole flight of steps, when, with a great rabble manhandling her, look—there was being dragged along, her hair streaming over her back and her face pale, the wife of aged Manasseh, Susanna.* To this man her father had united her, in the excellence of her beauty and the flower of youth, in an unwelcome marriage,* unwilling and sick at heart as she was. The people were calling upon her to pay the rightful penalty for sullying the good faith of her marriage bed, while a great horde of young men followed close behind them. Already the boys and the mob were holding stones in their hands.

But then, darting out in front of them in person, a priest held back their missiles, when he caught sight of Christ in the spacious colonnade. He went up to him, dragging the poor woman towards the threshold, and began to weave a trap for him. 'This woman', he said, 'betrayed her marriage and was caught cheating on the good faith of her bridal bed. Our laws command that a guilty party should receive the death penalty for such a crime, by means of a brutal stoning—but what unkindness is there in that? So we come to you, most gentle interpreter of the prophets, and we are all eager to know what your verdict is.'

So he spoke, and now he was nurturing idle hopes in his heart, supposing that his foe had been caught and entangled by these words, that every way out had been closed off and no escape route was left. For surely, if Christ were to let her off and save her from death, pitying her with his gentle heart, the whole crowd would waste no time in turning its stones and its vengeful wrath against him, on the grounds that he was illegally overturning the sacred laws of their race. But if he ordered her to be led away to punishment for her crime, he would expose himself to the bitter hatred of the mob for his cruelty. In hatching this scheme, the priest now inwardly assumed he was victorious, and the heart in his breast swelled inordinately with empty satisfaction:* just as a ploughman at one time appears to himself in a dream, while lifting the surface of the soil with his well-worn ploughshare, to have dug up a colossal weight of gold from the field he has tilled, and he nurtures a futile joy. Once sleep has abandoned him, he will perceive his poverty and will see that harsh toil is still with him, as he curses in his heart his dreams and his imaginary fortune.

The god himself found a way to spare her without damaging the laws, for no human trickery can stand against divine power. After keeping his eyes fixed on the ground,* he finally raised them and looked at the expectant crowd and said: 'There is no doubt that she has earned death by her crime. That is what our distant ancestors established in time past. So come, whichever one of you is free from any wrongdoing, let him be the first to take stones in his hand and strike her as she deserves. Will anyone come forward out of so many of you to inflict the first wounds,* freely declaring himself pure of sin?' Making this pronouncement, he kept all of them in his sidelong glance as he bent his head, observing them with a terrifying look and ready to write on the earth the name of the man whose conscience was unperturbed by any shameful act and free from fault. In the midst of their sight stood the girl, trembling, her eyes filled with the darkness of impending death, and kneeling on the ground she humbly entreated them, no less fear-stricken than a deer driven into the nets by the barking of hounds and worn out with the long chase, when her strength is now used up and she sees herself encircled on all sides by the enemy, and with no doubt in her mind awaits imminent death.

But when the people heard Christ's reply, without exception their unbounded rage rapidly died down, and their violence was overcome and fell silent. Each one went over his own life in his silent heart, and in turn they looked at each other and then looked away; nor was anyone in so great a crowd prepared to come forward. The stones fell from their hands and dropped silently, and they all went away and left the temple, every man mindful of himself. When the god saw the courts were empty all around, he removed the flaxen bindings from the shaking girl and sent her away with the guidance of these friendly words: 'Go on your way a better person, and extinguish the bad name of your past wickedness.'

Then, turning to his companions, he addressed them: 'Alas for the hard-hearted race!* Even when beaten, they cannot give up. They leave nothing untried, nothing at all undared.* For sure, on days of celebration, against divine and human law, I now bring help to the afflicted and restore the sick to health; I now welcome wrongdoers and those who of their own free will admit their offences, and I release their spirits from guilt and crime. Now my companions handle fruit and wine before applying water to their hands, while they bring comfort to their bodies with food and do not refrain from banquets, and do many other things which people cast against me as reproaches. Indeed, they even attack me fraudulently, resorting vainly to stealth, or try to bring me unwittingly into conflict with the Romans by their cunning, and they treacherously ask me whether it is in keeping with divine law to pay contributions of silver to the emperor per head,* as each person is commanded to do by decree. Nor do my mighty deeds, which could not be accomplished by human means or by any arts, have any effect on these people in their blindness. Robbed of sight, they do not see the force by which I set these things in motion, and they dare to stand in the way of the almighty Father's plans.

'I am not abolishing the old rites or annulling the laws; for indeed, a far different meaning lies hidden and uncomprehended within these obscure utterances. Far different mysteries are concealed beneath the obscuring cloud of words. Leaving aside everything else, why do you shrink from setting pig's flesh on the table, from which it is banned? It doesn't impose a stain on our transcendent souls to relieve our hunger with this thing or the other. It is the mind itself that injures you within, and terrible desire.* But since the bristly race of pigs rejoices in mud and filthy swamps, and lust is innate in this creature, the evil delights* of foul sensuality are symbolized by the pig. Moreover, the Creator, so that he could civilize through worship the spirits which he was gradually habituating to heavenly commands, and so as not to begin by keeping peoples who were at first untaught, and the unfeeling hearts of the race, without any religious practices, ordered them to sacrifice sheep and wet the earth with blood, and slaughter innocent bullocks on the altars. But all these things, to anyone who had a profound and active mind, were but a reflection and a dim outline of the religion to come later.'

When this was over, as evening was now closing up the slope of heaven, he departed and withdrew from the faithless city. Then, longing to speak with his Father before his approaching death and to hold secret converse with him face to face, he left his companions in ignorance in the depth of the valley of Mount Tabor, while he himself, gaining the steep summit of the mountain in his ascent, took his stand where the lofty cedars strike the stars. Out of the whole number only the faithful John, along with his brother James, and Peter had joined him as companions, since he had asked them. They were standing in prayer silently, and all together were directing their outspread hands* and their eyes to heaven without a word. But Christ himself, with great love, addressed his Father in these words:

'O Father, see, though guiltless I am now on my way to a terrible death—I, your offspring—nor do I refuse to endure so many undeserved sufferings, since this is your settled purpose and your fixed will, and the race of mortals is worth so much. I make no delay: here I am. But these men, choicest hearts, who have left their country and their people and followed me through all manner of misfortunes*—look upon them, at least, and steer them away from unseen dangers, blameless as they are. I am not at all afraid that human beings, that godless race, stand in their way everywhere; the mortal deeds of humans cause me no terror. Let them die, even, to the last man (that moves me not at all)—or rather carry them off by fire and destroy them, if you so wish, with your unforgiving thunderbolt, and smash their lives to complete oblivion; and put an end to such great toil,* Father, if it is so overwhelming a struggle to bring the human race to heaven* and to transform the world and return the ages to their former state. I pray only this: may the race sunk in the abyss of hell (that appalling outrage!), constantly devising plagues for men, cause no obstruction by its intrigues, wicked as it is. May it not lead them astray with unspeakable desires, caught in its snares, nor deceive their unwary hearts as it incites them to crime and urges forgetfulness of us. Now, right now, the unutterable enemy will be here—a race armed with trickery, their spirits not yet sated, for they have not yet avenged their grave distress. Even now they will launch their deceptions and set their craft in motion by deceit: what shapes will they not assume in their falsehood, putting on counterfeit bodies, in order to capture the innocent race and corrupt it with their pestilent poisons? You, Father, shatter their treachery and scatter everything to the winds, bringing it all to nothing. At long last impose your edict on the conquered, that they keep the peace. Let there be people throughout the lands to instruct the nations in justice and the love of religion after my death. Grant me this one favour, conceding it to the love of your son.'

These were the Son's words. The Father in turn replied to him as follows: 'My Son, your Father's true virtue and my closest likeness, no falsehood nor any of the snares which the master of the hidden realm is now devising will harm your people; put aside your fear. Frustrated in his endeavour, he is attempting everything to no avail. Let him put on a hundred appearances, a hundred forms: I shall be there, and I shall expose his tricks and scatter in confusion his columns fertile in fraud, blocking his way by my great power. Yet there will be one,* and one only, whose mind will be overcome by madness: unhappy man, now already in his doomed heart he is turning over an unspeakable crime and regrets his association with you, sick as he is. He chafes at himself for discarding the alluring love of mortal life in following your teachings, and for preferring to endure heavy labours under your leadership—but all this you have known, along with me, since before the world began. Yet I added this man, for all his unworthiness, to the number of your band of righteous men, to serve as a clear example to your people, since I was mindful of the prophets who had once foretold such things. The others, following a better path, will escape these snares: all of them, for your sake, scorning the love of life, will not shudder at death and will go gladly to their end, and by their blood they will generate for you an innumerable race, proud in their casting-off of life and their passion for passing away. I shall make them worthy of heaven at last after their bitter deaths, a mighty augment for the uninhabited sky.* What descendants you will see rising one day, my Son, from this religion!* What resolute hearts you will see! As for you, simply go on* and complete the toilsome course you have begun. These men, whom you see now barely following your commands in their unresponsiveness to teaching and ignorance of speech, will without delay conceive in their hearts a profound understanding, and they will intone with learned mouths the laws to be revered, being inspired by my divine power, and by their exhortations they will restore the boundless earth to a better condition.*

'Generation shall follow generation, and your holy descendants will bear your standards in triumph beyond the furthest barriers of the Ocean, which keep the spacious lands in check with their waves, and through the ages your name will everywhere grow in renown. Of their own accord unconquered kings will lay their sceptres and their arms before you throughout the world, and they will consecrate altars. And even that haughty Rome, pregnant with empire, which beside the wave of the Tiber that wends its way from the Apennines governs vast nations, supreme in her beauty,* will submit to you her insignia of power and the reins of the world which she controls. There will be religion, there a hundred gigantic temples, a hundred altars smoking in your honour, and a hundred ministers, and a priest to give laws to men far and wide and to kings themselves, and to stand for you in the place of highest honour on earth.* Yet if, as the years gradually slip by, some inferior age taints the ways of men and debased descendants arise as human pursuits become perverted, then disciplining them by hardship and toil I shall recall the fallen race to its former state. Constantly improved by its sufferings, it will raise itself to the stars. Often you will see that city which I just referred to practically uprooted from the ground and cut down by the onslaughts of invading peoples.* But the more she is chastened by sufferings, the higher she will forever rise and raise her head aloft among the stars. She will forever be renewing her walls, making them better and better, and will not stop until the earth is subject to her throughout its length and breadth. So it has been decided.* Let this be the seat of my divine power.'

So he spoke, and held his Son to him in an embrace. But look!—suddenly, hurled from the ruddy sky, there flashed out a thunderbolt,* together with a great crash, and the vast height of heaven rang all around. For the almighty Father in a clear manifestation from heaven displayed a cloud, lit up with rays of light and with fire. Everywhere around glowed far and wide.* Christ was caught up in a rushing whirlwind and shone brightly in the midst of the cloud; in his appearance he was revealed as a true god, and through the breeze he breathed out a divine fragrance* from his whole head, a paragon of heavenly light and the image of his Father. As he shone out in the surpassing beauty of his rosy countenance, shedding over everything around an unaccustomed light, it was just like when in the morning the newborn fount of light, the enormous golden sun, bathes the whole sky in a flood of radiance as it rises. In the mirror of Ocean its reflection gleams afar, and the gilded treetops of the saffron-coloured forest are flushed with light. This was what the hero was like when he presented himself to the sight of his marvelling companions in the midst of two prophets.* One of these once approached the heights of heaven borne on a blazing chariot, and sailed through the breezes of the sky in exultation, carried by his horses; while the other led the race of Isaac's descendants from the territories of the Pharaohs, the leader of a band of exiles, and gave them laws and the custom of sacred rites.* And that was not all: at that moment the immense palace of the heaven-dwellers seemed to be opened up close at hand, and the gigantic hall of heaven appeared. Then the Father, shining out in a raiment of glowing cloud, kissed his Son,* and a voice descended through the air: 'Here is my Son, here is my great delight. All you mortals, willingly obey him—and him alone.' That was all. At this the whole chorus of heavenly beings struck up throughout heaven with varied song and offered their ovation.

Then at last the hero, restored to his usual appearance, roused his companions, stunned and paralysed as they were by these portents and by fear, and he appeared to their sight with the mortal countenance of a human being.

BOOK TWO

MEANWHILE in Jerusalem the chief elders and the priests of the temple spent that night in sleeplessness, anxious at the turn of events* and blinded by a feeling of dread: so much did the uneasiness that afflicted them loom over their minds, and dismally allowed them no rest, worried out of their wits. Before the eyes of them all was the joyful vision of the god entering the city, and the jubilant acclamations bestowed on him by the youthful throng; and they saw his renown increasing far and wide.* Rumour took flight,* broadcasting on all sides the wondrous things he was doing. What were they to do? More and more now was the truth being revealed, which once the prophets of old declared would come to pass: that a king of heavenly lineage was destined for earth, at whose coming the temple and the kingdom of Judaea would finally fall in ruin, and Jerusalem would cease to bestow its sacred offerings as ancient ritual prescribed, its altars having been overturned. And so all of them were broken in spirit, and crushed by fear; they remained in their homes, each in his own house, shielded and shut in—just like bees, accustomed to flitting about and harvesting the flowery fields, who, when winter unleashes its fury and the heaven dissolves into pouring storm clouds and watery Orion holds sway,* pass their time in idle leisure and loiter woozily in their closed-up hives, or buzz around the doorways and in the entrance.*

It was that time when welcome rest sends slumber coursing through the limbs and brings on oblivion, with worries set aside.* And now the band of night-riders, sent forth from the depths of the abyss, shapes horrible to look upon, laid siege to the entire city in their frenzied gangs. Some swarmed down on the towers, some clustered round the summit and the topmost gables of the temple. The rest of the legion* swooped through the streets and among the high roofs of the houses, and clung to the beams in a long line along the rafters. Just so the birds, when they make their way back to Italy as the spring warms up, exhausted by their long journey over the blue seas, vie with each other to alight on whatever land first presents itself to them: in a dense throng they settle on it and fill the curving shores.*

First they sprinkled hidden venom and a viperous temper into men's hearts, breathing into them a blinding frenzy and leaving hatred and criminal instincts in their souls. Many even transformed themselves into human appearance and straightaway set the entire city ablaze with a whole range of rumours. Others crept into the houses and brought terrible dreams in a variety of guises to those who were lost in sleep, thereby deceiving human hearts with false impressions. And they entered the lofty portals of now this powerful man, now that, and incited them against the enemy, driving them witless by their words, and struck terror into their hearts by reciting things both done and not done,* saying that Christ was bringing torches and was bearing down on the altars, armed with a bronze axe; that he was threatening the shrines with destruction, and already fire had gained the upper hand in the half-razed temple.*

And not just this: falsely impersonating the very priests of the temple by their clothing, they went up to each house individually and summoned the elders to the holy portals for council. The commander of the dark cohort in person thrust open the doors, grating on their hinges of sounding bronze.* From this side and that they poured to the sanctuary, rushing together readily from all sides; the darkness of black night was no hindrance to them as they came on. It was just as if rumour were to announce that a city has been captured by trickery in the depths of night, and that with weapons concealed the enemy is bringing in troops and has already infiltrated the highest point of the citadel. Set loose on the rooftops, a deadly blaze devours the houses. In the packed streets everything is in turmoil, and in disorderly panic people rush this way and that, without any reason to guide their movements.* The terrible apparitions* went in front, supplying light from their monstrous torches and shedding illumination from the tops of their heads as they shook fearsome flames from their crests on all sides. And yet those poor people did not recognize them: without exception, the frenzy within them had snatched away their wits, along with the venom which had penetrated the very core of their being. Meanwhile twelve of their band were sent to Christ's twelve companions, in case they could bring down any one of them and deceive and set him on fire with their malicious raging. The disciples, however, filled with the warnings of their leader (for in his foreknowledge he had previously foretold to his followers that all these things would happen), preserved unyielding minds and hearts impervious to falsehood, for all that their enemy transformed himself into every guise* and sought to trap their minds by stealthy circling, making the attempt to no avail.

One only there was, who proved incapable of escaping these snares: Judas Iscariot, dedicated to unutterable iniquity*—Judas, that stain and plague upon the chosen Apostles! Once he had enrolled as a disciple, following the footsteps of the deity and leaving behind his country, his wealth, and those dear to him, prepared to incur the hazards of exile, to travel hazardous roads wherever he might go, and to submit to death on behalf of such a king. But soon he grew sick of these undertakings, and little by little he wearied of the harsh toil. Then he turned over in his mind, in silence night and day, whether there was some way he could extricate himself from these tight constraints and return to his old life—for he was resentful that his long toil had proved to be in vain. Secretly he planned now this way out, now that,* unable to tolerate the exertions and discontented with his impoverished existence.

When he had been tossing about on the swell of such cares and had been wavering in his mind for some time, the leader of the dark cohort himself came upon him. The joy that filled his spirits was no less than when a Gaetulian lion,* beneath a high mountain, tormented by a long-accumulated craze to eat as he gapes with dry jaws, sees far off, making its way to the fields—a stag! But first Satan turned himself into the likeness of Jora the Galilean,* who was Judas' own relative by blood, and advanced on the sleepless Judas with words:

'Do you wander in the silence of the night among the lonely mountains, you madman? Can you willingly endure the cruel chill under the open sky, and is your life spent at the bidding of someone else,* while you follow that man—what uncontrollable madness spurs you on?—who is both puffed up with pride and a destroyer of sacred things? The only people who approach him are the lowest filth of the world, girlish groupies and half-male hangers-on.* All the leading men are opposed to him and are on fire with unanimous hatred: they are devising death for this blasphemer. And now he will pay the price for his mad raving, and all that self-assurance will give way. That vaunting of his great deeds—which he falsely makes up—will be of no help to him. It will do him no good at all to spread out thick clouds in his defence, no good at all to arm himself with his usual arts. End this delay! Come on, snatch yourself from the impending disaster!'

So he spoke, and incited him to bitter hatred, setting him on fire. Then he struck Judas' altered heart with a sharp wand, and suddenly vanished, mingling into the blackness of night.*

After this, in his assault on the poor man he rushed right to the inmost parts of his heart, and entwined a terrible fire in the depths of his bones.* Now there came into Judas' mind all the harsh things he had endured under Jesus on his orders, and all the dangers he had drained to the very dregs. He was disgusted, and with his love polluted he pondered a terrible wrong: in his mind was planted the idea of betraying to the enemy his innocent king.

Ah, you poor, sick man, do you not feel God within your heart? Do you not take in the presence of his divine power with your eyes and ears? What overwhelming frenzy has altered you? See the summit from which you are now hurling yourself, the fortress from which you are falling in ruin! What are you devising?* Where is so deadly a desire* sweeping you off to, wrongfully taking possession of you while you lack reason and light? That lot which you are now throwing away is an irreplaceable gift: descendants in later ages will long for it a thousand generations hence. And those prayers you now so cherish, that hope you are nurturing in your mind, while your spirits are puffed up and swollen with empty euphoria*—all these the winds will pluck apart and whirl through the air.* While you can, cast out this unspeakable plague from your heart, and this care which now eats away at you in the very depths of your marrow!

And now the priests and the council from the whole city had all assembled in a secluded venue in the temple. The chief priest himself, Caiaphas, whose brow was encircled by a sacred headband, was sitting on a golden seat, raised above the rest. Then came other citizens in a long row; around them all pranced the hellish pests, sharpening their frenzy, bodiless and seen by none. There was no delay, no rest:* slipping into the hearts of all, they snatched away their wits and stirred fire into their souls. In their agitation they began to bring up many issues among themselves in varied discussion:* the gigantic temple rang with their mighty uproar. There were some who advocated doing away with Christ himself by whatever means, whether by violence or by trickery, and attacking with the sword the young man* who had recently been called back to the light from the shades of death and had come and shaken up the whole city with the wonder. Others, however, feared the people and the rage of the mob, for the hero had attached to himself vast crowds of people, some by his acts of kindness, others by the friendliness of his divine speech.

Among this gathering Nicodemus was the only one who remained immune to the evil contagion. He was not the least among the leaders of the people, and his mind possessed far better judgement;* but he did not have the courage to speak against all the others on his own. Once, in his ignorance, he had been an opponent of the god and had vainly striven against him with trickery. Later, however, when he had been prompted to recognize Jesus' divinity, he had been called back as it were from the depth of night into the light of day and had joined himself to him in devotion—but secretly, since he wished to avoid the bitter hatred of the resentful race. Then indeed, when he saw that what was at issue was Christ's life and blood,* and that a sorrowful death was being instigated against him in his innocence, he could bear his concealment no longer and in their midst he broke into speech with these words:

'It is not unclear, the matter we are dealing with, nor does it require elucidation.* No longer am I afraid to declare the truth for the sake of my country, even if I have to face the ultimate penalty. You see, all of you, that this man is guided by a manifest divinity,* that he is greater than human. Unless I am deceiving myself, the true offspring of God has been revealed, the true god, that one of whom the prophets, inspired by the breath of divinity, so often sang as destined to come, so that he might atone for our dismal wickedness,* making the race of mortals acceptable to its eternal parent. This is plain to see; it is no longer a matter for dispute.

'Through his aid, countless people who were oppressed by the darkness of night, deprived of the use of their eyes, now enjoy the blessing of daylight. Many too who were born deaf now hear and utter speech. How many sufferers have seen their health restored though they despaired of it, heaving around their impeded limbs in the grip of a wasting illness or seized in their bodies by a sudden sickness! Three times—as you know—this same man has brought people back to the light, rescuing them when they had already passed over into death: only just now Lazarus has shaken up the whole city with his report of this mighty portent. Ah, the errant minds, the unseeing hearts, of men!* These things cannot be accomplished by healing potions or by any techniques: a greater god operates inside, a greater divinity is within. How often have we stood in vain against him while he spoke divine words, fully equipped with all our arguments and ploys! How often have we dared to direct violence against him when he was unarmed, to destroy him with the sword or with hard rocks—to no avail! In a hollow cloud he snatched himself away, vanishing from our sight, and surrounded himself all of a sudden with a celestial guard of winged warriors. And would anyone not pay reverence to his proven divinity? What are we still trying to achieve? What is there left for us to do? No, since he has been sent down from heaven to help us, let us rather approach him all together as one, and let us humbly beg for peace from him, confessing our sins.'

Such was his insistent declaration. But a violent fury surged up in them all,* and a burning sensation spread ever more powerfully through their inmost being. Their rage intensified the savage seething, and little by little their spirits were bloated with grievous anger. They blazed up, every one of them. The pestilence lurked* within them and snatched away all light from the wretches, and as they surrendered to its polluting poison it stifled their minds with a black fog. Then at last it erupted, the wrath that had been simmering in them all;* every one of them roared and groaned. It was just like when, in the hollow of a bronze cannon, the deadly sulphur is consumed and the confined fire rages more and more with increasing violence and seeks an escape route. Panting, it can no longer contain itself inside—and yet there is no way out through the narrow aperture, and it cannot break out until it has got through all the material. Then, forced out in a cloud of pitch-black smoke, the iron bullet takes flight. There is a roar: you would think that the sky had split asunder and the heaven was falling. And now look—the missile has brought down towers and fortresses far off; bodies and weapons lie everywhere, and a path has been made through the enemy.* Just like this the elders were inflamed against Nicodemus as he attempted to give them better advice. They barred him from the temple and forced him outside the walls of the city.

Then indeed Caiaphas, once they were hushed into silence, addressed them as follows and set out the resolution which was planted in his mind.

'I'm not at all bothered, citizens, that even he has gone over to the enemy, snared by their unspeakable cunning—he who once willingly incurred danger so often on behalf of what is most important to us, and in defence of our ancestral laws; he who was recently pressing hard upon our foe himself, contending against him might and main with his arguments. So great is the seductiveness of the impostor, so great the force of his eloquence, that he can bring round anyone he wishes and overcome them with his poison. Am I really to believe it, then, that this man has been divinely sent from heaven and has come to help us, when he blasphemously claims to be the son of God and he wants to abolish the ancient laws of our ancestors and bring in new rites? He freely declares that he has come to destroy the temple, which our forefathers once built up at the cost of so much toil,* driven by instructions from heaven. What revolution is this? What religious scruple? What moral principles, I ask you? And what is more, to ensure that he has left no form of wickedness unattempted,* he grants pardon* to the guilty and to those whose crimes are a matter of public knowledge, and he has no reservations about entering the homes of criminals; nor does he abstain on days of rest, as custom prescribes. Come on then, men—get on and hurry to set your snares for him and bring about his death: he deserves it. Put out the growing flame, or it will soon leap up victorious to the roofs of our houses, feed on the rafters, and hold sway over the lofty rooftops. Otherwise he will subvert the entire city with his usual arts, triumphant in his sedition;* he will take the people captive and bring every region under his control through his deceiving wizardry. As a result this religion of ours, which has served us so well for so many years, will immediately cease, its altars overturned. Then I fear that the descendants of Romulus,* not tolerating such things, may demand back from our race whatever jurisdiction we still have left, and may order us to depart from our fatherland as exiles. Let one life be given in exchange for many;* let the death of one make atonement for all and procure safety in so great a storm. He's had it.* Let this better resolution* prevail, citizens; let these be the tributes, this the homage, that we pay to him for his divinity.'

Such were his words. As the frenzy goaded them from within, the elders felt its effect and began to roar in agreement. Their attitude was unanimous,* but what they wanted to know was the means or the method by which the scheme might be surreptitiously accomplished. Then suddenly, look—having stolen away secretly from his companions, there was Judas, appearing unexpectedly and to the amazement of them all. They received him with trepidation as he breathed fury,* and setting him in a seat among their leading figures they urged him to speak, burning in their uncertainty to hear why he had come. And so they fell silent.

Judas, swivelling his blazing eyes this way and that,* spoke as follows: 'I'm well aware, elders, that you view with dread the deeds of the crazed Galilean, who is bringing destruction on the laws of our homeland; and therefore I see you hatching all sorts of plans. If you promise me what I ask, I shall remove on my own the whole trouble that now preoccupies you so fruitlessly. I shall cause him to fall voluntarily into your hands this very day.'

So he spoke. Gladly they settled on thirty talents of silver—a memorable price for that extraordinary deed*—and eagerly sent him off, escorting him out of the doorway. He made for the mountains once again and returned to his comrades.

As it happened, the feast day* was approaching, solemnly observed by the people and the land, when in keeping with the observance of their distant forefathers they pass seven days in leisure, exempting themselves from work. In every home they feast on lambs and eat only unleavened bread, as they are bidden to do, and they swiftly produce hurriedly made cakes and pile their tables with rustic herbs, commemorating their happiness of old. On this day, they said, their early ancestors once went out of Egypt, prompted by signs from heaven,* with a great deal of plunder, and set out on their journey on foot through the salt waves of the sea.* At that time, therefore, there was a huge convergence of people upon the royal city from every direction, and the whole population came streaming to the ceremonies. Yet the crowd did not rush there in disarray or disorder, but each man went together in company with his leader and race and tribe. For although they all had the same blood, and were all descendants of Isaac sprung from a related lineage, and all obeyed the same laws, that single race nonetheless divided itself into twelve tribes and was spread out far and wide through all Palestine. The race had once been free and defended by a daunting force of fighting men;* its cities had prospered in their population and flourished in their wealth. But then, driven out of their ancestral territory, almost all of them lived elsewhere and inhabited the Caspian rocks. Of the twelve tribes, barely a couple remained intact and maintained their place in the land of their fathers: the race of Benjamin and the house that owed its renown to Judah himself, both still flourishing at that time in their numbers and their prosperity.

But just as lofty Rome had crushed* everywhere else in war and had exhausted all resistance by her conquering arms, so this region too she had added to her empire and was trampling in slavery.* Yet the conqueror had taken away from the city only its sovereignty and its weapons, leaving the men their sacred practices and their ancestral laws. Now the land lies deserted. There were once so many glorious city walls, so many towns likewise with their valiant inhabitants: some were toppled by war, some by the invincible power of time*—so devastatingly did the Father of the heavenly beings, powerful among the storm clouds, blaze forth in pitiless anger, and he did not suffer the death of his child to go unavenged. But, as consolation for so great a calamity, I myself shall not allow this ancient land to lack its share of renown (just so long as my verses survive), so that time may not completely erase the vanished race along with its name through the forgetfulness of the ages.* Let it count to the credit of those regions that the king of heaven was born there, and that he cried and first crawled beneath that sky.

You winged assembly, race of heaven on high, who tread great Olympus with light footfalls*—since you have often passed through this area when sent down from heaven, and have frequently enjoyed the hospitality of its welcoming people—be my guides while love whirls me onwards* in the course of my wandering through the whole region. May it please you to join me in bearing through long ages the names of the race,* which have now fallen into oblivion, and its obliterated towns and ancient strongholds of ancient renown. Afterwards, borne aloft to the heavens on your wings, I shall leave behind through my song the shores and sights of mortals.* You will conduct me, on my course along an elevated path, through the trackless places of heaven. Let it be my pleasure to lull the shining stars with cloud-scattering song on my winged chariot, to be the first to travel routes untouched by sickly mortals, and to seek a new kind of garland* from the high crags of heaven. All this will come to pass one day, so long as the breath of heaven does not desert me in my endeavour.

Now join with me in going through all the peoples who were making for the temple.* Never had a greater throng made its way there, either in numbers or in enthusiasm; and they weren't so much in search of the ceremonies as drawn by a passionate desire in their eagerness to see Christ. First those descended from great Judah made their entrance, a bloodline that had passed through many kings. This tribe forever stood head and shoulders above all the rest, both in its numbers and in its qualities, surpassing the others as much as a lion outdoes all breeds of wild animal in its unfailing courage and strength.

Countless folk came from coastal Gaza and Sheba. They abandoned Engedi and its secluded vineyards, the seat of Adullam's city and low-lying Raphain. Here were the people of Lydda and Shilhim and windy Jabneel and Hippa, of Ascalon and the strongholds of Ashdod, of Ekron and Socoh and Joppa, washed by the lapping waves, with its jutting cliffs and rocks that menace the ocean.* Elsewhere the citizens left ancient Damascus, where first (so they say) man was born, fashioned from the fertile clay, and burst out into the new breezes of heaven. Emaus too was deserted, and Nibshan fell silent, emptied of its inhabitants; Anthedon, nearest neighbour to the kingdom of Egypt, was left looking for its own people, and Bethlehem as well, the cradle of God's birth.

Then Gilgal was silent and deserted, and all Bethsura, and the fields where Maarath sits, where Hermon touches the clouds, and where Zoar marvels that the bride,* while she turned to look back at the fires, has kept her human features in the form of a statue and has all of a sudden taken on the hardness of solid salt. Silent and deserted too was the region where the water of the Dead Sea grows hot with notorious flames and the swamp sends up great spurts to heaven,* contaminating the atmosphere with stinking fumes of sulphur. Once there was a fertile crop here, and rose gardens in the well-watered meadows; but now the land stands idle, choked with brambles, and the fields are overgrown with thorns.* This is your doing, corrupting passion:* the inhabitants once attempted to inflict unspeakable violence upon the boyish angels,* captivated by their divine beauty and the bloom of their youth—and they would have done so, had their victims not slipped from their grasp and escaped up to the stars, relying on the oarage of their swift wings.* The Father who thunders on high did not tolerate this, and he enveloped the whole area in avenging flames and submerged it in the sea. The region is still a vast filthy wasteland of ash and decaying cinders; the land is sterile and the fields fruitless; the approaches are arduous and the recesses inaccessible. There, so the story has it, a tree puts out a gleaming flower, which young men and girls long to pluck. But as soon as it has disappeared thanks to the grievous gusts of the South Wind, its place is taken by apples coarse all over with shaggy bristles, which no young men, and no girls, ever desired.* You would think from their appearance that these were solid and whole; but inside there is a revolting mess, and they disintegrate at once, collapsing into ashes at a touch, and are completely unfit for human use. Similarly, when the pallid crop is barely white on the yellow stalks, the deadly breeze destroys the unripe harvest.

Hard on their heels came the peoples sprung from Simeon, men who dwelled in Sharuhen and Molodah and the region of Ziklag fertile in crops, fields abundant in moisture; those who dwelled in Sipabota and the stronghold of twin-peaked Ashan; the dwellers in Ether, hills once lavish in palms,* and Remmon and Ain, set high on cultivated slopes; and those whom the hundred towns of Edom support, where incense is gathered, and the countryside bordering the fragrant territories of the Arabs.

And look—the descendants of Issachar made their way in with loud tumult, seeking the shrines and acknowledging the altar: a race comfortable in their living* and satisfied within their narrow boundaries. Here were those whom Hermus nurtured beneath its peak, Hermus the producer of bees and producer of horses;* and those who held the high summit of Mount Tabor, whose home was the steep cliffs of Mount Carmel. This race once saw the prophet raised on high all of a sudden by a raging whirlwind through the expanse of heaven, and carried up to the firmament on a fiery chariot.* And there were those whom Sansannah sent, and Enhaddah; those whom noble Haphraim reared, cities thirsting on the heights of the crags; those who had left Shunem and Reboth and the Remethian fields, shores planted with vines and different kinds of fruit trees.

But in silence came on the race of those born from the blood of Dan, and with downcast eyes and downcast faces they made their way through the city to the temple. Just as when the first frosts issue their challenge to autumn, and winter has not yet shaken from the branches their glory,* the serpent turns its mind to hiding places and makes its silent way among the rocks, slithering soundlessly, and checks its hissing mouth and keeps low the coils of its tail. And even now you could believe that the men were sorrowful because prophets filled with divine inspiration had foretold that from that bloodline would come a leader to terrify the human race beneath the false image of Christ,* to probe into the lives and misconduct of men, when a debased age would invert right and wrong* and fire would bring destruction upon mortal affairs. Yet straightaway would appear, with many thousands in his train, an avenger*—the true offspring of God,* granted to the world as its true judge. That foe, as he vainly struggled and pursued his futile schemes, he would snatch up in a whirlwind* and plunge him into the lowest bowels of the earth.

There followed a cloud of young men,* the race descended from Asher, whose heads were all shaded with garlands of wheat, according to their custom, and entwined ears of grain sported over their brows. These sowed the fields of Betan and Ramah; these had Aphek as their seat; those Amad provided, while Rehob sent those. Lebanese Arctipus and Achzib did not yield to them in number. Next to them, bearing gifts, came the tribe of Zebulun, a race that dwelled by the sea and had the custom of burning myrtle from the shore late into the night. Some had set out from the seat of Japhtahel, some had come from Idalah. These had left Cana, which recently had marvelled at unmixed water blushing red, transformed into dark wine.* These Nazareth brought, those lofty Shimron; Nain in Galilee, which just now had witnessed a boy come back to the world of the living after experiencing death,* brought many thousands, and abundant Dothan the same number. Nalole and towering Katteh were deserted by their people. And who could have counted the towns of the sons of Naphtali and their numberless fortresses, and those of Kedar, and those which sacred Lebanon bore on its high shoulders, level with the limits of heaven? Here were those who lived in lofty Enhazor, and the city of Naphtali, a race powerful in their speech and eloquence, and abundant in truth, who greet the Jordan at its origin from two springs. The entire race of Galilee came, the entire race of Samaria abandoned its homes, spurred on by eagerness to see so great a man. Often the son of the heavenly king had spent time in this region and voluntarily disclosed his divine nature. Even now Ziddim and Capernaum remembered his miracles, and Greek Sebaste, which lost its ancient name.* Bethol came too, and Bethsaida, with its stronghold raised up to the stars, and those Gennesaret laps with its waves teeming with fish. And the sons of Levi, that holy tribe, made their way mixed in with everyone else; for to them no region of their own had been allotted for tending, but the leader who brought the laws* had previously shared them out this way and that to all lands equally, and had set them in charge of the altars as priests, and instead of the fertility of the soil he had granted them the task of sacrificing sheep and burning their entrails.

But Manasseh,* not content with the kingdoms and sceptres which he had acquired by lot in great number across the river, advanced his empire where Nepaca and Bersa rise up, and Dora, huntress and nurse of flocks and wild beasts. Under his rule too came Tenaach, and wooded Iblea, and Meggido, a land second to none in its populace and opulence; also the cities which Entappuah waters, silvery with its clear waves,* where spring is never-ending* and the meadows are forever refreshed by the fountains. Following these were those who sow the lush fields beyond the River Jordan, a tribe descended from Manasseh himself.

And still they came on: the sons of Gad and the descendants of warlike Reuben, who had been the oldest of all the brothers, all entered the city together, since of old they had chosen to occupy the same seat in common beyond the river, fields once ruled by indigenous giants.* And here came those who dwelled in the countryside of Argob and the region of Bashan—and your woods, Gilead, and the sixty conquered cities of Og, and the towns of Gilead: Jabesh and Shibmah and Baalmeon and Ramoth and Golan and Nebo and Ebar and Salcak and half-ruined Kirjathaim. These were their names then, but now the lands have another name.* Then came those who eked their living from the rough ground* of Aram, abundant in cedar, all of them crowned with foliage and all with javelins strapped to their backs. Here were those who occupied Bezer and Rabath-Ammon, those who worked Golan and all the region of Bethalto with their sturdy bulls, and those the Arnon waters as it rushes down from the mountains. Nor would I pass you by, you men who harvest the fields of fertile Abel and Elealeh and green Ashteroth and Sionian Heshbon, a realm bristling with rocks; and abandoned Kadesh, the cities cradled by steep Pisgah, those sheer settlements supported here and there by Hermus and by Abaris, from whose cloud-capped peak the shepherds once saw in wonder the Jordan slow down and stop,* the vast mass of its waves kept in check, and its streams giving way and turning back from their course until the house of Isaac's sons could gain the promised fields.

In last place came the sons of Benjamin, journeying from their nearby home; to them had been granted by lot the most fruitful land, the land of mighty Jerusalem, the regal home of the whole race, and lofty Japheti and the strongholds of two-named Luz,* and Bethany, which had lately been stunned by the calling back of its king* to the blessings of life on the fourth day after his burial. It was the home too of Taralah and Zemaraim and Gibeah, prolific in mastic trees, a race hostile to beasts of the wild: for this reason its young men advanced clad in the spoils of wolves, and with their hounds they wearied the woods,* which it was their pleasure to break up and fence in constantly with nets. Thus in the morning they bore on their shoulders the fresh prey from their tireless hunting,* which they rejoiced in sharing out when evening closed up the heaven, and they enjoyed the feast and held their celebrations amongst themselves* spread out over the fields. Here were those whose home was Mizpah and steep Hammon, hills hard to climb and ridges jagged with rocky outcrops, and those who had left Rakem and the elevated citadel of Beeroth, and Siloh that once delighted in its poor temple. And there were the people from far Heleph, and Aven and Mosa and Selah and the fields of Ramah, filled to their length and breadth with Rachel's cries of mourning.*

With them came those who had set out from the home of Gibeon and of Jericho. The story is that the natives there saw the sun halt for a long while at the leader's command,* forgetting its path and its habitual course, and the day depart late. Among these went a boy of notable appearance,* taller than the rest, who took his lineage and name from Saul of old. At that time already all the prophets with one voice declared that he would be famed for his surpassing eloquence and his deeds; yet with what great hatred and frenzy will he assail our people prior to that, his mind engulfed in darkness! Then the almighty Father will be at hand, and will instil himself deep in every part of the young man's heart and cast out his fury.* All at once, divinely inspired by the breath of heaven, he will fill the world with his precepts, and over all the wide earth he will call mortals to better rites by his teaching; nor will he shrink from death for the sake of his faith, and a bloody one at that.

Now the twelve tribes had entered the great city. Christ himself, in order to present the customary offerings in the temple and ensure he did not fail to perform such an obligation on so joyous a day,* addressed his companions:

'The holy day is approaching; every home in the festive city is getting itself ready for the feast. Will one of you head off to the walls in advance,* to find out whether someone with a surplus of wealth might be prepared to issue an invitation to weary folk, so that we too, before my departure and untimely death, may celebrate the solemn meal and the annual rites? You won't have to look very far for him: a boy will cross your path carrying on his shoulder a jar of water freshly drawn from the fountain. Note the direction he takes and where he ends up, and mark the place by following him all the way with your eyes. Let the same doorway receive you, and make your way into the house. Then speak to the master of the house in person and ask him for hospitality and for a modest venue for the celebrations, and give him my name. Straightaway he'll show you a vast golden chamber, magnificent with embroidered tapestries: set up the meal there and lay it out. I'll be there and will lead my followers to that same door.'*

He finished speaking. John and Peter set off to carry out his orders, and in sorrow they reached the walls of the great city. As they made their way uncertainly and followed everything with their eyes from a distance, a boy came up carrying on his shoulder a jar of freshly drawn water, on his way from a nearby fountain. They kept on his tail, following him wherever he headed, and when he entered a house, they themselves immediately entered it too. Here Simon, distinguished in his ancestors and blessed with seven offspring, always used to come from the country, whenever he was visiting the city with his dear children; for he took greater pleasure in spending his time in the fields and the countryside, disdaining civil honours and keeping them at arm's length. The shade of the woods was what was dear to him, and the streams cleaving the estates which he tilled with a hundred ploughs,* rich man that he was. On occasion, being a man of dignity, he loved the melodious lyre and songs on the banks of the river or beside a pleasant spring;* for he knew the rhythms and the measures and the paths of heaven. Often, filled with divine inspiration, he would sing to the farmers of what was to come, what the sun and the monthly phases of the moon had in store, teaching them the warning signs given by clear sky and rain.* At that time, then, he had come to the city, busied as it was with the sacred rites, in order to celebrate the feast days in keeping with ancestral custom. And while in another part of the house his servants were getting ready the feasts and gifts, he himself was singing of the deeds of his forefathers of old, running with delicate touch over the sounding strings of the lyre, now with light fingers, now with an ivory plectrum.*

In particular, he was recalling from its earliest origin what pious observance had introduced to the race in olden times this traditional feast and these annual ceremonies.* But look—as he was singing, Peter turned up unexpectedly and interrupted the sacred song. He said: 'We have a king, surpassed by no one anywhere in justice or piety.* Everyone calls him by the name of Christ. It is he who sends us to your door in entreaty;* we ask for a modest venue for the rites and for our meal.' When he heard these words, Simon rejoiced in so great a name, and without any hesitation in his mind he ordered the whole building to be opened up; then he commanded celebratory torches to be lit in every part of the house, and the halls to be fumigated with rich perfumes from the woods of Arabia. He led the men inside, into the very centre of the innermost rooms of the house. There he showed them a place of marvellous construction, hung about with embroidered hangings and with fabrics of glowing purple.* The paved floors sparkled in splendour; the silver frames of the couches shone with ivory, and the cups and dishes were fashioned from unalloyed gold; and on all sides the house gleamed with silver and with gold.*

Then Simon spoke as follows: 'This is not the first time this name has come to my ears; rather, his virtue has been known to me by reputation for a long time, though I have not received heaven's sanction to look on him face to face or hear his divine voice while he spoke. Let him come. Let him graciously make himself at home in my welcoming house. You wait here. I shall send men to convey everything that has been arranged and lead him to my doorstep. If only he may see fit to stay a long time in my abode and honour this house with a name for hospitality! May it please our descendants to recall it from time to time, and show this fortunate place to later guests! Meanwhile, let me pursue the thread of the songs which were interrupted by your arrival, and go back over the ancient glories of our fathers, until black night buries the earth in dewy shade.'

So he spoke, and joining his voice to the harmonious strings he began to discourse in verse. You would think that everything he sang had been painted in due order or represented by woven figures.* Indeed, in his singing he brought the race of Isaac's descendants out of the territories of Pharaoh, and he sang how the leader of the exiles,* seizing a rod, parted the expanse of the sea, and how without ships they passed unscathed through the deep waters and trod the depths of the ocean with dry feet. For the moisture dried up and hardened, and a path was cut far and wide through the watery waves. Behind them, from all Egypt, their foes were pressing on their heels with shining weapons, carried by four-horse chariots. And now he sang of the righteous ones reaching the high shores after making their way through the sea, and concealing themselves in fear in the coastal forests. Without delay, once the earth had been struck a second time by the sacred staff—look, the sea poured back and returned to its own bounds, though a path through its midst previously divided it with a vast track. Then you could have seen the enemy rushing onwards and their weapons among the saltwater billows: weapons and horses and the submerged bodies of men, sinking deeper and deeper in the swell, and chariots constantly disappearing as they seemed to be swallowed up. Those who struggled on the surface in the midst of it all were suddenly gulped down where they flailed by the tide of seawater.

He went on to recount how the almighty Creator of all things from the very heaven fed his people with celestial food as they wandered through the endless wilderness, pitying them in their need. And there you'd think you could see the feast of manna falling like snow all of a sudden from the sky to the earth, and the assembled crowds all ready to feast on the banquet across the wide fields. Then their leader, raising his eyes to heaven, began to strike the hard rocks with that same rod, and at once a stream sprang up and the stones spouted sweet water, and the people whom thirst had parched as it built up over a long period,* leaving their mouths hanging open, drained the draught from the new spring. Then he sang how the first founder of Jerusalem's stronghold* offered gifts of cultivated crops and cups full of newly discovered wine on those rustic altars which he had constructed from green turf and cut ash-wood.

Yet while everyone absorbed all this with ears intent, Christ, who knew very well what was going on,* had made his way down from the high mountains and had once again entered the hostile city. And now, as the sun was hurrying down the slope of heaven, in the company of his disciples he entered the house of his host, arrayed as it was in royal opulence and with the banquet laid out.* They all lay down for dinner, and among them sat dismal Judas, concealing his purpose and feigning love in his features.

And now the hero, taking unleavened bread and the hurriedly made loaves, broke it in his hands and shared it out to all. Then he filled a dish with wine and with fresh water, and consecrated the divine offering of the blended draught; and he gave it frothing to his companions,* speaking as follows: 'This is the true image of my body, this the true image of my blood, which I shall pour out, one man for all, as a victim consecrated to my Father, so that I may take away the contamination of ancient wrong. So you, whenever it occurs that you are entering on a dinner which has been set out—a sacred feast and due drink-offering—, will repeat with these things the sorrowful sacrifice of my death; and the glory of that deed will never disappear.' That was all. Ever since then, later generations have preserved this ritual in commemoration,* and on the altars we consecrate unspoiled bread and sweet juice from the vine, instead of the ancients' bulls and their fatty entrails of sheep. He himself, the ruler of Olympus, drawn out from the stars by the priests' words, enters into the bread,* and the sacred body of God is offered together with his blood. This rite has come to be held in the highest honour.

So when his companions' hunger had been banished, the hero quickly stripped off his fine tunic and, girded in white cloth, asked for a cauldron boiling on the fire.* Then, sprinkling cold water with his right hand, and with his left testing the water that bubbled around the sounding rim, he cooled it. After this, he knelt down and applied water to the feet of Peter and the rest of his company (though the former, astonished by this unheard-of action, was persistent in refusing), and he dried them with soft clothing, bending over them; thus he left his companions an example for imitation.*

Then, drawing a groan from the depth of his breast,* he said: 'See, my friends, the final day* has come for me, which so often I foretold was approaching; that bitter night is at hand. I shall leave you and, dying, I shall fulfil the commands of my Father. There will be one of you (barely, barely is it right to believe in so dreadful a crime) who will betray me to my enemies through his own treachery. His plan does not escape me. Already he is deceitfully harbouring that frenzy and is plotting treachery in his greedy heart. Is *that* what my great devotion and my labours have earned? But whoever you turn out to be, you won't rejoice for long in that glorious deed of yours. It would be better if you had never tasted the love of daylight, and had never entered on the threshold of sweet life. But you others, remain faithful and in turn obey one another willingly among yourselves (these things I have left you as examples), and with a spirit of humility cast out the haughtiness of pride. At such a crucial point, the dismal powers of Erebus* will not let up in their efforts to overcome your hearts with fear. Please, keep guard in watchfulness and take thought for what lies far off. For now, display that purpose and resolve which so often you promised me; don't give in to that scourge. Preserve yourselves, men,* for just one night—no more.'

At once they were all distressed and fell to groaning, on tenterhooks as to what man so blind and in thrall to frenzy the hero, with his foreknowledge of the future, could mean, as he concealed the name in his speech. The oldest of them* addressed him in such words as these, beseeching him: 'Glory of heaven, must we really think that so horrible a crime could occur to anyone? Who is that most shameful of beings? I shall bring it about this day that he may never trick us and get away with it.* Not so completely has my sprightly spirit fled along with my blood, driven out by lapse of years, nor does my right hand droop with such a chill.'

So he spoke, and as he did so, he freed his sword from its scabbard. The leader had exposed his enemy by clear signs, yet he snatched away everyone's wits and wished the truth to remain hidden until the deed was accomplished. Then he spoke as follows: 'No, out of all your number no one of you will fail to be unfaithful to me on this last night; I shall be left alone. You too, who have shown such spirit now and let forth such a flood of eloquence* beneath this roof, and who reach beyond heaven with your grandiose utterances, stirring all winds and all tempests—when you see enemies surrounding us on all sides and I am taken captive, you will seek a hiding place and will ground your safety in your lying tongue, energetic in the flight of your feet. And when the damp night has reached the turning point in its course,* thrice will you yourself deny, uselessly, that I am known to you, and an unarmed woman will strike fear into you.'

He had spoken. Peter, however, pledged more and still more earnestly the steadfastness of his spirit and the impermeability of his heart to shameful fear: 'Let disgraceful flight preserve the safety of others; don't you charge me with fearfulness until you see me turn my back on the impending foe. Wherever you go, I shall be there. I shall proceed even to the very end at your side. There is no force that will be able to separate me from your fortunes.'

When all this was over, the god left the meal and the city, and in the calm of night he made his way in private with his companions to the green hills and sought out an isolated spot among the olive groves, where he commanded them all to keep watch with him. But they, exhausted by the constant toils of both night and day, were unable to keep unconquerable sleep from their eyes; and lying down on the topmost face of a chilly rock, they exhaled deeply in slumber that filled their beings. Meanwhile the hero, worn down by gloomy worries, as if forgetting that he was born from heavenly seed, turned over in his despondent mind the undeserved outcome that awaited him, the undeserved punishment and the bitter manner of his death, and he shuddered. For from his mother's body he had inherited in his own mortal heart the fear of all those things that frighten men's mortal hearts. Nonetheless his mind remained unshaken* and his virtue unconquered; and so, again and again, he addressed his Father and, holding out both hands to heaven, he questioned him in these tones: 'Almighty Father, is it by such a death as this that I am to perish? Am I to atone for others' sins by sufferings as great as these? Save me from a gruesome death, turn your harsh plans in a gentler direction, and avert cruel torments from me. And yet if that is your fixed, unshakeable purpose and this your unchanging will, if you cannot be placated towards the human race except by the mediation of your son's death, it is not right that I be found wanting for the world's salvation. I shall go willingly, and I shall cancel the shared sin of humanity.'*

He finished speaking, and checked his grievous sorrows deep in his heart,* though his thoughts were in turmoil. At the same time sweat broke out and ran all over his body, together with blood too, or something resembling blood. But look—radiant, suddenly gliding down from the starry heaven, there stood beside him a boy with wings of vivid hue, bringing amid such great upheaval his Father's consoling words. He soothed him in his anguish and relieved his anxiety,* wiping away the running moisture from his whole body.

But Judas, the backer and deviser of the crime,* meanwhile summoned Christ's enemies from the high summit, as arranged,* and offered himself to them unbidden as companion and guide as they came. And so there they were unexpectedly,* seeking to throw him in chains; their bronze weapons glittered far off in the light of the wavering moon. Now their shields clashed, now the sharp points of their swords grated,* and their oily torches dispersed the night* in a long procession, along with splintered brands, which had been coated in grease by hand and whittled to a point with sharp knives.

A din arose; on all sides the whole mountain around them rang with a riotous clatter of weapons and the shouting of men.

The hero, undaunted, addressed them with these words, saying: 'Hey, stop now, men; I am the one you're looking for.* Why the swords* and flames? Openly in the city, for all to see, I preached my Father's commandments in the midst of a mighty throng. Why didn't you all seize me then, unarmed as I was? Why do I behold these armed columns under the cover of night? But if even so you are coming with your weapons to claim me for death, though innocent, and my glory is so objectionable to you, let these men go unharmed. They have deserved nothing and dared nothing. All they have done is carry out the instructions of their beloved companion. I alone shall be given up to satisfy your rage.'

These were his words; and twice he offered himself up unbidden to those who sought him. But each time they—amazing to see—fell flat at his voice, their weapons gave a mighty clatter as they fell to the ground, and deep night suddenly welled up in their eyes. At last they got up, like men weighed down by sleep and wine,* and stood rooted to the spot oblivious, until Judas (who had not lain down to sleep anywhere that night) gave a clear signal and cast his friend before the enemy. For masking that crime in the guise of devoted affection,* he composed himself and kissed him with a feigned expression.

Christ sensed his treachery in advance, and spoke these words in an undertone: 'Is *this* kiss really what my love has earned, most loyal of friends? Are you seeking any reward by so great a crime? This was not indeed the bargain I once struck with you.' Scarcely had he uttered this when a gang of young men rushed blindly around him* and surrounded everyone in a close cordon. Just as when a stag has been forced into thin-meshed nets, or a boar fearsome with its flashing tusks, and a band of shepherds rages around it, vying to pile on their spears at close quarters, and on all sides their hollering reaches the stars and the nearby mountains bellow back with the noise; so the raging troop pressed close on the young man, hemmed in by their far-shining weapons, and all loomed over their unarmed victim. Some seized him with their hands, others cast ropes of hemp around his neck,* and they led him captive now this way, now that.

Raving beyond all others and uncontrolled in his advance* was Malchus, who had been sent as a captive from the territory of Edom. He was unaccustomed to fighting* and combat, and had neither strength nor courage enough for it in his breast. But to display his excellence in arms to Caiaphas (in whose retinue he came as a servant, having been given to him)—for he saw that everything was safe and that here no danger stood in the path of one acting boldly—he behaved boldly, and disgracefully laid into a foe who was yielding willingly. Vainly he sharpened his windy tongue* for abuse, and scarcely could he contain his hopes, puffed up in his heart. Peter, quick-tempered as he was, could not endure this; he snatched up his sword, and bearing down on him, he inflicted on his temple an ignominious wound,* cutting off his broad ear faster than words could say.

Seeing this, the god suddenly stretched out his hand and lifted the severed part from the earth along with the sodden dust, and with a healing hand* he fitted it where it had been cut off, and fastened it in its place; it stayed put without any pain, and no traces of the wound were visible anywhere. Then, chiding his companion, who had been eager to defend him from violence by force of hand, he ordered him to sheathe his weapon and not to trust in his sword; that was forbidden. Had he not done so, the old man, burning with rage, would have driven his drawn sword through the ribs* of that pointless blusterer. 'These are not the means, this is not the force', he said, 'we rely on. I have a Father, who, if he wished to save me from bitter death and be placated towards the human race without his Son's blood being shed, could send to me from the starry stronghold a hundred companies, a hundred divisions, of angels to slay this hateful mob with the sword. Do you not know of the heavenly host and the wars it has fought, and its various powers and titles? Now let me obey my great parent's orders, which alone compel me. I have no time for human weapons.'

On hearing such words the old man scarcely ceased from his anger, unwilling as he was: just like if a Molossian hound happens to catch sight, in the middle of a city, of a stag tamed to follow its master's orders,* and rushes after it, thinking it wild; scarcely can the hunter check it with his calls as it goes for the neck with its rabid jaws. And so all of them laid hands on him (ah, the unworthy sight!), willingly defeated and not resorting to force, and they dragged him off in his weakness and pressed upon him with harsh words when he fell.

Almighty Father, ruler of those above on Olympus, can you witness these things with such composure and not merge hell with heaven?

Will you ever hurl from your hand the terrifying thunderbolt, if now the face of the unmoved universe is cloudless? Now let creation's law be broken, and let the elements toil in confusion and rush around abruptly; let the steep sky come crashing down.* Why is your hand not busy? Why is the earth not already smoking from your three-pronged firebrand? What uses is your devouring flame being saved up for? The human race is not worth so much, nor the palace of heaven with its complement of winged choirs, nor the golden race, distinguished for its devotion,* which soon will raise itself from here to the stars. Let not your care for us inflame you with such great love that you allow your only-begotten son to be whirled in such a tempest, abandoned, helpless and enduring the ultimate agony.

Christ's companions scattered in fear and took refuge in the woods, scared witless as if at the approach of a foaming boar or a fierce lion. Everywhere their bestial foe pursued them as they went. You could have seen this man, already taken captive, now slipping through their hands, leaving his garments behind, and making for the heights in a headlong sprint; and that one going deep into caves and whatever sheltered nooks he could find in the woods, and burying himself in hollows in the rocks.* There was no breathing space, no chance for rest:* the trackless groves seethed with scurrying movement, and the leafy hills resounded with endless clamour.*

And now they were making their way into the spacious dwelling of the High Priest; at once there was a rush there on all sides from the entire city. The foremost of the leading citizens were there demanding punishment, all of them hostile* to just one man, and fixing on him a look of savage hatred they intimidated and menaced him with cruel threats as he stood there bound. Then Caiaphas, the leader of the race, finally spoke as follows:

'You have done well today, men. This monstrous scoundrel* has not been able to escape by recourse to any wiles, and now he has no means of escape left. You must bolster your spirits and do what is left to be done. Now is that day when the greatest glory presents itself to us—but we shall need our wits about us as we hasten to get things done. Hear me, and grant me your silence and attention,* all of you. None of us has the right to condemn anyone to death; it is by the authority of the Roman governor that a man stands or falls. Let us first of all seek reasons and charges to procure his death, and then let us approach the governor once we are properly equipped with allegations, so that he may hear our case and sentence our enemy to death, with no possibility of defence.'

So he spoke. Then he addressed the captive: 'Are you he, then, the true offspring of the supreme god, the true god, whom prophets in times past foretold as destined to come into the world from the height of heaven?* By the divinity of the Father who sustains the stars, I conjure you: speak, and do not conceal your identity any further from those who seek you. Tell me now openly who you are, casting aside all clouds, so that we may not in our ignorance defraud you of the honour that is due to your divine status.'

He had spoken. Christ, however, standing weary and weaponless with all eyes upon him,* raised his eyes but slightly, and spoke: 'I am what you say. Why are you wasting your effort in putting me to the test, when you have made this same enquiry so many times? Spare your concealed traps and give up your trickery at last—you have been defeated. I declare it openly: there will be but a short interval before the shining expanse of Olympus on high places itself in my power and submits to my rule; now, even now, you will see me in the heavenly palace clasping my almighty Father's hand, and from there you will see me soon return to earth again, gleaming in a radiant cloud, with a thousand denizens of heaven following me* and beating the air with gilded wings.'

Scarcely had he said this, when the priest, tearing his tunic from his shoulders in time-honoured fashion, said: 'What further light does this case need cast on it, when it is clear from such a mass of evidence? He himself confesses his crime openly. Surely both right and law command that whoever dares to pretend he is the son of God should be punished with a pitiless death? Take him, don't just stand there! Hurry him off to the Roman governor's mansion, I order you, and demand the punishment he deserves.'

Meanwhile Peter, stricken by this cruel calamity, followed the proceedings with a heavy heart, watching his friend from afar.* And now he had come all the way to the entrance of the vast temple, the dwelling of the High Priest, and was sitting alone and sorrowful, his spirit broken, before the open doors; night had fallen. A slave-woman, who was tasked with keeping the door of her master's home, suspecting what was indeed the case, said to him: 'Are you too fleeing, then, you who were at that man's side as a partner in his crimes, and so are here as a spy in the shadows, when everything is at rest in the night?'

Peter froze at her voice, paralysed with shameful terror. Forgetting himself (yet why did he have so great a craving for life?),* he no longer knew, in his confusion at the sudden turn of events,* what to do, where to turn, what devices to employ: like a little girl, lulled by soft snoozing, when her mother has left her behind unawares in the deserted fields as she makes her way back home while day departs. All at once, her sleep punctured, she casts her tearful eyes around her and, not catching sight of her friends or her mother anywhere, she sees the abandoned places and is overwhelmed by panic, forgetting the way home; in her eyes, everything around her takes on a dreadful aspect in the black of night.

In such a state was poor Peter, baffled in his mind and rooted to the spot. But at last he disavowed the name of his dear friend, for whom he had only just now pledged passionately that he would willingly meet death. Indeed, he even put up with entering an enemy's home to protect himself, and had the folly to mingle among the servants. But he didn't succeed in passing unnoticed. They all looked at him with hostile glances as an object of suspicion, and assailed him with their words as he skulked in his hiding place. Three times he had heard the name and country of his master cast at him, and three times he had feigned ignorance with false assertions, when those crested fowl* whose habit it is to summon the dawn on the rooftops with their piercing voice began to give out the signal with their morning song that midnight had now passed.* Then, reminded of the last words that the hero had prophesied, he groaned and broke into sighing from the depth of his heart, and in his sadness the pain of remorse flared up deep in his brittle bones.* Then the poor man, reproaching himself and his dismal dread, slunk secretly through the doors, and groaned in solitude all through the city for the length of that night, without the blessing of sleep, as he tore at the white beard that fell over his chest. Indeed, they say that he always wept at this hour after that for as long as he lived, remembering what he had done. Often the rising sun, as it opened up the sky, and often the darkening evening found him in lonely caverns wallowing in grief and uttering those same complaints, while he allowed his grieving love no solace.* Constantly he recalled those final admonitions of the king he had deserted, and he kept thinking of how he had been stricken with terror by a woman's speech.

And now the time had come, when Aurora* had not yet risen and brought back the daylight, marking out the whitening regions of the sky. Already they were dragging the god, his hands tied behind his back,* to the seat of the governor, so that the one who had authority in this matter might make his own enquiry into the charges and might sentence the prisoner to a pitiless death. At that time Pontius Pilate, a Roman of distinguished family, was holding the reins of wealthy Judaea, having been sent at the command of Tiberius Caesar. A frenzied mob now advanced upon him with untamed uproar, shouting; 'Put this man to death! Fix him to the cross of shame he has deserved, this instigator of crimes and master of deception!'

They yelled these things over and over again, surging forward at the doorway in a packed crowd.* Pilate, however, kept his eyes and gaze fixed ever so intently* on the tall figure of the young man (for the fresh bloom of his youth had not yet disappeared at all), and marvelled at his extraordinary appearance and the remarkable graciousness of his features, and could not get enough of looking at him.* He acknowledged that this man was sprung either from the lineage of gods, or at least from the bloodline of mighty kings, and inwardly he pitied the cruel fortune* of his captive. Now he looked to help him, and silently deliberated whether there was any way he could rescue him without harm and free him from his chains, breaking those bonds. He addressed him as follows: 'Come then, tell me—what are these things you have done that now torment you, what calamities? From where has this squall suddenly rushed out upon you?* Surely no evil crimes have plunged and entangled you in such a mass of troubles? Can it be the gods' severe wrath? What home do you come from? What race do you claim to be sprung from,* or what rule do you aspire to? What kingdom is owed to you?'

Christ replied in just a few words: 'It is not because of any crime that I am being dragged here. My mind is guilty of no shameful deed, but I am following the orders of my Father, who is obeyed by the court of boundless heaven. Nor do I waste my time on mortal kingdoms, although I would certainly not deny that I come from a glorious line of kings.' This was all he said. Pilate, however, marvelling at his attractive and noble features, addressed him now on this topic, now on that,* and probed him in every way he could. But the hero did not favour him with any further reply, assailed as he was by a cruel tide of cares.* Finally the governor, to curb the resentful crowd, ordered him to be taken in and kept him shut away in the inner part of the building.

BOOK THREE

WINGED Rumour had now filled the neighbouring cities with the news that the hero had been captured by the plotting and treachery of his own people. Nonetheless, the report that spread abroad was still unclear and its author unknown;* nor had it yet reached the ears of his mother, despite her fear of everything in her prophetic spirit, which never left her free from care. Undoubtedly she had heard the fearsome forecasts of the prophets,* which filled her with alarm, that her son would willingly undergo a pitiless death to secure the deliverance* of the faithful.

But when the elderly Joseph,* to whom Christ's tender mother had been entrusted of old by orders from heaven, got wind that something was up, he left Nazareth and made his way to the city of Jerusalem. He had scarcely set foot within the city when he saw that everything was in turmoil, the inhabitants rushing together in great numbers through the shadows in the dimness of night,* and the city walls in complete uproar from the widespread commotion. But look—slipping out of the hands and weapons* of an armed patrol, the faithful John ran up to him, sorrowful and pale-faced. But in his panic he barely recognized his friend, flustered as he was* and with his mind fixated on his leader's cruel calamity. The elderly man said to him: 'Hey, stop there.* Where are you rushing? Where do our fortunes stand?* Where is your leader now without you—the son of God? What's this almighty hubbub in the city? Ah, I see that his anxious mother's premonitions have not misled her!'

So he spoke. But the young man, embracing and clinging to him, for a while just poured out tears and emitted groans.* At last he managed a brief answer:* 'Ah, our hope is dead, all of it, and our salvation wiped out.* The leader is cruelly captured and confined to a dungeon. In their envy, the city leaders are conspiring against him, demanding severe punishment and bloodshed.* All the faithful have taken flight, driven by dread. Where is his mother? Has the news already stung the poor woman's ears? If only she were now here with you in person: Pontius Pilate, seeing a parent's tears and groans, might perhaps bring himself to feel pity* at this undeserved calamity. Even so, we ought to go and beg for a truce and for pardon,* and make clear to him the people's envy and spiteful hatred.'

With such words he turned his step towards the mansion of the governor of Syria. The elderly man went along with him and they made their way together in sadness, like when a penniless farmer has lost his cattle, driven off by an enemy ravaging the fields; straightaway he embarks on a long journey to look for them, and his eldest son goes with him as his companion. And if by chance they both see cattle similar to their own wandering here and there through unfamiliar fields, they stand and weep and fill the countryside with their laments.

Just so were those men; and now they had reached the doorway of the building, which once had been the most ancient seat of kings, while the fortunes of Judaea yet remained firm and its kingdom undiminished; but at that time the Roman governor of the province occupied it. They saw everything in turmoil and commotion, and the elders in the very entrance quarrelling violently, and the priests now gradually withdrawing from the palace, to all appearances hostile towards the Roman and threatening dire consequences.

At this the newcomers roused their spirits* and began to calm their grief a little, starting to hope for some kind of salvation* for their predicament. And John spoke as follows: 'As I see it, some measure of hope is revealing itself here. Put aside your fear and speak to the man on behalf of your son—but keep quiet about his being the son of God, and come up with reasons for your entreaty.'* With these words they both entered the mansion together, and the older man addressed the governor, who, unsure how to proceed in this same matter, was requesting advice on this business in the midst of the leaders. Clasping his knees, Joseph implored him as a suppliant: 'Worthiest of the Romans, you whom the ruler of bright Olympus wished to keep proud Syria under control by your justice,* have mercy on the virtuous and curb men's wild frenzy. This has caused them to lose their reason entirely, and to resort to violence. I am the father of that man, who is the lone target of all the leading citizens' conspiracy and their attempts at intimidation on a false charge. And now he has been handed over to you as being the one man more monstrous than all others in his wrongdoing,* so that he may pay an undeserved penalty by his blood.* Yet only his own goodness and his services throughout the world have plunged him in these troubles,* while that savage race grudges him his superlative praise and cannot endure the honour awarded to one who is on the rise.'

Such was his plea; at the same time, tears soaked the old man's face in a generous shower.* Pontius Pilate received him with a kindly expression and comforted both of them with words of friendship,* and he himself sat the old man down in a comfortable seat* and proceeded to reply as follows: 'How welcome is your arrival here, just in time! And perhaps you will not regret having come. Now, father, just tell me a few things as I seek to establish the truth, and don't be afraid. It's completely right for you to trust in my good faith. I call as my witnesses the heaven and heaven's wandering stars: my greatest concern, anxious as I am, is now for your son. I am racking my mind to keep him safe for you, and as far as I could I have curbed the frenzy and rage of this unjust race.* Come then, tell me—for this is not the first time his name has reached my ears: what is this man's fortune, what home is he from, from what bloodline is he sprung?* Tell me your own family, and his mother's; for he certainly isn't descended from any humble stock, if my intuition is correct.* How he bears himself! How superhuman is his appearance, both in his face and in his whole figure! How full of distinction are his eyes, how majestic his movements! And then I marked his words: no mortal sound there. I sensed divinity in his breast. Surely he is either a god,* or not sprung from mortals. Speak, then; for he himself turned away from me when I made enquiry, and barely favoured me with an answer, silent in spite of my friendliness. He has a spirit that scorns both the light of day* and me.'

Following this speech, the elderly man stood doubtful for a little while, unsure whether to conceal his thoughts from his questioner further, or to reveal to him Christ's divine lineage and the true nature of his parent, without deception. Then his companion came up and briefly spoke in his ear: 'Offspring of kings, found worthy of glorious marriage* to a maiden, why do you still stick fast? Abandon your fear. Reveal everything now freely, dispersing the clouds. Lay aside your foreboding and cast off delay: I can see that all is safe.'*

He had finished speaking. Joseph, therefore, putting aside his terror, began: 'Indeed I shall speak, nor, governor, shall I keep great secrets hidden from you in silence.* But since you are resolved to learn my ancestry, I shall touch on that first, and won't keep you in doubt and perplexity. Although the poverty of my situation has driven me to turn to the labours of a craftsman, even so I possess a pedigree descending from the bloodline of kings, a lineage close in proximity to heaven, and illustrious ancestors. First of all, Abraham, that father and supreme founder of our countless race, has not failed, I believe, to reach your ears; it was he who gave the laws to our people and the forms of religious ritual. He begat Isaac, and from Isaac sprang his son Jacob, who then produced the twelve leaders after whom our whole race is divided into twelve houses and tribes. Among these Judah was distinguished above the rest, pre-eminent both for his devotion and for his outstanding offspring, and he called the land Judaea after his own name.* From this line, albeit with a very long sequence* of patriarchs in between, was sprung David, the father of kings; and from there comes the line of my own ancestors, extending from its origin through fourteen kings.

'But very different is the young man's lineage. Though he accepted mortal parents and was born in the mortal world, he is a divine being with a heavenly origin, was begotten by the fatherhood of God, and rejoices in a parent whom the sail-strewn sea, the earth and the sky obey.* But a woman never joined with man brought him forth into the airy breeze of daylight,* and even after giving birth her maidenhood remained intact, as in past times prophets foretold would come to pass.* For the almighty Father breathed upon her with fertile breath from above and filled her, and her womb swelled from heavenly causes. As for the fact that I am commonly believed to be his father, the true situation is not so: his tender mother was merely entrusted to me, to share the worries of her soul* and her gruelling labour. It was only later that, anxious about her reputation and unsullied chastity, she favoured me, undeserving as I am and unworthy of such an honour, with the name of lawful husband.

'To reveal the whole business to you and trace it back from the beginning: she was the most beautiful maiden among the girls of Judaea, desired by a hundred suitors, the only child of her parents, born in the city of Nazareth—they called her Mary. But she herself hated the idea of a union, because of her eternal love of maidenhood,* and had pledged herself at the altars. Yet her ancient mother Anne, well aware of the prophets and filled with knowledge of the future,* had foreseen that one day a child would be born from her daughter, wondrous in his deeds and a future king, destined to hold powerful nations beneath his powerful sway;* that, she saw, had been set fast by heaven, and was what the reverent prophets declared. Often in her dreams a voice sent through the air had instructed her to join her daughter in marriage and send for potential sons-in-law: already she was the right age for a husband, already marriageable.* Yet up to this point her parents had put off obeying the commands from heaven, when look!—again, in full daylight, through the air above was heard the voice: “Make haste and wed your daughter to a husband. You do not have to go looking far off for sons-in-law; let them be sought from your own blood, as is customary. Away with all slothful delay!”*

‘At once a report spread through the small city.* Then all the young men related to them gathered in hope of a beautiful wife; the girl’s house was full. I myself, being closely related to her father, came forward too, despite being advanced in age, to congratulate him, a friend and contemporary, on his daughter’s marriage. They stood there numberless, in all the flower of beauty and comparable age, unsure of the intended recipient of so great a gift from heaven; and each one longed for the lot to favour him.*

‘While their hopes hovered doubtfully, and the crowd of suitors remained clueless as to how things would turn out,* we all withdrew to the secluded part of the grand dwelling, where Joachim, the girl’s father, was in the habit of offering divine worship. There was an age-old altar,* which the first among our race had set up, consecrated in the fear of God; for full three hundred years our ancestors had tended it. Around this we all prostrated ourselves humbly on the ground, praying to the heavenly beings and their Father for peace, and asking that he might show his favour and give a sign from heaven above indicating his choice.* In our midst stood the dazzling girl, in tears, her blonde hair streaming, her eyes lowered and bedewed with copious weeping. A blush, seeping over her fair cheeks, had the effect of mixing lilies with red roses.* Just like a new moon, when it has bathed its virginal features in the sea and risen with stars accompanying it far and wide, makes its way through the blue expanse of heaven with graceful horns, so was the girl, thronged by a circle of young men,* as she called repeatedly on God and his winged ministers with her words to witness that she was not willingly being bent to this undertaking. Her father sought to reassure her in her distress and wiped her tearful eyes, telling her of the commandments from heaven and kissing her* as he did so.

'But look—being present too as matron of honour, in the midst of the throng her mother Anne, seized with a sudden frenzy, began to dance wildly* through the whole house, filled with divine inspiration (an awesome sight!), and to raise a deafening wail to heaven. On me alone she turned her gaze, and made her way towards me alone, though this was the last thing I was expecting and I'd feared nothing of the kind. Seizing me with her hand, she said: "You alone are chosen; to you alone has the king of heaven granted this union." Everyone was dumbstruck, but no one out of the whole assembly* grudged an older man the honour for which he had not bid. I myself, because my age was impaired by the passing of years, insistently refused, and I much regretted that I had come there; but trusted friends of my own age were there for me, both offering encouragement in my reluctance and putting spirit into me by their cajoling words. And so I was won over and gave way,* and finally I approached her full of husbandly solicitude, and in tears myself I led her in tears to my doorstep.

'And now night was at hand, studded with shining stars, spreading shadows over the world with its darkening wings. Together we both entered the secluded bedchamber. My bride was weeping, and the whole ground around her was wet with tears; just as if, when in spring the intensely fertile sap rises in the trees, an unsuspecting farmer, pruning the tip of a pliant vine, should chance to strike the stock with his curved sickle and defile the undeserving mother-plant with an injury. I was at her side and tried to console her in her wretchedness with gentle words, desiring not at all to pluck the first flower of her virginity. Then, drawing long sighs from the depth of her heart,* she broke into speech as follows: "No empty superstition induced me* to hate the idea of a union and cultivate an eternal love of maidenhood.* From within a heavenly force drives me, from within. Though the contradictory oracles and the threats of the prophets worry my aged mother, I too have my own opposing orders* from the prophets: not to give in to any stain, and not to bow my virgin mind to any marriage.* Before that would the Jordan reverse its flow and hurry backwards to its original source, and the wandering stars would halt their course!"* This was what she said; and as she spoke, jewel-like tears of virtue began to swell up from her eyes and rolled all down her cheeks.

'Immediately a sudden terror then ran through me and shook the very depths of my frame. My knees gave way and began to totter, and a deep night rose up before my eyes. Three times I tried to stammer out a few words, but three times my tongue was thwarted in its attempt to make a sound, and the words did not follow.* Then too a voice was heard: "Refrain from marital bed and bridal chamber waiting ready; yet preserve the marriage permitted to you." I got up, and after fixing my eyes for a long while on the formidable girl,* at last I spoke in such words as these: "Who joined you to me, maiden, against heaven's will? Who enravelled me undeservedly in such monstrous business? I didn't seek out this marriage. It wasn't this kind of mockery that my father the prophet once foretold to me as a boy, elderly prophet as he already was then, and priest of the temple. No, he prophesied that there awaited me either no union at all, no marriage at all, or that I would surely be famous* on that score. But come, I shall reveal the resolve that is rising in my mind,* since those above have joined you to me and yet those same beings frighten me off with their portents. You are free, and always will be free, to preserve the flower of your virginity, your body untouched. But I wouldn't dare to undo those bonds of sacred wedlock unbidden. We shall pass our lives in the same home, I as a father to you and you like a daughter to me forever, and to that degree I now take you into my embrace, come what may.* This is what your devotion would wish, and likewise my advanced age." The girl agreed to this arrangement and slept apart in another part of the house. I pass over all the portents and amazing dreams I experienced, as I shuddered, through all the course of that night.

'And now the day was glowing red as it made its entrance, the darkness now driven off, and the sun had dispersed the dark shadows with its rosy torch. I roused myself from bed and made my way to my bride.* Scarcely had I pushed open the double doors of the bedroom on their hinge when a light—look!—an intense light suddenly filled my eyes.* The panels of the ceiling above* shone with its rays, the beams shone, and the bedroom seemed to be on fire. The girl herself, bathed in gold, was sitting in the middle of the chamber like one stunned, and she did not favour me with a reply, though I had many questions. She was wholly unaffected by my speech.* She merely fixed her eyes on heaven and held out her hands, like a star or like the glowing dawn. Ah, how changed she was from her usual form!* How great the glory of her eyes, how great the splendour conferred upon her face! Just as if, when the sculptor's hand has fashioned a statue of maple wood from the forest to be set up in a sacred site for all the common folk to venerate thereafter in humble supplication, after he has shaped the image from the trunk by his art, polishing it smooth, he should place upon it the final adornment by applying a layer of gold on its surface. As she sat motionless, the luminous cloud completely surrounded her, blazing with the sun's rays,* and shining stars seemed to be grazing around the golden temples of her head,* while the gleaming moon seemed to shed light beneath the goddess's feet.

'I was petrified, and struck senseless by the wondrous appearance of things* I came out with words like these: "Almighty Father, release me from these supernatural happenings. The heavenly ones are not bringing these things to pass without your divine will.* I recognize these portents and visible signs as yours. Look favourably upon me, breathe inspiration into my soul, and instruct me in my doubt what course I should pursue or what is your fixed resolution." That was all I said. At last the exquisite girl returned to herself, sighing as if stirred suddenly from sleep, and bathed her breast in welling tears.* I went up to her and asked her humbly, in the name of our recent wedlock and that love of hers for eternal virginity, which alone she cherished,* unspoiled in her chastity white as snow, to admit me as a partner in her cares, reveal without fear the great secrets of her life, and trust me with everything.

'She kept her face and shining eyes downcast* on the ground, like a rose drooping its head with the morning dew, and hesitated. Finally she unsealed her lips and began as follows: "Indeed I shall tell you,* father. I shall not allow my joys to lie hidden from you. But where shall I start, how shall I begin?* For who would believe someone who told of such miraculous things, such wondrous events? By these tears* which my boundless happiness wrings from me, I beg you, store up in your heart the things I shall tell you, so they may not begin to go creeping in among the fatuous crowd before God himself has broadcast everything by other signs.

'"Now Dawn, the superintendent of tasks, had put the stars to flight, and the sun was beginning to light up with its lamp the pale earth.* I myself was pondering the utterances of past prophets,* recalling their words in my mind. But at that time one thing beyond all others happened to remain motionless or fixed before my eyes—and I don't think it was without a definite design* that it occurred to me. This was what all of them equally foretold would come to pass above all else, when a royal virgin, without intercourse, without experience or possession of a man (marvellous to tell), would bring forth the king of the heaven-dwellers into the air of daylight,* at whose coming all things would rejoice throughout the globe and straightaway a golden race would arise through the whole world.*

'"Silently, to myself, I called that woman blessed whom the almighty Father should load with such honour, and already I revered in my mind the one who would be God's mother, and I was starting to prepare gifts for the infant god, in case he should chance to be born in these days and in this land. But while I was contemplating such things privately, unaware of how things would turn out—look! An unfamiliar light suddenly met my eyes.* I looked up, and cast a sweeping glance around the cloudless, clear air. I shall tell you a marvel: I saw heaven parting down the middle* and a winged host, the inhabitants of happy Olympus, rejoicing in the skies and glorifying the king of angels. No closed doors, no building ringed with wall of stone, stood in their way. I saw the fiery stars of heaven and the starry spheres, the golden dwellings of those above. Then a boy, gliding down from Olympus before my eyes, like a god in his countenance, came to me on radiant wings; and calmly proffering in his hand white lilies, he addressed me as follows, uttering joyful words: 'Most pleasing to heaven beyond all other* mothers, the mighty ruler of Olympus is with you, his power close at hand. You alone are more fortunate than all women.'

'"At this, though I had scarcely heard these few words, an intense trembling suddenly gripped my limbs, frozen with fear, as I marvelled. Then he strengthened my spirits as follows with a divine assurance:* 'Put away your fear,* maiden. You alone out of all have found favour with the king of heaven, for him to make you the mother of his child.* And now you will conceive a son, being pregnant; he will be mighty, and all ages will call him the offspring of the supreme Father. And since he himself will one day bring salvation to many and will save the faithful, you must call him by the ancestral name JESUS—a name which is now already a source of mourning in the infernal realms. You will see him raise himself above all people, above even the very heaven-dwellers,* glorious in his fame and his exceptional feats. For the almighty Father will restore him to the ancient rule* of his ancestors, and he will reign far and wide and will sit on the throne of kings. He will receive no limits to his kingship in space or time; over the whole earth he will reign for ever.'*

'"He had spoken. But I myself, as my fear gradually departed, responded: 'But in what way can this thing you speak of come about? For my purpose remains altogether fixed and unmoved,* never to impair my virginal chastity, and I have always shunned dealings with men.'

'"With these few words I finished speaking, and with these he answered: 'The heavenly Father will breathe upon you from above with divine breath;* filled by this breathing alone, without any human intercourse, you will give birth to your child when the time of your pregnancy has been completed. And therefore, the one you bring to birth will be counted as a god, born from the eternal Father who rules the world. So you do not think these words empty,* you know how your kinswoman, Elizabeth, has so far been lacking in offspring, and how for a long time her worn-out old age has deprived her of all hope of giving birth and producing children, barren as she is from long years.* Nonetheless she is pregnant by her husband and will bear a child,* and the moon has already completed its sixth cycle since the start of her pregnancy. For he who is sending me to you from heaven on high can accomplish all things, the king and creator of starry Olympus.' So he spoke, and darted off to heaven on his pair of wings.

'"Looking up to heaven, I answered him with words such as these: 'Whoever you are, most beautiful of heaven's youths, I eagerly obey, and with all my prayers I desire what the king commands.' Meanwhile a cloud, stippled with specks of gold, descended to the earth and embraced me in its yellow wings.* Rays of light gleamed within, and scales (so to speak) flashing with fire sparkled all around in different configurations, scales and stars glittering with the sheen of gold, such tints as the misty rainbow imitates in the light of the facing sun when it divides the heaven with its colourful garment,* once the drenching showers are all poured out. As soon as the almighty Father breathed through this cloud from on high, at once there rushed—look!—whirling from the shimmering stars, a mighty wind; and wherever it went, far off, from all sides, all around, sparks of gold leapt out from the flickering beams. I was caught up in the wild whirlwind, and that force, the almighty force of the wind, was spread through all my limbs, and the heavenly energy permeated my whole body,* and my heart seemed to melt with a love intensely sweet—just as the earth, through the hidden compact of nature, conceives and grows heavy, filled in secret with its varied young, when the sky descends in abundance into the mother's lap, and the spring breeze wafts its fertile warmth.* At this the winged throngs sounded clearly through the upper air in varied singing and gave their applause.* Then the heights of Olympus trembled with an awesome thunderclap, and throughout the heaven, on this side and that, frequent flashes of fire flickered out."*

'Such things the girl related, and as she did so, happiness covered her cheeks with tears.* Then I stretched out my hands to the stars, praying intently and wavering in my mind. I could not believe her* as she reported such wonders (so wayward were my senses),* considering that young men are very often in the habit of devising traps for unsuspecting maidens and dishonestly deceiving girls too easily inclined to lend an ear to their words, alas! Still more, at one point I even contemplated (criminal as it was) leaving her, in my madness. But then in a dream the same vision appeared to me of a boy returning, strongly resembling in face and attire that figure my spouse had just reported as having spoken to her. His rosy shoulders were bare; on the shining left one only a cloak hung down, which a polished triple gold clasp held tight below the waist, and a red girdle hung with close-set ornaments.* Soft feathers gradually grew from his back and rose by degrees from his shoulders to form two wings. Beyond that, he wore jewelled boots, but was otherwise bare.* The great distinction of his face and the graceful movements of his body bore witness that a boy not of our race was at hand, but the offspring of heaven and a nursling of the starry palace. No less remarkable for its amazing workmanship was his actual clothing, tricked out with pearls along its upper edges. Below ran a band of gold fabric with a double meander,* an astonishing work. Here three embroidered boys* were happily passing unscathed through the flames, and together they were singing praises to the king of the heaven-dwellers* as they turned towards the stars. Fierce fires could be seen* in the heart of the furnace sparing their bodies, and flames retiring to a distance.

'I was silently marvelling, when that most beautiful youth addressed me thus as I trembled: "Scion of the bloodline of kings,* what crime so terrible has slunk into your mind? Don't all the signs convince you that these things are not coming about without a definite design?* Do not be in doubt,* since the most holy virgin declares the truth. Already now, though never joined with any man, she has conceived a child, made pregnant supernaturally by the breath of heaven; for the almighty Father breathed upon her from the celestial stronghold,* and divine power filled her womb, gliding down from the stars. Her unsullied faith receives our worship. Cease from your fear. These things your prophets once proclaimed would happen,* but they wrapped everything up in the concealment of mysterious riddles. For she indeed is that mighty portal in the lofty sanctum of heaven, forever closed and impassable for any human being.* Only almighty God himself passes and repasses by that way,* and he does not open the unmoved bolts. This woman the ruler of highest Olympus entrusts to you, joining you in stable wedlock*—but avoid union with your wife. Let your bride pass her life free from care in your company, even though the virgin is already now safe under God's protection."

'Speaking thus, he suddenly vanished into the insubstantial breeze,* hastening in swift flight through the clouds to the airy fields; and as he did so, he struck enchanting love into my breast,* and just as the hardness of iron softens in the glowing fire, so I felt my heart grow soft with a quickened pulse. I got up and, turning towards heaven, prayed for forgiveness, reproaching myself witlessly; and the light returned to my mind.* And day by day, the sublime schemes of heaven were more and more clearly revealed, all of which God once disclosed to the ancient prophets, wrapping the truth in riddles.* This virgin is that bush, which the horned seer saw ablaze far off on the mountain, burning with a crackling fire,* although the harmless flame licked it without touching it* and its leaves were undamaged and grew green upon the stalk. This same woman was the fleece of snow-white wool,* once impenetrable by rainstorms, though everything far and wide was drenched by the pouring showers all around and the moist earth was swimming—unless the prescience of the ancient prophets is hollow. I pondered on these things, and from my whole heart the darkness was completely driven off.

'Without delay, the truth of the matter was established* by mighty portents. Now a report spread abroad through the towns of Galilee declared that there had lately been found (a mighty wonder!) among the high mountains an old woman who, though already afflicted by extreme old age, had become pregnant by her husband and given him hope of a child, although even in her youth she had been barren and infertile. Then my wife said to me: "The boy sent down from the bounds of heaven foretold this to me, for I remember everything.

This is the old woman, this my kinswoman Elizabeth, for whom the moon has already completed its sixth cycle since the start of her pregnancy."* That was all she said. At once she wanted to go and visit the old woman who was closely related to her, and we both made our way over the heights and sought out the lofty abode of the prophet Zechariah far off. Scarcely had I set foot on the doorstep when—amazing to tell*—the old woman ran up trembling and gave the girl as she entered the embraces she desired.* As she embraced her, God entered into her, a sudden heat ran all at once through her inmost bones, and in reverential awe she uttered words such as these:

'"Uniquely blessed are you far above other mothers,* you and the burden of your womb, most holy virgin. What has caused such great favour from heaven to come suddenly upon me? What has caused this glorious season to shine upon my late old age?* Behold, it has been granted to me to look upon the mother of God, and speak in her presence to the one woman chosen from thousands, who has graced this house and freely set out to my home. For you had scarcely set foot on this doorstep when my heart felt a jolt, and leaping up in my womb the child gave a sign. Blessed divine parent, most pleasing to the king of heaven, tried and proven in your flawless faith, you who did not hesitate to believe the words of truth while you had as yet no foreknowledge of the joys that would be yours. See, the promises of the winged boy remain sure for you. Already now be at hand and look upon the world's misfortunes, queen of heaven,* pitying the toils* of humankind."

'She had spoken; and like a rose full of tender modesty, the shining maiden, not at all carried away by feelings of pride, began joyfully to sing praises to the king of heaven,* since in his goodness he had looked upon her so closely from starry Olympus, unworthy and lowly as she was, deserving nothing of the kind. And in her exultation she prophesied the honours that would be hers, promised of old to her forebears and ancient ancestors.*

'What great portents and prophetic manifestations terrified people's minds after that throughout the boundless world, up to the point when the almighty babe was reaching the threshold of life—it would take a long time to recount all that. Already at that time the Caspian realms were shuddering at the prophets' responses, already the Nile and all Egypt trembled,* and all the cities of the East. Even your own people (if the report is true) had heard throughout the bounds of Italy that an unconquerable king was on the point of issuing forth into the air of daylight, one to whom the world would surrender itself on every side to be ruled, and who would bring himself, mighty through his father's powers, and his people to Olympus on high.*

'By these signs I was at last made sure, and I humbly revered my expectant wife like a deity and willingly obeyed her. A winged boy used to bring food and divine drink from heaven to the pregnant woman; I often saw him entering her chamber in clear daylight.* And now with fervent spirits I was ardently awaiting the time of the divine birth, but a cruel delay tormented my hope and often I would return inwardly to these reflections in the eagerness of my heart: "If only, if only that heavenly boy might not shrink from revealing himself to me face to face before my death, since everything the dazzling maiden told me about herself was true.* Cull shining flowers and bring gleaming white lilies in handfuls;* prepare gifts for the god as he comes to the threshold of light, and come to visit the royal child. Ah, if only the final portion of so long an old age might remain for me as well, enough to allow me to witness your deeds, holy child, when you bring peace to the world, all dread removed, and reign as a god in your Father's Olympus. Then bountiful peace will nurture the earth, along with devotion and good faith, and religion which now is faltering; and the world, altered for the better, will behold with amazement justice rising up again on every side.* Then the savage sword will be melted down into curved sickles, and the golden age will begin to make its entrance in the world."* Like this I often used to comfort myself inwardly for the delays, and the hope that had been kindled grew ever stronger in my heart.

'As it happened, Augustus Caesar, who held supreme power in the world, was holding a census* and gave orders to carry out a registration of the peoples. I myself therefore made my way back to the walls of ancient Bethlehem, where my family comes from, in order to include myself in the roll of the citizens of that city, giving my name and the name of my people. My wife followed me, setting out from our home* in Nazareth. Scarcely had I entered the walls and scattered dwellings* of my homeland, when night with its sleep-inducing shadows stole away the light of heaven. There is a deserted shelter as you go into that humble city, roofed with rough straw and rushes from the swamp, once a most welcome lodging* for any farmers detained in the city by night far from their ancestral fields, for it was secluded and set back at a distance from other residences. Here then we both made our way together, exhausted,* whether by chance or because the ruler of Olympus had so decreed (as I rather think, and consider it fitting to believe so).* For he not only wished his Son to pass his life among all the most serious hardships* and to experience unworthy misfortunes* on earth, but also wished for him to be born under a pauper's roof and in a humble home, pitiable and lacking in everything.

'First of all I stabled the crooked mule at the stalls, the beast that had assisted us in our journey and lightened our load;* and next to it in the straw the glorious virgin set herself down, the inner part of the house being fully occupied. There was an ox on the left, breathing warm breath from its mouth, which a poor ploughman used to put to work in the fields by day, turning over a few acres of soil with the curved plough; nor did he return home from his rented plot until late at night, so he could get through life by his own toil and ward off hunger from his small children.* And now night had achieved the midpoint of its course as the hours passed, when, as I lay motionless against the stone with my eyes defeated, sleep left me—for at that point no deep slumber held me fast,* sunk in sleep. Look: an intense light filled my eyes with a sudden gleam.* The hut shone far and wide within, and the mean bed of straw, which only just now had been lying roughly strewn, you could have seen transformed into gold. I got up. Beside the stalls I saw a naked child all lit up and gleaming with light; this tender babe the poor maiden had just delivered on the hard straw, without any pain or struggle afflicting her. Standing by silently were the ox, on this side, and the dawdling donkey, on the other, and forgetting their fodder they held their heads high as one. The mother herself was resplendent with rays of light, kneeling on both knees,* her shining eyes lowered. Ah, with tears welling up she gazed at her naked little one, and stretched out her clasped hands as the light streamed over her.

'Just like the aspect of the stars in the damp darkness after the rain, when chill Boreas comes up on parching wings and scatters the hollow clouds as he storms the heaven;* such was the appearance that had come over the maiden's face. What was I to do? Beneath the two of them I placed a part of my mantle, and I spread out the hide of a smelly sheep in place of a painted cradle, in place of dyed sheets and gold. Poverty and the gloom of night prevented anything else. Not yet had the brightness of day dawned on the submerged world, but now shepherds were there in a close-packed throng, and they decorated the doorway of the cave with flowers and assorted garlands,* piping a rustic strain on their perforated reeds. When they entered the stable, they bent and turned their eyes to the manger, knelt on the ground,* and worshipped the deity.

'I wondered inwardly in silence how this report had suddenly got out through the fields, and I started to make enquiries of the shepherds themselves. One of them took up my query, addressing me as follows: "We are shepherds; we all graze our flocks in the neighbouring pastures. It being our custom to pass much of the night sleepless, keeping safe our gathered flocks, at about midnight there appeared, as we kept watch, a vast light over all our heads; and as we stood stricken with terrible panic, a voice like this was heard through the air: 'Do not be afraid, men;* I bring you new-found joy.* The one so often promised of old by pious prophets has been born today in these lands—a god. He will bring the human race out of darkness and return it to its original condition.* It is granted to you to look upon him in the neighbouring city, cushioned on a bed of straw and lying by a lowly manger.' Prompted by these tidings, we turned our eyes to the neighbouring city. And look—an airborne host with wings of vivid colours, heavenly children, were seen riding on clouds throughout the sky above through the limpid expanse of the air, and opening the festivities in wondrous fashion in their swift-moving throng. And when three times they had moved through the heaven in their threefold troop and threefold dance,* wheeling in full formation, they made for the height in harmony. Far and wide the steeps of Olympus echoed in answer, while the sky burst with joyful celebration."

'Such things as these they recounted, and they could not get enough of the shining infant's face, rooted to the spot as they contemplated him intently with their eyes and intently with their whole heart.* The child beamed from his face, his eyes and his whole body, filling the space all around with a divine radiance, just like the flower of roses opening up with its crimson face, when first it comes forth into the heavenly regions of the daylight, or when the glory of a spring day is revealed and gleams abroad as the sun rises anew in the rosy regions of the East. Meanwhile we, although we knew beyond any doubt that he was a divine being and a god, in need neither of support nor of milk, nonetheless fed the little one as if he were sprung from mortal seed; as he drained his mother's breasts we cradled the child, delicate and feeble in his limbs. For upon his creation he inherited the mortal part of his being from his mother's mortal body, and for that reason, as the ancient custom of our distant ancestors prescribes, we marked him with the sign of our race, trimming a small section of skin in the area of his genitals with a fragment of Samian pottery.* And we gave him a name, remembering to call him JESUS, as the winged boy sent from heaven had previously instructed us. Moreover, since he is a priest from the bloodline of kings, among the Gentiles he is called by the Greek name Christ.*

'Furthermore, although his mother remained undefiled by any physical union, she nevertheless remained inside the building until she observed forty sunrises.* Then at last we made our way to the holy city of Jerusalem along with the child, so that the royal maiden could purify herself, and in keeping with custom we brought with us to the altar a pair of collared doves. At the altars themselves there stood a priest bearing ritual objects,* girt in white linen and wearing a two-pointed headdress, preserving the unsleeping flame in the sanctuary.* Around him before the altar the unshorn circle of his sons were pouring from bowls the blood* of a bull-calf (as it so happened), which their father had sacrificed to the king of heaven to atone for the sins of the guilty race, and praying for pardon he was offering the accustomed gifts at the altars in supplication. Ranged around him were the leaders of the race, all of them touching with their right hands the garlanded head of the bullock. And now he, pouring out the spilled blood, had sprinkled three and four times with a light finger the holy altar, the flame placed upon the altar, the seven lights in a row,* and the broad cloths by which the secrets of the rituals are concealed.

'And now the rituals had come to an end, and the tired priest was getting ready for the lavish banquet together with his sons. At that point the virgin went up with humble step to the altar, carrying the infant in her left hand and the birds in her right. Why should I mention the signs the Father sent from high heaven, acknowledging his true offspring? Or how much the priest himself shuddered at the sight of the boy? Or how wondrous a light suddenly shone around the altar with unfamiliar flames? Three times he threw incense on to the lighted fire in worship; three times a colossal flame suddenly flared up beneath the dome. Even so, he sacrificed the birds according to the inherited custom, wringing their necks and pouring out their blood in due order; and he offered up their feathers and the entrails of their sliced gullets, turning from the sun's setting to its radiant rising, and broke off the wings. Then he heaped the consecrated fire with their flesh. A cloud went up to heaven with welcome smoke, and the blazing altar exhaled eastern fragrance.*

'But look—people's hearts were thrown into disarray by a sudden occurrence. There was a man oppressed by the weight of years who bore the name of his ancestor,* Simeon; no one in the whole city was more devoted to the cause of righteousness* than he. To him, since he had foreknowledge of what would happen* far into the future, the almighty power of the heavenly spirit had once promised that he would see God and the instigator of salvation, long awaited by the world, before he left the air of daylight. And now he was weary of life, and in his infirmity he longed to put an end to the hard toils of old age by death;* but that hope still remained fixed in his zealous heart. Therefore, when through divine possession he sensed in advance that God was at hand, he was like a dog when, accompanying his master's step* through the fields, he happens to sense a hare far off by his power of smell.* At once he pricks up his ears and sniffs the air with his nostrils, and breaking off the journey in hand he strays from the path and, scanning with his eyes the uncertain tracks of the animal, directs his course now this way, now that,* turning and returning in his uncertainty; far and wide the fields resound with barking. Such was the appearance of the old man as he rejoiced in the temple. Then he caught up the boy in his trembling arms and embraced him, clasping him tightly. As tears welled up in his eyes, he proceeded to speak as follows:*

'"Hail to your goodness,* child, undoubted offspring of God, the world's saviour—you who come unbidden to wash away our sins and those of our ancient forebears in the abundant stream of your blood, and to open up the limpid ways to the stars of heaven. Much desired you come*—and your mighty promises have not failed me, supreme Father. Finally it is permitted me to die. Now, ah now, you are letting me go off* to rest and an end of my labours, freed from the chains of the body, as once you promised;* now my eyes have seen the one you have sent to the world as its succour, to be a light in the darkness* for the Gentiles, and a new glory for the descendants of Isaac."

'After speaking these words, he then turned to the mother and addressed her: "Ah, to whom can I compare you in your beauty? To whom can I match you in glory?* What thanks can I give you,* you who alone have brought forth salvation for ailing mortals by your fruitful womb? Though I foretell that this birth will bring death to many, and a time will come—an unhappy time—when a sharp sword will pierce your freezing heart, poor woman, and your maiden's dowry will be great grief,* and the Jordan will flow discoloured with altered waves. Then the day will rise late and lethargically, and reluctantly and with difficulty, pale and wan, will it display to the world its grimy face. And the earth itself will pray to be released from the burden of its own mass and slip through the void, breaking its compact."*

'When he had said these things, he immediately drooped his eyes as if they were giving way to sleep, and on the spot he passed into rest by a peaceful death.* The others were astonished, but we, who knew the rest of what he had said, were still more terrified; and in turn we both asked anxiously what the swords were that he foretold for the mother, or whose destruction the boy himself would compass.* But not for long did the matter remain in doubt* thereafter: the outcome fully enlightened us both and freed us from our perplexity* as we pondered—unless even now still greater blows remain for us* and other things, ever more grievous, are being lined up on top of the rest.

'In those days, from the furthest reaches of the East, three kings mighty in their sway had set out and journeyed here, bringing lavish gifts for the boy: gold, lumps of incense, and liquid myrrh. To them the power of the stars and the configuration of the revolving heaven had revealed that a king had been born in our lands, before whom the sceptres of heaven and earth would be set as his due. Therefore they made their way here in their eagerness to see the holy birth. A star trailing its gleaming light before them constantly as they went was their guide, and it marked the way with its ample radiance,* just as of old the fiery lamp showed the way by night to our ancestors through the trackless desert, running ahead of them, as they returned at last to their homeland from Pharaoh's country, and in its brightness it shed upon them from above a wondrous light.*

'And now they had entered the city and went up to the palace of the tyrant Herod; and they informed him of the reason for their journey, thinking that this offspring had been born to him, since he was the king in this territory. At once he was stunned and terrified in his heart; without delay, dreading that some foreign boy had been found to succeed him as his heir in his ancestral kingdom, he gave orders for native seers to be gathered within the walls of his palace and for them all to seek out the time and place of the child's birth, and he asked them his country and his home. And they told him that all the proclamations of the ancients portended Bethlehem, from where a leader would arise and one day raise himself up, immense in his fame, immense beyond heaven in his glorious deeds.* Then more and more was Herod tossed on a surging tide of worries, his fretful mind afflicted with vain terror.*

'At last he sent away the kings from the East with these words: "This same cause, men, which brings you to our lands* has long kept us in anticipation, eager to behold the birth of the boy, which has been promised by so many prophets. Not far from here, founded on an ancient rock, is the city of Bethlehem, inhabited by our people.* Seek there the king who has been born. Then, I bid you, send from there someone to report to us that he has been found, so that the boy may be heaped with honour from us too." So he spoke, and feigned new-found joy with his deceptive countenance;* yet he was devising something far different in his unfriendly heart, that madman, who could believe that the king of heaven, whom the stars obey,* is at all concerned with mortal kingdoms on earth.

'And so they resumed their journey, rejoicing in the sight of the star. And now they were approaching, with a great throng pressing round them,* when suddenly above the roof the mighty star came to a halt, casting its beams and filling the hut with an ample radiance—just like comets, when they foretell the shifting movements of war or the deaths of kings, let stream their menacing hair in the angry sky, unless they ominously glow mournfully red.*

'And so I, a poor man in straitened circumstances, received three kings under the beams of a lowly roof.* I saw them, gleaming with gold and splendid in purple, prostrating themselves humbly before the feet of the boy, and falling at his reverent mother's knees, while each offered his own gifts in the order allotted. Meanwhile their barbarian entourage waited before the doors, and a charger, standing by draped with fabric dyed in Tyrian purple,* champed on a bit of smooth gold. Then, having completed their homage, they went away and joyfully followed the star that appeared,* casting its beams, on their long journey. But having been warned, they did not go back from there by the same way, keeping the walls of the palace far on their left, lest they should come again to the seat of the Palestinian king.

'Herod, however, when he finally realized that he had been deceived, flared up with rage* and sent to the suspect city a thousand men equipped with weapons, whose task was to enter the walls by stealth at night and slaughter all the young infants they found, seizing them from their mothers' breast;* among so great a number, the royal heir would also fall. But I myself seemed to be warned by a voice in a dream to hurry in headlong flight, and to leave familiar places: "Come on—get up, break off delay,* snatch up the boy and his mother with you, and make with haste for the streams of the sevenfold Nile.* After that, inhabit a land not far from this region; and don't come back from there unless I myself summon you first. For the king is contriving a cruel death for the child."

'I got up, and full of these promptings I revealed everything to his mother. You could have seen the girl drained of colour* and scared to death, rushing about this way and that in her panicked departure, scarcely trusting even in the darkness of night.* Already then a sharp sword pierced her breast, poor woman, and her heart was shaken with unbearable grief. We slipped away and silently left behind the treacherous city under cover of night, and with hurried steps we made for the trackless woods. And now our course had brought me beyond the passes and the heights of palm-bearing Edom, now past the walls of ancient Elusa and where Mapsa, abundant in olives, divides all Asia from the shores of Libya. I entered a kingdom untouched by rain, the kingdom of Pharaoh, the first land to recognize the power of heaven, the stars, the sphere of the moon and the paths of the sun.* On all sides I hailed unknown mountains, unknown rivers, observing cities crowned with towers as my course took me past them; and now I was making my way along the banks of Anthedon, producer of papyrus.

'Every breeze struck terror into our trembling hearts, fearful as we were for so precious a being.* Yet the laurel-leafed forests lulled the child with their murmur and bent their heads over him, flexing their branches; and the light breath of the breezes* favoured him with its whisper. Even the very crags, the very mountains, seemed to sport before us, lightly swaying their peaks, while the talkative pools* all around appeared to give signs of their joy. You could have heard the water, wearied with its wanderings, babbling softly and splashing among the rocks in its gentle fall, over rocks damp and green with gleaming moss.* Above all, the birds that frequented the banks and channel of the river were caressing the breeze with their fluid warbling,* and their bodies resounded with the beat of their wings as they struck their sides. Rejoicing in the sight of God, the earth proffered itself to us with bountiful bosom as we came by. Every kind of grass breathed its own fragrance, and the marjoram tree stretched out its soft shade.* Nor indeed did the Nile, hiding away in its unknown source, fail to give distinct signs, its stream leaping up as the god made his arrival;* with joyful waves it raised itself up, stirring its hidden pools, and was laid bare in its deepest bed.

'As we came to a fork and bend in the road, there appeared in the sky all of a sudden, jangling with his shield and shining sword through the air, the most beautiful winged being; and he showed us the way through diversions known to him,* so the enemy might not catch us on the direct route of our journey. His back glowed red, covered with dark markings, much like that one who previously rebuked me as I sought to dissolve my marriage, and who put the darkness to flight from my mind. Above us others, hanging in the air on their wings, made their way and would ward off the lingering damp of night from the sleeping child's face, covering him with their feathers.

'And now I, pursuing my wandering way, was skirting and had almost within my grasp the trustworthy fields which echo with the sound of the sistrum,* and now the child was safe, far from our own land; yet still I struck into the innermost regions of Egypt, and no land seemed to me safe enough or sufficiently sundered from the wicked king's domain. In my mind I feared everything, even when all was safe.* And I was not satisfied with Hermopolis, nor did Thebes, accessible through a hundred gates, seem far enough removed from such great danger. Therefore Memphis received us, famous for the towered tombs of kings; at last, in this place, I rested in safety beneath the impoverished roof of an old friend.

'But now a report, spread abroad through the lands of the Nile, suddenly broadcast on all sides the news* that the Palestinian king had deprived the thriving city* of its newborn posterity, sinfully taking their lives in wholesale slaughter, for all the good their innocence did them as bawling they left the sweet light of life.* His terrified mother grew pale and pressed the child to her bosom, while the vision of that atrocity frayed her spirit.* What can have been the weeping then among the people, do you think, what howling from the mothers roaming desolate through the city cursed with carnage? The earth dissolved in blood, the emptied houses were afloat. If it happens at some point that a storm has arisen without warning to the shepherds and has suddenly fallen upon all the fields and all the woods, the number of lambs seen laid low on the ground by the terrible hail beside their stricken mothers is not so great as the number of boys' bodies which then lay strewn on all sides throughout the squares and streets of the city. So it turned out that the child, as the prophet had foretold, was the source of destruction for many;* even now the bereft mothers are mourning for their offspring. Yet even so, that villain did not long take joy in his atrocity; for he was seized in his limbs with a filthy disease that wasted them away, and shortly afterwards he breathed out a life which no one thought fit to celebrate.

'I myself, once again, was impelled by a divine voice in my sleep to leave behind the sevenfold streams of the Nile, that cradle of wonders; and I returned to my homeland, carefully noting and retracing the steps I had taken,* and bringing back my son along with his mother. Perhaps you are also keen to know* the boy's interests, his cast of mind, whether he displayed a virtue in advance of his age or attempted anything beyond the capacities of a child in the years of his childhood. If I had leisure to recount to you all the amazing things I observed back then, while his youth was flourishing in its first flower* and growing to maturity, the very power of speech would desert me, worn out in the telling, and night would close up the sky and bury the day.* How often that young lad startled us both with words that were beyond the grasp of mere mortals! How often we were scared witless at the sacred fires,* balls of flame, and terrifying flashes of lightning* with which the boy's shining hair frequently seemed to be ablaze as he sparkled with heaven's brilliant light! I shan't tell you how often we heard him address his Father in private, uttering unfathomable words. His caring mother, as she wove fine thread at the loom with shrill shuttle,* was often petrified to see throngs of heavenly beings entering the house in human form, fondling the child and offering him their gleaming feathers to play with, or covering him with violets and swathing him in a cloud of roses. All the while, even so, he treated us, his guardians, with humble reverence, carrying out his dear mother's bidding and mine, and he fulfilled the love of his true Father* as vigorous energy and solid strength came to his limbs.*

'And now as he grew he had passed full twelve years, and had not yet revealed his identity to the people by any sign. It was then that his power first began to appear in public through the towns of Judaea and was revealed openly. It so happened that a day had come which is sacred to our race and is revered in this great city beyond all others; the royal maiden had come with me too, and the marvellous boy followed, holding her hand.* And now, with the rites duly performed, I was returning home together with his worthy mother. We were tired from the exertion of the journey, and the first day had already passed; night had enveloped the sealed sky in pitch-dark shadow. Then the boy was gone: he had slipped away from his mother and me.*

'Thereupon I made enquiries among my relatives and friends, but to no avail; three and four times I retraced my route and filled the way with my shouting. His most lovely mother wept, blaming only herself, as her golden hair streamed over her ivory neck. Yet tears enhanced the beauty of her face, and tousled hair suited her neck, just as when a tender marjoram plant in a maiden's pot, beaten by the combined forces of the rain and the buffeting winds, droops its leaves in distress, but then rises up again and presents its face to heaven, recalling its former glory.* And while I retraced my route, she came along with me against my will, an afflicted companion. For three days we wandered in bewilderment* through the city—in vain; on the fourth day, at last, he was just about found. For when all hope was completely gone from me and his unhappy mother, the idea came to each of us to make our way to the temple again and offer prayers at the altar. I had scarcely stepped over the threshold when at once—look!—we both spotted him in the midst of the priests (the first elementary foundation and indication of his future power), reviewing the weighty pronouncements of the prophets, asking the leading elders about obscure matters without any prompting, and teaching them himself.

'They were all amazed at him as he disclosed things that were not common knowledge, with an understanding beyond human perception, comprehension, and mental capacity, for he owed his instruction to no human power, no teacher's art,* and displayed a maturity of spirit beyond his boyish years. And he was no less pleasing to all the onlookers on account of his distinguished looks: they could not get enough of gazing at the beaming features of the god,* his eyes more charming than the cloudless daylight, or the combed gold of his hair and the bloom of his gracious youth, which had as yet scarcely begun. For in whatever direction he turned his noble head, more beautiful than the newly risen sun or a golden star, everything in the stilled world began to laugh with joy, and from every inch of his frame he cast sweet love*—just as the purple narcissus shines amidst the grasses of the untilled field when first it protrudes from its leaves and unsheathes its head, its covering burst; or as the warm glow of a gleaming emerald twinkles when enclosed in a thin band of silver or gold.*

'From here came the first spark of our suffering:* from then on the boy incurred envy from the leaders of the city for his awesome goodness, and he stirred their cruel hearts. From this kindling was a huge fire then lit,* and day by day the fury and madness swelled and grew. Seeing for myself that all these things would come, and fearful for the future, I begged him, for he had no fear, not to be careless of his life and lay himself open to the enemy, lest he surrender himself to ruin unforced. But sooner would fortresses lurk unseen by day on the mountains,* or fire be concealed on the tops of towers by night, than his goodness could lie for a long time buried and without recognition.*

'Yet never did he cause their hearts to blaze with bitter hatred more than when, now become a man after the passage of thirty years, he turned water from the fountain into Bacchus' dark liquor.* As it happened, he had come with me to the city of Cana in Galilee (and his mother was there too) as I fulfilled the wish of an old friend who had summoned me. He was preparing to unite his maiden daughter in marriage to a son-in-law in the time-honoured way, with a great gathering of leading citizens. And now all of them reclined round about, with the tables set in place, and were enthusiastically feasting and happily calling for more wine; nor was the banquet yet ended, when a sorrowful murmur arose on all sides and was heard throughout the house—the flowing wine, the source of their joy, had run out, the casks had run dry, and everything seemed to be thrown into confusion. At this point the kindly mother, feeling pity for the girl's reduced circumstances, made a sign and entreated her son in a lowered voice, asking him to help. I saw the young man at first grow troubled in his expression, but then he agreed to his dear mother's prayers and came to the aid of our distressed friend. He ordered six casks (that being the number they had there) to be filled immediately with water and set on the tables; as soon as the god looked upon them from nearer by—behold, in all of them the liquid was seen to change suddenly and grow dark,* and in astonishment we drank wine in place of untainted water.

'You have heard, governor, both the lineage and the birth of my son, and the god's first beginnings. To save you the trouble of asking about the rest, he has stirred up this whole region with his blossoming deeds. But if pleasure prompts you in your heart* to hear these things, this man can tell of them far better' (at this point he gestured with a look towards John, who was sitting by); 'for he saw everything in person, constantly following the tracks of his leader as he went on his travels, while my concern to look after the maiden kept me at home.' So he spoke, and bringing his speech to an end here he wearily fell quiet.*

'By all means,' said Pilate. 'Go through from the beginning the reasons for that birth. What religion is this? If I have observed correctly throughout the region, Judaea worships no more than one eternal god, born not of mortal seed, and keeps the native divinities away from its altars. Tell me the other miracles of this god who is known to you, recalling them in order from that point; for the strength in this man's body is failing him,* and he himself bids you come to his aid.' These were Pontius' words; and everyone kept their eyes fixed intently* on his addressee.

BOOK FOUR

THIS young man, unsurpassed in his good looks* at that time, still at the age of adolescence as manhood was making its first entrance, first spent a long time pleading to be excused and insistently declining, keeping his words firmly in check. Then, gradually leaving behind all mortal things in his mind and forgetting human concerns, he entered in his consciousness the innermost sanctuaries of divinity and roamed through heaven, enjoying the blessed sight of the celestial beings* and the overpowering atmosphere of ether. Granted admission, he fed in radiance on the heavenly light, and dwelt fixedly on God with his whole consciousness; just like the queen of birds,* when she soars aloft and is borne up from the depths of the earth, ranging through the wandering breezes, wheels round with a beat of her wings and disappears into the clouds. And now she presses on weightlessly through the ethereal expanse, and directing her keen gaze she looks up at the light of the flaring sun, fixing her eyes unwaveringly on it in a piercing stare.*

Meanwhile they marvelled at him as he kept silent, all of them turned towards that one man who remained as if lifeless or heavy with sleep,* and they crowded round to shake him out of it. At last he returned to himself and with a groan began to speak as follows from the depths of his heart: 'In the beginning* the almighty Father, creator and fount of all things, ruled everywhere alone, vast and measureless. Not yet had he forged the starry orbs of the universe; not yet did the world exist, nor yet did the seasons go forth in their round. No lights shone in the dusky firmament.* Whatever existed was God, encompassing everything everywhere, the whole contained completely in that one being. There was just his Son, born not of any goddess nor of mortal woman by an ordinary birth, but the eternal Father had conceived him, eternal, in his eternal mind, miraculous to say.* He had no earthly limbs or mortal parts,* but was without body, as having been conceived by the profound intelligence of the supreme Father, lying hidden in his secret heart as the Word, which no utterance had yet brought forth into the winged breeze—the almighty Word, without end and beginning, by which was formed the sea, the earth, and the boundless sky.* And as the Father was God, no less was his only child God as well. But you should avoid the error of believing that there are therefore two gods: the same godhead is shared by both, and each is the one God. Moreover, the love by which both are joined together (for from each comes a shared mutual devotion)* we call both Spirit and God, equally almighty, which breathes upon the seas and the lands and the deepest recesses of heaven,* at which breath all things take on vigour and all things are set in motion. We say that these three are one God, and that the one is a divinity threefold.

'And to astonish you still more, this God, whom we ourselves have seen made human and born from the mortal body of humans, now reigns in the palace of heaven together with his Father no less than before, directing all things in company with him through the same divine will.* For he is constrained by no locality, no space; and present and the same in all places at all times, escaping our sight and removed from our perception, God fills all things and infuses himself into all matter—just as the light flooding the low-lying earth with radiance comes from the sphere of the sun and encircles the fields laid out below, but nowhere is it sundered from the heavenly sun and goes its separate way, however distant the regions it reaches. So there is no light without its sun, nor any sun without its light.

'What drove God to undertake such great labours* and to endure these things, as he wandered in danger of death—these things I shall tell, and I shall set out the remote causes, going back over them from the very beginning.* The heaven and the heavenly orbs you look up at, along with the lands that lie below*—these the universal craftsman* had scarcely hammered out,* when the Father, enflamed with eternal love,* created all at once the winged peoples and holy angels, a host thrice threefold and a swift race without body, to dwell in the very spheres of the sevenfold heaven.* This he did so that the pleasure which he alone, together with his Son, enjoys for all eternity might be shared and granted to many. Straightaway, no small part* of those who by right ought to have been singing the praises of their creator and God and paying him thanks were invaded by a mad desire for power (who could endure it without taking vengeance?) and were impelled by frenzy to hanker for precedence over their sovereign Father, ungrateful as they were, their wits overthrown, and blinded by delirium.* The almighty Father could not endure it, and armed those who followed the better cause against them. Without delay, he thrust down from heaven the depraved beings who had ventured such things to the very depths of hell, among the blackness of terrifying night and the eternal gloom.

'As a result of this the first man was born, whom the supreme Creator set as master far and wide over the earth and the watery waves, so that in the future he might occupy the stars and their abandoned dwellings in place of the heavenly ones who had been cast out. To man alone the Father himself made subject every race of his own creatures, the generations of living beings of every kind—the shoals of scaly fish, the brightly tinted forms of winged birds, and every species of wild beasts that roam the mountains.* When God placed man in charge of the flowery fields, he commanded him just to keep off the fruit of a single tree; but seized with forbidden longing for the ill-omened apple at the encouragement of his wife,* whom the serpent had ensnared by trickery, he thoughtlessly broke his covenant with the king of heaven, alas!

'Scarcely had he defiled with his greedy mouth the fruit he had snatched, when the Father who has dominion over the rain was now heard to thunder from above from a ruddy cloud, and angrily to pronounce the punishment which in the future he and all the line descended from him that would come into the light of day* would expiate. At once barriers were set before heaven's vast expanse; then for the first time a godless brood shot up suddenly and the earth was immediately polluted with unspeakable wickedness. Out came deception, out came criminal lust. Consequently, gruelling labour was added* to the human lot, and together with the wellspring of cares, the doorway to grim death was unsealed, along with diseases and pain, famine and shameful destitution*—though the human race could have passed its existence without cares and outlasted many ages in its life on earth.* From that time on, men spent their lives in the fields without civilized customs or laws; all they did was seek to appease the king of angels by shedding blood, so that he might graciously lend his support to their flocks and to them and might ward off the violence of heaven from the fields they had sown. They were uneducated, ignorant, and empty of reason.* And that had been the general condition of the world for two thousand years, when increasingly the best of fathers forgot his ancient wrath and began to grow a little gentler. Not yet had he opened heavenly Olympus to man, however, but fashioning the human race and sharpening it by his instructions, he gave them laws and observances and sacred practices;* and he laid it down, prescribing it by law to our race as a means of distinguishing it, that we should circumcise with a sharpened potsherd* that tiny part in each man's body which makes us men. Then he filled the hearts of prophets with the truth of what was to come, so they might prophesy to the nations that at last that happy day would be at hand when the door of heaven would open of itself and grant entry to the faithful.

'But meanwhile the chaste spirits and the souls of the pious were waiting beneath the earth, sitting in a shadowy vale. Now, mindful of the prophets, they were reckoning up the times* and were stretching out both hands to the stars in common entreaty, pleading with the king of angels to cease from his anger and refrain from annihilating the whole race for the transgression of one man. "Spare us, spare us, almighty Father," was the one cry of them all.* "Take thought for us and admit us to that heaven once promised to us, from which we are far sundered,* with no share in that comforting light. Not in vain did you bring us out to the light of day. If, however, any traces of ancient fault survive,* wash them away graciously with your dew, and uncover the divine springs. Oh, may some one of the heavenly beings at last sprinkle upon us kindly the celestial streams, the celestial showers. You, gliding spheres of fiery heaven, cast your dew upon us! Wandering clouds, come to our aid; pour out on us your longed-for rain, your blessed dew! And you, for whom so many ages have now been waiting,* promised to their prayers, for whom the walls of the infernal world lower their heads, true offspring of the highest Father,* golden rain of heaven, break off delay*—come, swiftly break off the course of the starry spheres, burst the gates of heaven, and glide here in full force!" Such were the prayers of them all, and all made the same proclamation.

'The almighty Father of the heavenly ones, who was already planning to mend what had been ruined, took pity on them fully from the citadel of heaven.* Although he could surely have opened the gates of heaven with a nod and sent one of the angelic citizens instead to free the spirits from those dark realms and bring them back to the seat of the celestial beings, the starry spans, he sent from highest Olympus his own Son, made human, to atone for everything, in order that he might keep men more mindful of him and bound to him by still greater services. Even so, to prevent him appearing unknown to ignorant mortals and unfamiliar to his own, and to prevent them driving him out and keeping him away from their territories* for claiming against the ancestral laws that he was the offspring of God, he sent ahead of him an excellent prophet born in that region, named John. This vessel of divinity the barren Elizabeth bore in extreme old age to Zechariah, to proclaim as herald to the nations that God had been born, and to display its own hope to the weary world.

'He, avoiding the tracks of men from his earliest years, spent his life unkempt in the lonely mountains—the mountains and woods and deserted shores. The rough caves were his home; with no form of cultivation the earth supplied wild berries for his food, or honey seeping from hollow tree-trunks. The gushing springs supplied him with drink. His clothing was an animal skin, rough with shaggy bristles. He took pleasure only in spreading glad tidings,* addressing the groves and mountains and shores of the sea. Yet such great goodness did not remain hidden, even so; the man's vast renown took no time to make its way to the surrounding cities.* And already the peoples believed that he had been sent down from heaven, as once so many truth-telling Sibyls sang,* to lead the human race out of the terrible shadows. And now in a great throng the peoples went up to him* to find out who he was, where he came from,* what he had for them and whether he himself had arrived from heaven, the one who would one day come to bring help to the afflicted nations: these things they kept asking him over and over again.

'But he, from his shadowy cave, kept repeating such words as these: "Rejoice, ye peoples who have long been shrouded in darkness and black clouds! Behold, the longed-for light approaches! Do not—no, do not—believe in your ignorance that I am the promised light: I do not seek to steal honours I do not deserve. I am only as the morning star which appears before the rising sun and announces the day with its shining sparkle; I prophesy to you, in no time the full blaze of your sun will be among you. Now, now, the god will be here—look, God is here* in mortal regions, like a mortal! Run to meet him with joy as he comes, strew the roads with festal foliage, the fields with woven carpets, and in worship acknowledge his divinity with worthy honours. Meanwhile, learn justice* and accustom yourselves to righteousness, and under my guidance wash off the stain of sin* in the flowing stream. But he himself will wash away divinely with heavenly breeze every evil and all the infection of ancient fault, and the Golden Age will come into being* for the world he has transformed."

'After hearing such things, the neighbouring folk made their way from all the cities where the Jordan flows in its pleasing course, praying for peace and voluntarily confessing their sins. The prophet baptized them naked in the pure stream, duly pouring the holy water on their heads from his hollowed palms.

'But look—God himself, even, like the rest of the crowd, made his way in secret to the river in keenness to purify himself through baptism, so that in his mortal body he might leave nothing unexperienced* that is both right and necessary for a mortal man to have undergone, lest later generations should feel reluctance to imitate his deeds. At first the prophet refused and shrank from his touch,* and recognizing God, he held out both palms in supplication,* bending low before him as the very waters marvelled. Then, however, he obeyed, as he was bidden, and trembling and shaking he bathed the divine limbs in the flowing stream. All at once the Jordan shone out with golden current, and the heavenly abode on high thundered with a deafening crash.* And from above a dove descended from the bright peak of heaven through the clear air, its back silvery with gleaming plumage, but with wings all golden and glowing. And now, marking its passage far and wide, it stood above them both, and as it hovered on the heavenly breeze it infused each of them with the breath of divinity. At the same time the voice of the mighty Father was heard from the glowing sky, bearing witness to his tender love for his Son. Meanwhile winged youths, the race that inhabits the heaven, were there as commanded, hovering on the streaming air round about, and were bearing linen garments and white robes*—their allotted task—to dry the wet limbs of their master's Son and his hair dripping from the sacred stream. When this had been done, the god made his way out and left the river.

'The prophet pointed him out to those who were spread around the bank in a long line, and as Jesus departed John called after him:* "Behold, the one who I so often promised was on the brink of appearing—our God! Behold the god,* who like a lamb slain at the altars as they burn with incense will atone for our sins by his death and will fall as a willing victim offered to his heavenly Father.* Choose *him* as your leader,* choose *him* as your teacher." From then on the prophet, leaving behind the woods and the wilderness, began to go through the midst of the cities and proclaim to the peoples that God had come, that the promised deity was at hand.

'The matter was believed by few, until the god himself began to reveal his nature among them* as more than human through his mighty exploits. For first of all he chose twelve friends out of all his company, so he could share with them his concerns* and gruelling toil and could take them with him into all eventualities;* before that, indeed, he had spent thirty years alone. But lest you suppose that his favour alighted on us out of the many thousands because he had ascertained that we were practised in wiles and masterful skill,* or powerful in wealth and from an illustrious family background—the origin of all of us is obscure, our homes undistinguished and our fortunes humble, and our livelihood is not obtained through our wits. Five of us were born in paltry Bethsaida; our art was to set traps with our curved hook for the scaly creatures along the rivers where fish abound,* and to sail the saltwater and the teeming fishing-grounds. Even then, when he first called us to him, I was patching up dripping nets on the sand by the shore; James, my brother, was taking care of the fish that were still thrashing about on the beach. Not far off, Andrew and Peter were at that time cleaving the salty shallows in a small vessel,* brothers sharing the same occupation, and in the same stretch of water. Then Philip, who shares with me his country and home, was summoned and left behind the fish and the twisted nets. There joined us as companions* Thomas, Thaddeus, and Simon (in the same line of work) who was born in Cana in Galilee—a friend to his ancestral rivers, a foe to the mute swimmers;* for James, his blood relation, the son of Alphaeus, had joined him earlier. And as we are almost all from inglorious origins, so too you see our names are harsh, unusual, and rough to pronounce. It's not just our faces that are coarse with their uncombed beards!* Three others, of no significantly better fortunes, also joined his company: Matthew and Bartholomew, already encumbered by age and next after Peter in the feebleness of his years, and the deviser of evil himself*—Judas.

'I could scarcely tell of all the miracles I saw with my own eyes, all those I heard of with these very ears,* in recalling everything he did in so short a time (for the third winter has barely passed since I was first by his side, deemed worthy of the name of companion); nor would it be right for me to set my course now on so vast an ocean. But a few out of many—and those not easy for me to relate—I shall go into, even so, and briefly I shall set them out,* in obedience to your orders. I shall leave aside the enduring achievements, great as they are, that he recently left behind* throughout the neighbouring cities (I think these are known to you), for he has honoured the whole region with his magnificent deeds. Who does not know of the king of Bethany rich in palm trees,* recently recalled to the blessings of life, on the fourth day when the sun had seen him dead and laid in the tomb—to say nothing of countless others for whom he was there on the threshold of extinction and wrenched them from the jaws of unpitying death? For sooner could I reckon up the tally of all the waves that foam on the boundless ocean through the impulse of the winds, all those that deluge the shores with sand, than the number of those to whom he brought succour when they were suffering from a whole range of bodily illnesses and came to him in supplication, and he sent them away healed and happy. Many were blind,* many born without the use of their hearing, preventing them from being able to hear or utter speech; others were lame, and could barely make their painful way with faltering steps. For some, paralysis had put to sleep their long-motionless limbs; for others, spreading sores gaped open on their half-eaten bodies and putrid pus oozed from their arms and legs. There were also those whose insides were swollen and whose afflicted belly had brought on a stinging thirst for those poor people, which no treatment and no quantity of water could quench. Then there were those whose limbs were constantly shaking with the knocking of continual tremors and would give way beneath them as their body trembled; those whom burning fever or fluid in their infected bodies,* or indeed the unknown force of a hidden illness, caused to twist and turn on their beds as it permeated their whole frame;* and those who had lost their senses and were tormented by ill-treatment at the hands of a Fury. To all of them the god brought help, by a mere look or touch; at once the illnesses left their bodies, and unaided the sick rose straightaway from their beds.

'And so wherever he was seen as he made his way, a huge crowd was always waiting for him, lying prostrate throughout the town squares and along the roads and at the entrances to the holy temples. Not yet had he called back anyone from the shades of hell after their death,* however, when he was travelling back from the coast of Sidon and entered lofty Nain in the company of his followers. But look—a vast procession advancing with a long line of flaming torches:* that was what we saw, and we heard mourning throughout the sorrowful city. Then at last we observed the reason for this mourning: the pitiable body of an outstanding young man, placed on a soft bier, whom that day had plunged in an untimely death* and deprived his flourishing features of all their glory, though he had scarcely reached adolescence in the sweetness of his age.* He was like a hyacinth that droops slowly from its weary neck when an ox has trampled it with its hoof as it leaves its prints in the field; or like a rose which a maiden has left behind, fallen among the thick thorns in the sunlight, after plucking it with her delicate fingers.* His poor mother was rushing frenziedly all through the city,* tearing her hair and defiling both cheeks with her bloodied hands. All around her, in the labyrinth of streets, mothers likewise assailed the stars with their wild lamentations; the citizens themselves pitied her in her bereavement—he had been left to her as her only child, the consolation of her widowed bed. When the god saw the pallor of the dead boy's youthful body, and his cheeks flecked with soft down,* he bade the procession cease from lamentation and come to a halt, and coming up close he stroked the motionless body with his hand and attached its soul once more to the cold limbs. Then look—up got the boy and (a miracle in the eyes of all) he sprang forward into their midst and left the bier empty, and comforted his mother with his voice as he embraced her.

'Furthermore, not many months later, he also restored the light of life to a remarkable girl, from whose frame all warmth and breath had fled, drifting away* completely into the breeze of the air. The girl's own father Jairus bears witness to the deed, a man generous with his fortune,* and influential both by his speech and in popular favour.*

'Why should I speak again* of when he turned fresh water from the living fountain into wine,* taking pity on a friend's circumstances? And once, as it happened, when he was looking down from the peak of a soaring mountain and the sun was starting to sink at the close of its passage through the heaven, he saw that an enormous number of followers had flooded in, mothers and men,* whom he had led through the desert, without a thought for themselves and for their own people. He stood there and pitied them; for he saw that three full days had now passed since they had had any taste of bread. There were no crops here, nor any nearby towns from which they could obtain food for money and buy supplies—and summer had not yet ripened the fruit on the trees. At last, with difficulty, a boy was found among so vast a gathering who was carrying with him as provisions for the journey five loaves and two fishes, wrapped in myrtle and fragrant herbs, which his caring mother had given to him as he was setting out. But what use were these for so many thousands? His companions were despondent and began to mutter and grumble, but Christ consoled them benevolently with friendly words,* calling them together and then addressing them briefly as follows: "No one from so great a number will depart this day unsatisfied."*

'Then in supplication he prayed to his Father like this: "Supreme parent, by whose aid the earth nourishes all things, and who makes the fields fertile with sunlight and pouring rain, if ever you bestowed on the race of Isaac's children* divine sustenance* from heaven on high as they made their way through the wilderness, if all things you have created exist without seed and the sky, the seas, and the earth were once nothing at all, be with us now and stave off loathsome hunger* for so many thousands." That was all. Then he instructed the spreading assembly to lie down on the grassy plain and prepare themselves for dinner. After that he cut the loaves of bread into tiny slivers, with a cheerful expression, and shared them out among all the people* (five thousand individuals were sitting there on the plains needing to be fed). Look—incredible to hear and astonishing to see, the minuscule portions were seen to grow in the hands of all, and everyone dined quite amply on the feast. And their desire for food and for drink was satisfied equally; not only that, but twelve hollow baskets could scarcely hold the heaped-up leftovers from the meal, the remaining scraps.

'And hear now another thing which we saw just a few days ago. There was a tree in a deserted field, very thick with foliage, from which a thirsty traveller used to be able to pluck the hanging fruit. The hero, who happened to be making his journey this way covered with dust from the road, looked for fruit on the tree, but in vain, since it just extended leaves and shady branches, unproductive and running wild all around. He could not endure this, and cursed the barren tree with bitter words. All at once—this is the truth you are hearing—the tree dried up, and fallen leaves fluttered in the airy breeze.

'Nor does he have less authority over the deep expanses of the sea. For him alone all the waves rise up, and the billows sink to rest at his sole command. I have seen (yes, I've seen it myself) the raging wintry north-westerly gales cease on his order, and all the force that roughens the goaded waves with its blasts.* Not yet had the full moon completed its course thrice over when suddenly, catching us on a calm sea at around midnight as we drew in our nets, there arose a squalling storm, and the deep grew black and rough as the billows rose up and the waves crashed together. The swirling surge had very, very nearly swallowed the distressed vessel. We were trembling with fear,* almost on the point of death,* when far off—look!—our leader, whom we had just left behind on the high shore watching the breakers smashing against the rock. We spotted him making his way unharmed through the midst of the waves, suspended; he didn't even dip his feet in the swollen sea. We shuddered at the sudden vision,* and I couldn't have believed that I was seeing his real form, and not just a likeness of his figure, making its way so quickly over the waves without oars, had he not voluntarily revealed himself in cheering us with friendly words: "Where has your confidence in me disappeared to,* in such sudden retreat? Let all fear be gone.* Finally get out of the habit of doubting my words." So he spoke, and leaping on to the ship, which had already surrendered to the waves overpowering it, with just a nod he calmed the swollen seas,* and the ocean put aside its threatening rumble. And so, with the waves stilled, we sailed to the safety of land unscathed, skimming over the surface of the water* on our speedy course.

'Without delay, when he had barely set foot on dry land after reaching the shore—look!—something else, yet more amazing to say and see.* Some officials, you see, were there on the shore, sent to call in the revenues which we are, each one of us, bound by ancient law to pay to our rulers every year. He received them unperturbed, and while he detained them in conversation he called Peter to him and bent down to whisper in his trusty ear: "Go, and inspect closely the first fish you catch from the sea with your cast hook, opening it with a sharp knife. Inside will be what we are both bound to pay the king."* The elderly man did as he was commanded: he drew his prey ashore on the hook, and gave to the men the silver coin he found in the fish's mouth.

'I shudder whenever there comes into my mind the thought of a man hounded by cruel goads, whom I saw at that time possessed by madness, his features raving uncontrollably, while I was sorting the fish laid out on that same shore. He was (so they say) the child of parents joined in a forbidden union* and unlawful wedlock; for they entered the marriage bed despite God's rites forbidding it, at a time when our whole race takes part in mournful displays.* But the pair did not take joy in their crime for long. For all at once, in the very course of their joy and embraces, the adulterer breathed out his godless life into the insubstantial air, unhappy man, and the same night was the first for their appalling offence and likewise the last, with scant space in between.* The woman, moreover, was seized supernaturally with flames of fire from heaven* when the burden of her now ripe womb was pressing, and the same hour would have consigned the two of them to death, had not the mother been cut open and the child removed from her belly. The sisters of the baby's father then raised him. He himself, though he had done nothing to deserve it, soon paid the penalty for the wicked deeds of his parents: he was deprived of the cheering light of the eyes, and his ears remained completely blocked—he had the power neither to take in nor to give out speech.* Furthermore, as soon as he reached manhood, straightaway a frenzy, the untamed violence of the infernal race, caught the afflicted man in its grip. A hundred furies, a hundred scourges harassed and overcame him (it was woeful)—a legion issuing from the lairs of Erebus;* inciting sobs from the man's mouth, they emitted awful cries and fearsome bellowings.* Everyone shrank from him as he bawled and roared inhumanly,* and they swiftly took refuge in their houses in alarm whenever he monstrously burst his bindings and chains* and got away free through the carelessness of his guards. And now, forgetting his brothers and sisters, he no longer set foot within his father's house, but like a wild beast he spent his life* in the woods and caves, wherever there were hollow rocks* or tombs wasted with age; he was blackened, penniless, and naked, having thrown away his clothing.

'In such a state, then, with his hands tied behind his back in a knot, his kinsmen and those closest to him were dragging him* with great force into Christ's presence, to see if he might take pity on the man. The captive strained against them, however, trying to burst the knots, and raised awful cries to heaven; just like when a battling bull is being haled to the altars with long ropes, it bawls through the city with wild cries and foams at the mouth and gores the air with its curved horn.* From this side and that the attendants press on and heap a thick shower of blows upon it and brandish their staffs over its back and shoulders; the crowd scatters in panic, and once they have reached safety among the colonnades they take pleasure in watching the danger from afar. Such was the appearance of the young man as he raved monstrously. Finally, exhausted, they set him before the god, asking him to bring help—to release him, at any rate, from such grim furies and cast out the cruel fiends from his mind.

'At this point the hero raised both hands to heaven, and formulating prayers he called on his Father to grant his appeal. And look—great, sudden, and wondrous: a miracle!* As if wolves were heard howling, and dogs barking, such were the dreadful cries the maddened man hurled from his lips. Not so monstrous a sound would issue from an enormous cascade of waters,* as the waves shattered on their descent from the high rocks, if the lofty barriers of Lake Velinus happened to burst and all its elevated pools rushed down into the depths of the valleys, with the result that the whole region became a sea* and the towns round about were plunged in the water and started swimming, and Rome was overwhelmed and feared for its sacred temples. Now they mimic the crashing of heaven, when the king of the celestial beings hurls his lightning and shakes the golden expanses of the sky with his thunder; now it's the sound of iron, or the ghastly grating of chains broken by a gargantuan mass, or the rumbling of the ocean. The whole earth all around and the whole heaven round about bellow back.*

'God pressed on with much force, chiding them for their delay. And now they started to panic within* and beg for peace: "Why now, true and undoubted offshoot of God, are you forcing us out of this body which has been given over to us for punishment? At least let us be allowed to come out and occupy these animals" (as it happened, at that moment some bristly swine were feeding near those shores). "Don't plunge us like this in the awful chasm, nor command us to enter the hidden places of the lower world."* He agreed. Immediately you could see far off—look!—the dark herd straying in different directions, now this way and now that, driven by the ungentle goads* of the Furies. There was no delay, no respite:* within them the untamed violence raged until they hurled themselves headlong into the deep pools and all lost their lives together beneath the waves. And the young man suddenly collapsed, his limbs exhausted, his arms finally freed from their knotted bindings. He remined prostrate on the ground, gnashing his teeth and still sobbing; an uncontrollable gasping made his chest pound, and as he panted the afflicted man expelled the air from his lungs.* The son of God stood close beside him, and touching his face with his right hand he opened his eyes and ears; and now the man saw and spoke, and his heart, forgetting what he had suffered, settled down. A cry went up to the glittering stars* from the exultant crowd, as they declared that Jesus was both offspring of the supreme Father and himself God.

'But what could he not do? He even sent us too with orders to bring aid to the sick and to relieve their pain with help* on the spot. Many we called back from death's dark jaws, not by any human capabilities or any particular skill,* but at the mere invocation of our teacher's name three times over, they got up from their beds and went off cured. Out of that whole number there was just one man who came to us, however, hounded by cruel goads and blind frenzy, whom we tried in vain to heal and were defeated; with ever-increasing intensity the violent force within drove him on. Soon that superlative deity brought aid to the man in person, annoyed that we had so little confidence in him, saying: "It is easy to expel infestations like these from people's bodies; but you must abstain from food and seek help from heaven. Nor is this capacity granted to you alone, but whoever has broadcast my name may attempt all things, if only he does not lack faith in me. That man can even move mountains with their mighty bulk at his command and bring meandering rivers to a halt, changing their course.* Go, then, be confident and reassured in your spirits, and do not falter with unsteady faith. Cast everywhere the golden seeds of truth; flood with your light the world shrouded in darkness and lying buried in deep night. You are the light of humanity,* you the lanterns to light this dingy world." So he spoke, and brought others to join us, so that they might share in such great undertakings and be companions in our labours. And though he chose seventy,* he was yet unhappy at so meagre a number, and declared that so many were not sufficient for so great a task; like a man who turns the soil with a hundred ploughs* and works his ancestral fields with hoes, when the ripened crop now grows bright with golden ears of corn, if people are lacking to store up the abundant harvest by their labour, he worries and hires men from other regions.

'Why should I tell of how he can see into people's minds and observe their hidden cares, which surely couldn't happen without some divine power?* Often, as we nurtured empty fears in silence, he would rebuke us for our inner doubts and rouse us with reproachful words as we stood there in astonishment. How often in the past did he declare even to his very enemies what treacheries and ruses they were devising in vain, while they were being spurred on blindly by cruel hatred?

'Nor did it escape him that a woman had suffered for twelve whole years from a stream of infected blood issuing from her body. She, indeed, worn out by the pain of the burning ailment, was following along behind him in case she could touch some part of him, thinking that this was the one path to deliverance that remained for her. And so, while the young people poured in from all sides and their ranks streamed round him, she crept up* and lightly took hold of the edge of his garment. At that touch, the chronic illness fled from her body, and now she was secretly preparing her departure, thinking that she had escaped notice; but the god sensed it and addressed her kindly as she panicked and tried to cover herself up, imparting friendly advice.

'I myself recently saw him before my very eyes* stripped of his mortal frame or flooded with light from on high, emitting from his body a light not less than the glare of the sun. By these and many other signs, which I saw in abundance,* he was revealed throughout the earth as God.* Yet even so he never forgot that he had been born a human being with a body that was destined to die; he endured many things, too, that mortals must endure, and he did so voluntarily, leaving behind examples for our imitation. Often he attended merry dinners and parties, nor did he disdain gatherings of people in the city, benevolent as he was. Often, too, as he fled the snares and the anger of a race hostile to him, as a man would, he left the entrance of the dangerous temple and flung a hollow cloud around him,* concealing his form, and disappeared from their sight, hidden away in dark retreats, while his foes roared in vain and readied their stones.

'Indeed, I remember* (for barely a whole year has passed) that lately, when he learned of the recent killing* of John, whom the king, warned to give back the wife he had snatched from his brother,* had beheaded by the sword in a dark dungeon, he prudently went off and left the cities round here, distancing himself from the population. The deep woods welcomed him as a fugitive. But the very king of Erebus,* the human race's foulest foe, who is always striving to turn our minds away from what is right, did not give up or let our lord and god be.* For at one point the hero, while seeking refuge from the clamour of his companions and the crowd of his followers, had secretly slipped away from human company and was spending time in isolation in the deep glades. And now he had passed forty days without taking food and had endured hunger in the wilderness for the same number of nights, when now—see!—thinking it was time for inflicting harm,* immediately his foe, the lord of night, was at hand with a host of thousands, whom he was leading from the caverns of Tartarus, tossing the flaming adornment of his half-bestial head. Already he saw in hope—but to no avail—the reward for his cunning; and so, plotting fruitlessly to trick Jesus with his words, he accosted him like this: "You are the sure offspring of the heavenly Father, and the true God; all things obey you. Why do you go on enduring as your body wastes away with hunger? Why don't you try to turn these enormous rocks that you see around you into as many spelt loaves,* all at once?" But his tricks did not escape the notice of the deity,* who replied as follows: "I have, in place of the mortal blessing of baked bread, the speech of my Father which I have heard, and his divine words; whenever I think on these and recall them in my mind, all hunger is repelled and flees at once, and my desire for food is forgotten."

'He had finished speaking. But after hearing this his foe did not leave off, though defeated in the first encounter, and he returned to the fight, pressing on with one assault on top of another; and three times he tried afresh his ruses, frustrated in his endeavours, each time a new tactic—but to no avail. At one time he tried to lead his opponent's steadfast mind astray with empty longing* for dominions, at another with the hollow desire for praise; as when the East Winds lift up the troubled sea* in billows and the wave beats relentlessly and rages with menacing blows against the raised shore, but is dashed against the rocks and is turned back.* But the god, although he perceived these efforts at once, did not fend him off in his attempts and permitted him to weave his web of tricks for him, pointless as it was. Now he willingly allowed himself to be ushered up on to the gables of a marble temple, now up on to a cliff edge and an irregular rocky outcrop, and he kindled in his tempter a hope—an empty one.* And just when his foe thought he had won* and was nurturing feelings of terrible glee, gawping in deluded delight, all at once the hero, affirming his divinity with manifest power right before him, invariably evaded his frustrated wiles and exposed trickery; like a horse, when it has got away over the level ground after shaking off its reins, runs free and makes mockery of the attendants who pursue it from all directions, often pretending mischievously to come to a halt here and there, and periodically grazing on the grass it comes upon along the way—but when it now sees them coming closer, it slips away and shoots off way ahead, covering a vast stretch of terrain.* When the gruesome foe finally realized that he had attempted this scheme in vain, he went away defeated and left the god behind attended by a hundred swift-winged angelic assistants who had been sent at his Father's bidding to bring him help.

'But if you're looking for the causes and the germ of such great hatred, why it is that an entire race is set in opposition to just one man—that's for them to know. Certainly he has not committed such acts as they fabricate against their captive, driven as they are by cruel hatred. There is no one friendlier among men, no one superior to him in holiness;* he embraces all in his forgiveness. Enemy and countryman are treated by him with no distinction.* Many have cast slurs against him with impunity as he has put up with things both deserved and undeserved,* when he could have destroyed them all with just a nod. Once, late at night, when he was travelling through the region of Sidon and was tired, the uncivilized folk shut us out of their little city and refused shelter to the hero when he appealed to them. We were upset and began to entreat the supreme Father to look down from heaven and not to let his Son go unavenged, but to strike that heartless population straightaway with fire from heaven and cast down their unwelcoming walls with sudden flames. But he did not tolerate this and rebuked us indignantly with stinging words, and instead he pitied the spiteful city.

'Often he even used to keep company with criminals in full awareness of what they had done, and would enter disreputable homes and dens of iniquity, so that they might be warned and strip off their pride and evil ways* and begin gradually to accustom themselves to what is right. That's how it was with Matthew, that's how it was with our friend Zacchaeus himself,* the wealthy landowner, and with a hundred others called to better things. Even so, so long as this was something he did frequently, there was always someone around who thought that he was unwittingly being deceived and would reproach him, as a serious offence, with not shunning the taint of wickedness. But he himself, in order to bring medical assistance (as it were) to the sick and drooping, sought of his own accord through the whole length of the city, wherever mortals were oppressed by mental darkness,* people he could rescue from night in his goodness and call them to the light, taking pity on their grovelling in the darkness with blind hearts. That, he would say, is what is really pleasing to those on high and to the Father of those on high, and that was the reason he had been sent from bright Olympus.

'Moreover, he also taught us what great joy filled heaven, and with what great rejoicing the race that inhabits the heavenly realm received the news, whenever some perpetrator of wrong* in mortal regions, a despiser of holiness and equity, began to cultivate justice and have regard for what is right; just like an unwary shepherd, who has lost one sheep out of thousands when it forgot to leave for home with the flocks late at night,* if by chance, after searching sorrowfully over the rocks and through the tangled thickets for a long time, scanning every spot with restless eyes, he finds it at last grazing in a sequestered valley. All at once he snatches it up, and bearing it on his shoulders he delightedly carries it back to the fold. As he comes in his sweet children run up to snatch kisses,* and the whole house receives with rejoicing the one returned. For this reason the hero did not refrain from conversing with women, and just recently, while passing through the countryside in the territory of Samaria below the ancient walls of the city of Sychar, he happened to see a girl coming to a fountain. He begged her for water as a suppliant and drained the gift of the well—he who commands the ocean and the sonorous streams,* and waters the broad earth with ample showers, and at whose command the rock once turned to liquid for the thirsty peoples,* flowing abundantly with water. Meanwhile, in seclusion, we all marvelled; but once she had received instruction and freely confessed her sins, he called her out of darkness and deep night into the light of day.

'Often devout mothers, fearful of everything, committed to him boys and girls in blooming youth, their hair crowned with flowers and tied back with soft leafage,* so that he might implant in their young minds a love of fair virtue* and fill them, while still inexperienced, with honourable impulses. Addressing the youthful throng in a kindly manner, he gave them instruction and purified them by his touch, so that wicked incantations might not harm them and no violent force issuing from the infernal regions might subdue them.

'Furthermore, above all else he used to chide with stinging words those who were haughty in spirit, and by his actions he left them examples to follow. Once his companions were making their way together with me, as we searched for him when he was away, and we all sat down tired from the journey before the mouth of a cave, which a host of elm trees overshadowed with their thick foliage and shielded with their bending branches.* Here we wasted much time pursuing empty questions* amongst ourselves—which of us was pre-eminent among the whole number,* or was more loved by or more pleasing to the teacher himself. I'll tell you something amazing: as soon as he himself saw us in the entrance, he stopped and glared,* and asked us again and again what our talk was or what kind of contest we were engaged in. We however stayed silent and didn't dare to open our mouths, all of us being ashamed of our words as we recalled them; we had gabbled so much and so pointlessly. Then suddenly, indicating a boy whose tender years meant that his mind had as yet no awareness of praise and inflated conceit, he said: "No one may rightly aspire to the blessed assemblies of the heavenly ones without learning to put aside empty pride and discarding completely and with scorn the love of fame—just as this boy has no longing for praise in his heart. Under no other conditions could admission to heaven be granted. Sooner could clouds exist in the salt sea or fish survive in the fields,* or tree trunks burst into leaf in the districts of the air."

'My mind still shudders at the thought of the time when my devoted mother asked him in vain for special honours for me and my brother—namely, that when he should sit on his lofty throne in the heavenly palace of his Father on high, in the very midst of the denizens of heaven, each of us should take our seat beside him, the one clasping his right hand close by, the other clinging to his left.* All at once he, stern and harsh with a reproachful look, scolded not our mother (for what rebuke did our mother deserve by her devotion?) but us, berating us deservedly with no soft words, we who had set her up to it unawares by our vain ingenuity. So we were told that God constantly puts down the haughty and decisively rejects the proud who are spurred by desire for fame and commendation.*

'He, though not at all unequal to his Father and fully capable of those same things that his Father can do, nonetheless often turns the lips of those singing his own praises towards the Father himself, declaring that he ventures on nothing beyond the capacity of a human unless the almighty Father inspires him with strength from Olympus on high. For that reason, as a rule, he forbade anyone he had cured of serious illness to publicize the deed anywhere. And in order to conceal his powers, although he could have banished the wasting sores from people's bodies by his nod alone, he nonetheless often used to send off the sick to healing springs, so that they might free themselves of every taint through the power of the salutary water. Why should I tell of how many peoples, how many cities, sought to claim him and wanted to set him over them as king,* sending him the royal robe, the sceptre, and the holy diadem?* Even his companions often pressed and enjoined him to arm himself and invade the territory of Syria, to make it his kingdom: soon, they said, it would result directly in his bringing beneath his yoke by force of arms whatever lands Ocean encircles with its winding rim,* and in his reining in the boundless world with new laws. But when they put pressure on him by their incitements, immediately he hid himself, taking flight into the high mountains.

'Yet those monstrous people are now rising up against him through their envy and cruel hatred, and are clamouring with one voice for punishment: all of them are after the head of just one man. You know with what frenzy they have dragged him here, with what uproar they have filled the whole city in their commotion, as if it had been captured by enemies. He himself, obeying his Father's injunctions, has borne everything, resolved to suffer all kinds of things;* for he freely offered himself* to them when they came looking for him, and though he could have protected himself by taking advantage of the darkness of night,* twice he openly gave himself up to them. Even so, I have seen them fall flat in amazement at their captive's voice and lie stretched out on the ground in a heavy fall.

'And yet he doesn't take away respect from rituals or from the temple; he hasn't remade the laws of our race or the decrees of the ancients, though he prescribes that from now on we should forgo the offering of flesh and sacrificial entrails,* and should no longer make atonement by bloodshed. But he points out that very different rites and sacred practices* lie hidden beneath the obscure mystery of words, and he unveils the pronouncements and the intention of the law-giving teacher.* And for your even greater amazement, they know—and they admit they know*—that a prophet will come forth into the light of day, the only one who* can unbar for us the impassable gates of heaven and bring the spirits of the righteous out of the darkness to the stars on high. That was what was promised to our fathers; that was what all the prophets had in mind; and he is the one people are waiting for now, in firm assurance. Wretched are they to whom it is not granted to recognize the light at hand in the pitch darkness, and who thirst in the very midst of the ample river's flow.* For whom would the man's supreme virtue, his innumerable accomplishments, the glory of his appearance not move, unless their feelings were completely unreceptive?* I myself, as soon as I saw him and took in his words as he radiated sweet love from his whole figure,* I left behind my fortune, my homeland, my mother, everything I had. That was what his other companions did too. And I have had no regrets about following him subsequently: as much as a vast conflagration often rises from a tiny spark and grows ever fiercer, so much my love for him seems to grow with each passing hour,* and my heart ever to blaze more and more with sweet devotion. All those who have come into contact with him just once are bound to him by mighty bonds.*

'And don't believe that he tricked us with gifts or with words, ensnaring us with enticing promises. He gave us his word that everything would be harsh, that scattered exile awaited us all as outcasts, wandering about everywhere.* Nor has the trustworthiness of those promises proved empty: a crowded forest of evils is continually sprouting up in constant succession.* Just one man's head he spares from the sword; one man (whoever he is)* will close his eyes in peaceful death, while gruesome slaughter—he says—hangs over all the rest. Meanwhile he bids us despise our possessions, share out our wealth,* and spend it on the destitute throng of wretched folk beleaguered by sickness, cold, and hunger; he tells us to endure poverty and get used to deprivation. Thus many have seen us on numerous occasions stretched out slumbering in the fields or on a bare rock, or in our exhaustion plucking the ripe ears of corn and relieving our hunger with the produce of the wild, lying on our front by the deep rivers or any springs afforded anywhere by the parched earth, and swigging water from our hollowed palms. Not if a hundred tongues supplied me a constant voice in an iron breast* could I run through the enormity and the character of the miseries, the magnitude of the toils we drained to the dregs under his leadership, holding out in equanimity. For though from time to time the scarcity of food pressed upon us* as we wilted, lacking those things that necessity requires, even so we constantly judged our elevated spirits equal to the wealth of kings,* and in our meagre circumstances each man possessed a mind unparalleled in its riches.

'Furthermore, an enormous number of new companions could always be seen arriving, matrons and men, all with the same purpose and with their mind set on following him.* It was just like when a mighty king has declared war on some city: now he stirs up arms, now he gathers his troops, bringing defeat and destruction to the region and ruin to its peoples. Not just the sworn-in guard and enlisted cohorts march out, but also those led by a terrible yearning for possessions,* eager for enrichment on the varied spoils of war—these too congregate in large numbers and follow the camp* unbidden. Both the broad ways and the spreading fields were not enough to hold such masses of people, willingly following wherever he might go. Often the hero removed himself from the vast multitude, making for the mountains and seeking the deserted woodlands.

'And indeed I remember* one occasion when he had set out and was making his way beside the shallows, and a vast band of people lined the shores and was pressing in on him even more thickly than usual. He snatched himself away and leapt into a little boat which happened to be standing ready, and suddenly giving orders to cut the cable, he advanced into the watery expanse to within a spear's throw* of the shore. There he stopped, and looking out at the land and the packed shores all around, he began to address the throng with divine words, disclosing the way of justice and the path of righteousness. On this side and that they stood with ears pricked up, all of them, cut off from him by the waves, and they gaped at him in astonishment in a long line, their spirits enraptured by his amazing sweetness. As for him, he stood there speaking, while around him the surface of the sea settled into stillness, though only a moment before it had been whipped up on all sides by the breath of the gusty winds;* and the forests, leafy homes of the birds, stood motionless without a murmur along the curving shore round about. Yet even in the midst of this the aged mothers did not hold their speech; they all marvelled at him while he spoke as no one had spoken before, and cried that his mother was blessed in her womb, blessed were the breasts of the mother who had given birth to such a being and had offered her swollen breasts to his tender lips.*

'For he used to instruct the mortal race to raise their minds to heaven, grovelling shamefully on the ground and trapped in darkness as they were,* and to look upon the light and shed their habitual vain preoccupations. Then he would urge peace: "Above all things, men, choose in gentleness the serenity of peace, and cast aside puffed-up conceit;* humble in spirit, and with no craving for empty praise,* scorn mortal riches* and honours—scorn them, and endure poverty, training your life to hardship and blessed with a little.* Brief is whatever pleasure that life of yours holds, and nothing is long-lasting for sickly mortals. Your home here is not your true home: long granted to you, a kingdom awaits, a better one, when death has loosed your heavy limbs from your soul.* The best of fathers will receive you directly in his court set with stars as you arrive with joy in a better region, where there is the stillness of peace and an abundance of all things, untroubled rest* and pleasure that will never perish. For such a reward, would anyone hesitate to endure short-lived toil and to follow me, freely leaving the earth behind? Strive to pass through to your true wealth, to pass through to your true honours, which no stroke of chance, no passage of time, can take away. Be reverent; maintain a kindly spirit towards one another, and in tranquillity of soul take pity on each other. Moreover, keep anger far from you, and refrain from hatred through endurance; scorn the changeable chatter* of the mob. No one may rightly give a blow in return for a blow received; it would be better to offer yourself willingly to those who strike you, and to wait for a blow to the cheeks—a second one.

'"Let others compete with weapons for empty glory; let them sharpen their deadly steel and seek a beautiful death through their wounds.* You, though, learn to love all mortals without distinction, and desire peace for your enemies, though it leave you inglorious; let the rumblings of blustering renown hold no value for you. Above all, let everyone's mind be free from the terror of death, and let no impulse make you hard-hearted and lead you astray from what is right. Sometimes humans may be able to snuff out earthly limbs and mortal bodies,* and destroy them by the sword; but the soul itself remains safe, not being subject to cruel death. And the almighty Father is looking down on you from heaven on high and keeping you from evils—without his authority, not a single human being can pluck a hair from your heads. In humility it is your duty to revere him alone: it is he to whom you must offer prayers in the appointed manner, he to whom you must direct fit offerings, the one whom the sea, the land, and the air with its spreading plains* obey, and before whom the clear expanse of the shining heaven* trembles. For him prostrate yourselves on the ground, to him set forth your prayers as you lie stretched in supplication, since he has the power to crush you with everlasting punishments even after death, guilty as you are, in the awful pit below. And let no one feel fear at going up to unleashed lions, or the race of spotted panthers,* unrivalled in its savagery. Go forth, shielded by the protection of my name; go to meet danger without trepidation. At once bears will grow tame and lick your wounds with their tongues,* sparing you from harm. Indeed, put from your minds lowly anxieties* about how you will live. Look at the race of cattle, the race of birds soaring on high: no arts are theirs, no care for the future touches them. And yet even so they lack nothing by way of shelter or supplies of food. All things are nourished by the universal Creator in his bounty, all things receive his care. It is he, too, who clothes the earth with grass unbidden, tinting the sown fields with flowers of assorted colour; he adds leaves to the trees* and shadows to the mountains.

'"Have nothing to do with deceit, trickery, and shameful lust, and don't delight excessively in feasts spread before you, but drive sloth and idleness from your hearts. Don't hanker after prohibited unions and forbidden intercourse, and put an end to thirst for others' gold. Live content, each one of you, with your own resources, and freely put aside illicit hopes and vain desires. But so as not to go through all the varieties of wrongdoing* just now, what should I say of those who take pleasure in deceit and embrace dire lust, and yet feign virtue with a counterfeit expression, concealing their true nature, and proceed by tricks and draw a veil over their wickedness? Don't, I command you—don't allow your hearts to become accustomed* to such a scourge. Nothing remains so well hidden that time itself cannot uncover it unprompted. Furthermore, keep your eyes in check: don't go voluntarily in search of things to harm your souls. From now on, curb your love of talking; often in the past has an unchecked tongue sunk the unwary. Learn now, therefore, to utter henceforth no falsehoods, and now, after being cleansed, clothe your minds in new habits. If any traces of ancient fault remain,* however, wash them away and vanquish the infection with holy water. I myself, like the purest spring, shall supply the running water. Make haste to the waters; drink deep in your thirst right away, mothers and men,* from the flowing stream. Come this way, all of you. There's no need of gold or silver for those who drink: the water of *my* spring is open to all. In this way may you avoid the paths of death; this is the way to the stars* and the starry dwellings, the unchanging realms. These things my Father declared to me, so that I might proclaim them with the voice of truth; from that source come all my words."

'Such were his words, and above all else he bade us sue for peace from the king of heaven, who is to be appeased not by the offering of entrails, nor by blood from slaughter, but by vows and prayers. And he himself proclaimed to us what our manner of prayer would be: "Almighty Father, whose abode is the gleaming heaven, so may your name and your praises be celebrated everywhere and the ages promised to the world begin to go forth, when the mortal race fulfils your commands on earth no less than the denizens of heaven obey you in the sky. Restore us today with divine nourishment from heaven on high. Grant us mercy hereafter in your goodness, as we ourselves forgive our enemies, and cast us not in the way of adversity, defenceless as we are, making trial of us, but keep all dangers from us."*

'And prophesying things to come,* he added that there would be a time one day when the wandering sun would be shrouded in a dense glow and cast off its radiant aspect, and the silvery moon would be suddenly extinguished in the starry night* and cease to dispense its brightness to the world, its blackened face strewn all over with blood-red blotches. The stars which now are borne on a fixed downward course or in a set position would hurtle headlong in disarray from all quarters of the teetering firmament. And that force which stirs the restless spheres of heaven would cease, he said, causing all things to be whirled in indeterminate motion and the universe to recoil from its near wrenched-off hinge, until like a scorching thunderbolt through the void he himself would make for earth once more, and making his entrance with a train many thousands strong would hold his enquiry into the lives and offences of humanity. And as soon as creation caught alight with the promised fire and the flaming tempest spread over all the earth, directly upon the renewal of earth and heaven he would summon the lifeless souls back into their bodies,* back to the enchanting light, and he would raise the nations from their tombs and lead the righteous with him to the stars, those who from the very beginning of the world the Father foresaw would be his own and whom he marked out for lofty Olympus. Winged youths will go forth and fill the deepest recesses of heaven* with a fearsome blare, calling out the peoples on all sides with the sound of the trumpet's curved bronze* from the direction of the four winds.

'Through the whole sky there will be a hurried progress to the judge's throne. He himself, raised on high and shining out as adjudicator on the topmost peak of the mountain, will cast about him his awe-inspiring countenance; he will set apart the righteous* and place them on his right-hand side, but on his left he will round up the guilty, the largest throng. Just as when, after winter has run its course, the smiling pastures with their soft grass call the herds from their opened stalls, the shepherd divides his flocks before sending them into the glistening fields: first he picks out the placid sheep, counting them off, and bids the reeking goats remain at a distance. Then it will be possible to see shining afar through the shimmering air the beaming bodies of men, from which the almighty Father will wash away all that is within the grasp of dismal death, and they will remain forever, no longer subject to any chances of this world. Let no one hope before that day for the abode of heaven in the flesh, with a few exceptions whom God himself, when rising from the tomb, will personally carry with him to the regions on high. Until then, the souls alone will enjoy such a situation; but the guilty, by contrast, will be pressed down by darkness and night everlasting,* and will pay for all eternity the penalty they have deserved.

'All these things he foretold to me not long ago, late at night, while I rested my head weighed down with sorrow on his lap, reclining together on the same couch, often drawing closer to him as he spoke: this was the solace for my sorrowing love. Why should I repeat what he often declared by the waves of the wandering Jordan, what he proclaimed beneath the lofty mountains of Judaea, now choosing to envelop the truth in obscuring riddles,* now stating it clearly and openly in unambiguous speech, while the people stood around and crowded round him in great numbers?* At one moment he would declare himself the beginning and end of all things;* at another, the fount of truth and the light and the way for all people.* Fortunate are we to have been born at this time, happy the earth and joyful the age that has given us birth! To our lot, and ours alone, has it fallen to hear the divine voice of God regularly close at hand as he utters divine words. Clearly an age will come hereafter, as the years glide past,* when our distant descendants will long to have witnessed these same things.'

Such things John persevered in saying,* to the amazement of all, when suddenly—look!—with a deafening uproar a sacrilegious band of Jerusalem folk burst in, appealing to the city governor and with one voice clamouring for punishment. Joseph and John both fled; they resolved to go to his eminent mother, but to conceal everything from her for a long while, unaware as she was of such momentous happenings.

BOOK FIVE

THE prisoner was innocent, and the Roman sought wholeheartedly to spare him,* casting his mind around in all directions.* The man's renown and his manly qualities and the glory of his remarkable face kept coming back to his thoughts; there was no longer any doubt that his lineage was from the gods.* Everything tallied with what he had heard. At last he turned to the people of Jerusalem, who were filling the whole building with their uproar,* and said: 'Go, and turn up here again in a little while, when this contest has been settled. Let someone be chosen out of your whole number to speak on behalf of all and put your case, explaining what crime this man is to be punished for with death and setting out in due order what terrible offence is to be held against him, innocent as he is.' As soon as he said this, they went away at once growling, determined in their hearts never to back off while Christ still lived.

Elsewhere, the one who had shamefully betrayed his king to the enemy returned to his senses and recognized his crime—the faithless Judas. Ah, poor man: how he would have wished it could all be reversed and made undone! No rest came to his mind;* avenging Furies* raged in his breast and wrung from him the unseen punishment for his wrong, and he could not contain the frenzied surge of anguish in his breast. Senselessly taking with him in his hand the money that had been the cause of his crime, which the Jerusalemites had given as arranged for his valuable service,* he came to the hallowed portals of the priests, shouting: 'It's yours, this silver; this payment is yours—take it! Here, I give back the deadly reward for my crimes.* Oh, what was I after,* mad as I was? By what price was I induced to commit the awful crime? He is the true offspring of God, and the true God*—now at last I see that. The darkness is scattered and gone, and my sense is restored to me.'* As he spoke in this way, he hurled the silver at them; but they laughed at him as he wept, perceiving all too late what he had done.

Sunk in unhappiness, he went away. Then, senseless and blinded by frenzy,* he entertained all kinds of thoughts; his mental torment doubled, the pain raged in the depth of his heart, and he could not bear to look upon the vault of heaven.* Then he spoke to himself, turning his flaming eyeballs this way and that:* 'Ah, what shall I do,* unhappy me? What age to come, so very distant, will ever forget and keep silent about so monstrous a crime? Shall I go back again as a suppliant and confess my fault, and should I dare to hope for pardon for this unspeakable crime? With what countenance can I look upon him, with what speech can I address him—the one I previously deceived, though he was innocent and did not deserve it? Shall I flee far from here, then, as far as it's possible to go, and live out my life unknown in other lands? Whirling winds, bear me away from here, away, to where the day flees from us when its light is finished! But what place will be safe, after all? God sees everything, he's present everywhere, and he terrifies the earth on all sides with his thunderbolt.* And in my case a guilty conscience and compounded anxiety will follow me, whether I hasten my journey on foot or by boat over the waves. To whom? From whom? But I'm wasting time, and dreams are playing tricks with my mind. I entreat you, mighty earth, open wide now to receive me.* Why am I hesitating? Now your sinful crimes are coming home to you, unhappy Judas! It was then that you ought to have thought about it, then such considerations were fitting,* when it was right and proper to check your course and oppose this scourge. Now die, and freely avenge so great an abomination by your own hand; willingly leave behind both daylight and humanity!'

Such were the thoughts he cast about, now resolved to break the thread of his loathsome life* and bring his cruel pain to an end* by death; this, he thought, was the one way to conclude his anguish and his travails. He vacillated, and constantly seemed to himself to be swallowed up by the earth or blasted by devouring fire from heaven. At every moment the image of the prisoner loomed before his eyes. A pallor crept over his face, his eyes were shot with blood, and a tremor ran through his freezing limbs—all symptoms of impending death—while thick night hovered round his features, enclosing them in shadow.* Everything began to grow dark with the shade of blackening gloom.* That madman, who didn't dare rather to hope for mercy by confessing his fault—for the king of angels is swayed by prayers* and benevolently forgets his righteous anger.

And so he, persisting in his enterprise and holding fast to that same position,* went away and slunk trembling into the murky woods that put forth their leaves in abundance beside the royal residence. There, while he shuddered with dread, unsure by what form of death he might finally find rest (should he bravely pierce the hiding place of his soul* with a sharpened sword, falling forward and burying it in his chest? Or should he hurl himself in a headlong plunge from a high place?), those Furies who forever led him on in his bewilderment, fixated as he was by the desire for death, and tormented him as they went ahead, showed the way by tying a horrid loop of rope to a bending tree.* From there he hung by the neck, as he deserved, and pursuing his own end by the shameful noose he shut off the airways of his breath,* constricting his throat; and as he hung there his whole body instantly wasted away.

The expanse of heaven was not yet glowing red, washed with colour by the new dawn, and already the priests were standing there near the entrance, filling every inch with their cluster, and growling fiercely throughout the length of the colonnades; for by ancient custom it was not permitted for anyone to set foot over a tainted doorstep* on a holy day. At last the Roman emerged with a crowd of young attendants packed close round him,* majestic with his ancestral rods of office and purple garments, and took his seat before the doors, raised up on an ivory throne. The elders too likewise sat down next to him in order, and for a long time they kept silence. Then the governor finally began proceedings and spoke: 'Tell me, then, for what crime you are demanding this remarkable young man be sent to his death. I myself have made enquiry into his background and life; nothing was found deserving of death, but rather report holds him up for his mighty achievements. The moment I saw him chained close at hand and heard him speaking, I was astounded;* for he seemed to me to emit no mortal utterance, and to resemble a god in every way—in his face, his voice, and his eyes. Either he is surely a god,* or the surest offspring of a god.* Give it up. Don't refuse to recognize your king.'

At these words resentment flared up in their very marrow, deep within them all, beyond all measure.* They all roared and groaned. Then the elderly Annas,* their most accomplished speaker, rose to his feet in their midst and launched into speech with such words as these: 'If this matter were not fully apparent to you of itself from other indications, Roman, it would be readily recognizable to anyone even from this fact (and you in particular ought to be greatly struck by this, as governor), when you see so many citizens have gathered here, assembled from all sides, to oppose the crimes of one man. This deviser of rhetoric has deceived many by his speech, and by his respectable appearance—don't fall for his tricks—he makes a false pretence of virtue. Deep in his heart he conceals his love of crimes. Don't you see the goal of this new religion,* the aim of its secret celebrations and congresses and night-time get-togethers? Gaining influence through sedition,* he is stirring up the cities of Judaea, and has the nerve to call himself everywhere the king of the world and offspring of the supreme Father, whom the very stars obey.* And so, like a god, he grants forgiveness to those who readily confess their sins and frees them from the fear of punishment after their deaths: this crime he cannot atone for except by death—that's what our ancestors decreed. But he even goes about repealing the old rules on his own authority, and has established new laws through his feigned divinity,* instituting new rites and new practices through the cities for our distant descendants to observe for centuries to come.

'Indeed, he threatens unequivocally (for shame!) to cast down the very altars, and to consign the temples to the flames*—the temples that were once raised at the expense of such gigantic toil. And any moment now he'll want to put out the sun itself and lay siege to heaven and draw down the stars by his words.* Yet he has not been able to conceal his wickedness for long with his deceiving heart, for he doesn't shrink from entering the houses of criminals or steer clear of forbidden gatherings, despite being warned, and his companions are enthralled by sumptuous banquets.* And not just that: periodically, if by some report an ungodly man is identified in all the city, one known for his criminal behaviour beyond all others, immediately he loses no time in going straight to him, rejoicing in those like himself, and doesn't rest until he has joined the man to himself in friendship. So great is his love of crime, so great the affection he has for deceiving. And then on holy days, when it is right and proper not to engage in any exertion, he nonetheless dispels diseases and heals the sick. Why should I mention how his associates feed on forbidden foods with impunity in people's homes, and handle bread and wine without washing their hands first, with a disregard for cleanliness wholly free from custom or any law, and defile everything with their touch?* Obviously the almighty Father would go back on rites which have found favour for so many generations, and change his mind!* What is this new upheaval? Can heaven be subject to such inconsistency? Give him up to execution! Let him not destroy the altars where incense is burned, the object of his threats; that will guarantee that no one dares such things hereafter. Give him up to execution! Let the sinner drain to the dregs the just punishment for his wickedness. Keep unspeakable fire away from the holy altars.'* He finished speaking, and they all roared their agreement in unison.

The Roman, however, remained entirely unmoved by any words; it wasn't as if at this point he was hearing new charges for the first time. All of it, he knew, had been cooked up out of terrible hatred while Christ's glory and boundless virtue were tormenting these wicked people with bitter goads.* He said: 'The word in public is that you've made these charges against him all too often, and he has always stood up to them with a ready defence and has refuted them triumphantly with true reasoning. He himself does not deny that he is the offspring of the Father on high, who—as you are fully aware*—was promised as destined to come from heaven one day at long last by divine dispensation to bring help to afflicted mortals. He would do this to soften the Father's ancient anger, reconciling him to your race, and to wash away the guilt of your forefathers in person by his own virtue. This is the tenor, as I understand it, of the teachings of the ancients, and this, I gather, is what your fathers foretold; and he himself confirms it by the facts—so greatly, in the course of his travels around the towns, has he stirred up the whole region with mighty portents, of which no human arts or force are capable. Furthermore, he has even recalled some people to the light of day from the shades, of whose whole frame death had already taken full possession and had loosened the clinging bonds of the soul from their body. So come, you poor people, get out of the habit of unjust hatred; don't fight in vain, but come to know your god.'

He finished speaking. But more and more the violence flared up among them all.* With a deafening uproar they pressed on, raging all together with nothing to curb their fury, and tore the cloaks from their shoulders. The anger swelled in their blazing spirits just like when farmers strive to restrain with the barrier of a hastily constructed blockade the Adige or the Po* as it prepares to flood the fertile fields with its waves; yet the current surges on still more in its impetuous course, rushing over the obstacle and triumphantly laying low the lofty bulk of the barricade in its advance.

As it happened, at this time the king and scion of kings, Herod,* had just arrived in the city in his enthusiasm to take part in the religious rituals. Through the gift of the Romans, a part of his ancestral kingdom which had been lost had been restored to him, and he now held the towns of Galilee. Once the Roman governor learned that he was there, he sought to free himself at last from an unwelcome duty and passed the captive Galilean over to that other Galilean, ordering him to conduct an enquiry himself into the man's life and crimes—if indeed there were any—and to determine a punishment for him in accordance with his deserts. Then, on hearing Christ's name, the king gladly ordered him to be led in, possessed as he was by an overwhelming desire to speak to the man and look upon his real face at close quarters.* He proceeded to make overtures to him on a variety of topics, but the captive said nothing in reply and kept his eyes resolutely fixed* on heaven. And so Herod, not at all amazed by anything superhuman in him, actually mocked him and ordered him to be taken back into custody, and although innocent he was returned once more to the keeping of the Roman, who was far from happy about it.

At this point my spirits fail me, and my mind grows sick and starts to waver. I shudder to recall* what evils the true offshoot of God endured as God made man, the creator of Olympus, whom the sea, the land, and the stretching halls of the empty expanse and the shining span of boundless heaven* cannot contain. Almighty Spirit, restore my strength by your descent, sent down as a breath from heaven, and sustain me here by your power. Every time I strive to set forth these things, my resolve is overcome, and everything starts to grow dark* around me. I see the stars become pale and the sun hide its rosy head in pitch-black gloom* and the sorrowing sky dissolve into tears. Did such great piety, such great love, glorious light of the cloudless heaven, drive you, in pity at our sorry state, to choose to endure these things so grievous and harsh to suffer, though true offspring of God and true God* sent from heaven, and to subject your divine being willingly to so many evils, weighed down by earthly load? Would you accept this reward, to erase *our* sins by *your* death in your goodness? It was we* who picked the sweet fruit from the forbidden tree, you who paid the cruel penalty, hanging on the unspeakable trunk, o you who pitied our struggles too much.* You, despite being God and the undoubted offshoot of God, are now compelled, alas, to undergo human judgements one after another in chains and to feel awe before the face of a judge, you who one day will come as the judge appointed for the whole world.

Pontius, when he observed the prisoner being returned again to his door and saw that he could not get out of the grim judgement, was beaten and battered by wild waves of care.* With one line of approach and then another he tried again and again to hold back their cruel spirits and their hearts incapable of mercy, but all in vain; and he stood against them to no avail with futile fervour. The more he strove to set their spirits right by his speech, now imploring and calm, now severe and with harsh threats, the more agitated the anger became in their inflamed hearts.* At last he said: 'At the return of these rites on fixed days (the age-old empty superstition* of your forefathers), I have been accustomed to give up one of the many people confined in prison and to let them go unpunished from their constricting chains. Do you bid this man be set free for you, then, innocent as he is? For whom could I release instead? Already there has been sufficient punishment and more than enough savagery. Either I release him, or you take him away from here and sentence him undeservedly to a dismal death, as you please, without any involvement from me.' But the horde couldn't stand this and broke him off mid-speech,* amplifying their false charges and yelling for greater punishment.

As it happened, in those days Barabbas, hated by the people and the elders, unsurpassed by any in the enormity of his wickedness,* had long been in custody awaiting harsh punishment. He had no hope at all of escape,* no way to salvation. So the governor asked whether they wanted to spare him or Christ, hoping in this way to be able finally to get out of it. But they, overcome with hatred and blinded by frenzy,* demanded that Barabbas be let off and all called for mercy for this one man, while they strove for Christ to be put to death, resisting the governor's wishes with all the force they could muster.* So he gave directions for the divine body to be thrashed with cords and switches of willow—a lamentable sight. 'Perhaps,' he said, 'in this way I shall be able to extinguish their thirst for innocent blood; like this his heartless enemy will pity him,* and when they see him up close lacerated over his entire frame they will be sated and need no further prompting to steer their thoughts back from death.'

Now Christ's defiled body was streaming with a copious flow of blood—his whole frame soaked in gore, his limbs beaten black and blue, his neck and arms, and his ribs laid bare by the lash; from his rosy lips he spat gobs of blood. In such a state they set him in sight of the people, his bare shoulders soiled with blood, along with his breast and both legs from the knee down—for a linen garment covered him in between with its white fabric.* Heaven grew pale at the sight; in terror the silvery moon fled beneath the earth, its horns blunted,* and for a long time disappeared from view, skulking with its face obscured in cloud. At the same time, stars were seen falling from the clear heaven. Yet even so he did not satisfy with his blood the penalty* required by his enemies; no, their hearts were fuelled more and more* by entreaties, hearts that no skill, no force, could soften. They strained every sinew to inflict death on one wholly undeserving of it, and in their bitter hatred they demanded the ultimate punishment;* the towering halls rang with their cries. All vied to rouse each other to rage.* The Furies and hellish agents sent from the infernal gloom, insubstantial souls and beings without a body,* circled around them and sharpened piercing goads for the inflamed mob, snatching away the light of sense from those poor people and driving them on in their frenzy.

Meanwhile the Roman's own wife, scared witless by visions in her sleep, warned him not to pollute himself with the young man's blood and to keep his hands off the prisoner; a god, she said, threatened imposing portents in her dreams. 'It was him,' she said; 'he was that white lamb*—empty dreams never deceive me—which encircling dogs and a whole bunch of shepherds with stakes were after. And soon everything, the pastures and the fields along with their familiar groves, was mourning its death. But the Father who thunders on high, roused with evident rage, vented his fury from above upon the perpetrators of this slaughter. All at once heaven seemed thrown into confusion and to come rushing down on all sides,* as rough hail* shook the fields and the woods far and wide. Then suddenly a voice was heard from on high, piercing through the air: "Spare the god, Roman,* and curb the anger of men." I really believe (and it does not escape you too) that this man's lineage is from the gods.* Refrain from staining your hands with crime, husband, refrain from* shedding pious blood! May the serene denizens of heaven themselves bring these portents to nothing, and may they go after the Jews alone, threatening that race.'

After hearing such things, the descendant of Romulus* pressed the people of Jerusalem still more earnestly, firmly resolved to resist their fevered frenzy.* And now he assailed them with threats and no longer used gentle words to keep them back as they raved and roared unbearable things. And now he seemed to want to remove the man's chains and let him go, and to free himself at last from such a weight of care. In the depths of Erebus the awful ruler of the shades* sensed this, as he nursed perpetual anxiety in his fixated heart.* He groaned, and felt resentment in his bitter spirit at the thought of being beaten. Straightaway he summoned dreadful Fear from its hidden lair—a dark, hulking, inescapable monster.* No scourge in the shadowy regions is gloomier, to be sure, or more grudging towards the glorious enterprises of humanity. Shivering is its attendant, and Sloth with downcast features. Immediately he ordered this sluggish creature to ascend to the air above, where the shaggy mountains of the Phoenicians rise with their gentle brow, and to enter the high walls of Jerusalem to sway the stern heart of the Roman governor, dislodge him from his defiance, and compel him to abandon his resolve through fear. It carried out his orders, fitting itself out with the black wings of nocturnal birds and gathering itself into a dark body.* And now, after completing the long stretch of its journey, this revolting fowl fluttered backwards and forwards over and over again in front of the eyes of the eminent governor (look!), pestering him as it wheeled about all around and made a noise.* Now it struck his breast, now his face with its black wings, filling him with icy fear and freezing fast his heart.

The governor went rigid at the sudden sight and turned white; his hair stood on end and a freezing shudder ran through his bones. His knees weakened and began to give way, while his voice stuck in his throat.* As soon as the citizens noticed his unaccustomed fright, the pallor in his cheeks, and the complete transformation that had come over him, they seized the moment* and at once piled into him with these words, yelling: 'That man dared to masquerade in public as a king. He aspires to royal power and lays claim to the honours of a king. If it so happens that you prefer to save him from execution and are unmoved by such grievous crimes, he will go on to turn the cities of Judaea away from Roman laws, gaining influence through sedition,* and will induce all Syria to cede from the authority of Rome by his arts. So, if you have any concern for the Roman state and the honour of Caesar, get on and remove this plague from the upper world; make him drain to the dregs the punishment he has deserved, and not just for one crime, to prevent this awful infection spreading through the whole people.' Such was their persistent roar,* all of them with one voice. The governor, who had learned from experience that they were an intractable race,* grew pale at the name of king (for the hidden contagion raged in the inmost recesses of his heart)* and no longer resisted their overpowering advance any further. Defeated, he gave up and retired, powerless to keep up the fight against their senseless frenzy.

Just as when in the midst of the surge the East Winds, striking full-on, set themselves against a beaked trireme,* at first the captain wrestles from the raised stern and exhorts his men to lean to their powerful oars; but at last, when he sees that he is straining to no effect against the intolerable force of heaven and that the raging winds are getting the upper hand, he changes course in whatever direction fortune calls* over the sea with its many paths, and obeying the breezes he rows limping along. Yet even so Pilate did not refrain from speech or spare his voice.* 'I am beaten, certainly,' he said, 'and your rage is incapable of taking a step back.* There's no delay on my part:* let him die, condemned on a false charge.* A sorry punishment awaits you—and close at hand, I hope. You and your distant descendants, you wretched people, will pay the due penalty with your impious blood.'* With this pronouncement, he ordered water to be brought quickly to him in a full vessel, and washing his hands he added these words: 'As now all stains are gone from these hands, so no wrongdoing attaches to me in this bloodshed,* and I release myself from all transgression.' So he spoke, and rising from the throne he retired inside the residence. But they replied: 'May God keep this for us and for our children, and may he impose a heavy penalty according to what we deserve.'

While these things were going on in the colonnades in front of the entrance,* as the populace looked on, inside the house the governor's armed attendants mocked the prisoner* and laughed at him, while he said nothing. Because the people had wanted him as their king throughout the cities, they adorned him with purple robes and glowing garments dipped in dye, and set him raised up on high on an elevated seat. In place of a golden band* around his head and a royal crown, they covered his fair temples* with sharp thorns. In place of a glorious sceptre was given a reed from the river.* Then they cheerily displayed him at the open gates* to the whole populace with great applause, and hailed him as king. Just so do boys at play, when they have chosen one out of them all as leader to give orders at will to his subordinate friends, all stand around bunched up in a cheery throng, and rise up without exception and fulfil the comical commands of their proud monarch, and their boisterous shouting goes up to heaven;* in such play as this did the attendants indulge within the residence, a savage gang. Then they covered the young man's eyes with a blindfold of cloth* and beat his divine head with their hands and with a rod. This one pulled with his fingers at his beard, stiffened with blood,* while that one vilely spat in his starry eyes from his unclean mouth and defiled his handsome body with dirt.* There was no pause, no respite:* they whirled him round and harried him, while he endured it all and uttered no words of complaint at his ill-treatment, and they did not allow him to close his weary eyes in sleep. Ah, the agony, the disgraceful spectacle, unworthy to be seen! The woods do not lack foliage for the birds, the mountains are not without caves for the four-legged creatures, where they can hide themselves away for the night and bring up their young. But for the Creator of the universe, on whom the court of heaven waits, there was no place in all the earth, in all regions, for him to lay his head and rest exhausted in death.*

Then indeed the people of Jerusalem, their victory complete, prepared every kind of torture and sought out all forms of punishment so that he might endure brutal agonies to the full in his cruel death. And now they hastened to stretch him out and fix him on an upright plank, and to destroy him little by little with a slow death. Without delay they split apple trees; the axe resounded as it was driven into the wood,* and a towering cross was created from the split timbers as a form of torture.* With this penalty the kings once used to punish crimes of sacrilege, despatching the guilty by this type of execution—a harrowing death for those poor people, with protracted agony.* At that time the infamous cross possessed no honour or glory;* but now it holds a hallowed power and we all humbly pay homage to the venerable wood.* We who were born in later times place it, overlaid with silver and gold, on our holy altars, and from that time on we have kept its memory alive and celebrated its honour with joy.* Moreover, it will shine in heaven like a celestial lamp and illuminate the whole world with its light,* when a single day gives over all living things to destruction* and fire brings an end to mortal creation.

Scarcely was the nurturing daylight showing its face on earth, when already from all sides the youth were rushing through the whole city, prompted by their eagerness to witness the spectacle.* The streets were full, and every spot was seething* with the massing of the crowds. And now, stripped of his purple robes, his mocking insignia, with his hands bound, they were dragging him with an uproar* to his awful torment, with a great throng in attendance. Through their midst he went, hauled by long ropes, half-conscious, his limbs trembling, and bloodied from the night's blows. On his shoulder he himself bore the double plank, weighed down with shorn-off knots and the sturdiness of the cruel wood, on which he would leave the mortal world in unspeakable torment and end his harsh labours with death.

Armed men stood around him, and ranks fitted with shields pressed in close beside him;* their spear-points shone far off—their spear-points and the hollow helmets on their heads, with their red crests—and the bronze bugles blared with answering blasts.* Some followed on foot;* others rode glittering on high horses; the neighbouring hills rang with their rumpus.* Yet many, whose judgement was better,* were weeping: in particular, devout mothers and gentle girls, when they saw him struggling over the rough rocks with bare feet and frequently stumbling on the uneven ways as he heaved the cruel weight of the wood up the opposing hill. To them the hero spoke as follows, with a sigh: 'Don't weep, mothers, don't weep for me as I endure such indignities, devoted as you are. Weep rather for the destruction that awaits you close at hand, and the remuneration due* to your children hereafter.' So he spoke, and with faltering steps* he left the city.

Meanwhile the king of angels, at so crucial a moment,* went up on to the towering stronghold of the celestial summit to see in person the cruel death of* his mortal son—a spectator of his own self.* The race that dwells in heaven, those winged beings, thronged round him in formation and went with him on his way. On the soaring peak of Olympus there is a temple made from solid gold with sparkling jewels set into it: a vast, gigantic edifice, the inner sanctum of the supreme Father, looking down over the stars of the firmament gliding beneath. In its midst rises a slope crafted from unyielding adamant, gradually narrowing to a point like a pine tree; around it a great range of seats is set out above and below, rising above the heavens in nine tiers.*

Here the denizens of heaven assembled, and singing of their king they made their entrance in their troupes; then they all settled in their own seats, circling the mound all about in their flashing ranks with a ring* thrice threefold, all separated into distinct orders—for the status of all was not equal, nor their strength matching, nor their power the same. Rather, as some had precedence over others, so they were duly positioned in their own station, each one happy in their own office and blessed in their lot. In their midst the almighty Father, gleaming with gold on a high throne, held his sceptre and scanned everything round about far and wide with his gaze, his whole being resplendent with light,* sparkling all around with flashing fire, and blazing with beams that flickered far off. Soon, however, he fixed his eyes exclusively on the ill-fated lands of Judaea,* and before all else he kept his sight on that sorrowful hill. As he did so, the mournful race of Olympus also looked upon the unhappy hill that appears first as you leave the holy city, white with human bones.* There the perpetrators of crime used to pay their penalty with a hideous death; dead bodies hung around on all sides from tree trunks, ghastly with sun-baked corruption.*

As soon as the pitiable hero, on completing his journey, reached this place, recognized that the cruel torment was being made ready for him, and saw that the unspeakable plank was already set up, he cast his dejected eyes this way and that, surveying everything,* to see if maybe—just maybe—he could spot one of his companions among the ranks of enemies. A loyal supporter in sight? None: he saw only cruel columns of men, and the plains were ablaze with the gleam of weapons.* All those dear to him had deserted him, scattering in every direction; just like when a shepherd has been struck by lightning from the heights of heaven or slain by the stealthy attack of a wild beast in the glen—immediately the sheep are dispersed through the fields in every direction,* unguarded, and the countryside echoes with their bleating.

And now, ascending the unspeakable beam and hanging in the air, he shuddered and—as if forgetting he was God—felt terror at this dreadful kind of untimely death; he was in inner turmoil and divided his wavering thoughts* between intense anxieties, musing on many sorrows in his mind, while over his whole frame, as it grew pale, sweat ran darkened with mingled blood. Frequently he recalled his Father's palace in heaven, and then, looking up to the sky,* he uttered these words from the depths of his heart: 'Oh why, supreme Father, are you deserting me in my ultimate peril? Where now is your care for your son?'*

That supreme Father heard these words; the whole choir of angels heard them, too.* The Father himself, pondering all things inwardly in the depth of his mind, and not forgetting that the matter was assuredly proceeding at his own instigation, stood motionless and kept himself in check. But no force could hold back* unbidden the throngs surrounding him, the winged race of high heaven. All of a sudden, anguish flared up in all of them;* in all of them a towering rage seethed. They wanted to come to the aid of their lord's son, to prevent the abomination and make a stand against the cruel swords. War is what they incited—arms, they all cried over and over again with increasing fervour, arms!* At this a boy, by no means the lowliest among the winged race and unsurpassed in his skill at summoning the ranks with the curved bronze of the trumpet,* rose rapidly in swift flight* above the soaring pinnacles and then, taking his seat at the very pole, at the height of the glowing heaven, he sounded the signal for war. On all sides broad Olympus quaked, and the stars trembled with unaccustomed movement. If there is anyone the damp moon detains far off in its remote sphere as it advances with subdued tread, even he heard the sound. They heard it too, those to whom the safekeeping of our race on earth was once assigned by lot, and the vast earth immediately trembled, shaken by the thunderous din. Then those whom the king of angels had sent on assignments to different regions travelled back through the expanse of the air, leaving behind their commissions unfinished and hurrying swiftly to the heights of heaven—just like doves which had left their lofty seat for assorted feeding-grounds, when at a storm's sudden urging the sky starts to churn with an unseen rumble and black clouds have enveloped the heavens. Straightaway they abandon the fields on all sides and make for their sheer homes on the wing, swiftly taking cover in their hollow towers.*

Now all was in a rush on the summit of huge Olympus, and throughout heaven the horror of hazardous warfare was piling up:* chariots covered in bronze resounded, and the groan of wheels could be heard, along with an almighty clang of weapons above. Both poles of the universe marvelled at such vast commotion; so too did the stars and the spheres of the revolving heaven marvel, though these are insubstantial souls and beings without a body,* possessing a nature far removed from our senses.* Yet often, whether they are sent to mortal regions or need to take up arms at some point against their rebellious brothers, each one fits himself out with the wings* and airy limbs of an assumed body, fitting on an image for his use,* so that the spirit can be susceptible to human sight. And so they wrap their solid bodies in a raging whirlwind* as they come within the range of even our senses, and around their glittering shoulders they put the unaccustomed arms* they have hastily taken down from heaven's bronze-resounding portal:* the spoils of celestial citizens, memorials of that unspeakable war* which once they waged against their crazed associates. This good angel arms himself with javelins and brandishes a beam-like spear;* another snatches up a torch; another grabs arrows and hangs a curved bow from his blazing shoulders, while yet another slips both hands into boxing gloves. Some wind smooth slings round their hands. All of them have a golden sword hanging at their side in a scabbard of ivory,* in keeping with custom. Some drive chariots* through the blue expanse of heaven, while the rest balance their nimble forms on wings stippled with colour; even the power of flight is not the same for them all. They thrive on different means of movement:* some skim along on a pair of wings, each shoulder rising and falling in turn; others raise themselves into the air by means of a threefold arrangement, their feet being fully winged. They do not have one single appearance, nor do all have the same colour; for you might see these shining out with scarlet plumage, flame-footed, resembling fire in the reddish flush of their backs, while those recall the look of grass and green emeralds, and yet others have backs which gleam suffused with saffron yellow.* Others have their wings painted with a hundred other shades; as when after summer's ending the year adorns itself with fruits of many hues from every tree, and comely Autumn displays its worthy head.

And now the winged army was making its way through the rippling expanse of the air,* and was enveloping heaven with its airborne formation, such thousands as had never, from the very beginning of the nascent universe, been seen assembled in the human world—thrice three divisions, and thrice three commanders.* Overtopping all by a whole head was the commander, that mighty warrior recently arrived from the summit of Monte Gargano in Apulia,* whom once the glory of his ancient battle raised up on high far above all others.

In their midst he made his way exultant,* gleaming gold in his helmet and proud crest, and blazing with jewels shining far off; even now he displayed the spoils and tawny hide of the conquered dragon with its vast coils, and treading on the beast's back he subdued it with his feet and his spear. His armour shone far off, while the golden boss of his shield spewed fire and his sword flickered afar, glinting with sparkling jasper.*

They had reached the gates of heaven. Here the wrath of all flared up still more, as the memorials of an earlier war met their eyes; for they saw chariots hanging from high towers and bronze items suspended from the doorposts—spear-points and shields, weapons taken from their defeated brothers who once (an incalculable sin!)* rose up in heaven with cruel designs. In vain these aspired thoughtlessly to the sovereignty of happy Olympus, their wits overcome and puffed up with vanity;* against them had stood those very beings, who followed the better cause, and they had beaten them down in the struggle and driven them from heaven. This battle the handiwork of craftsmen* had once carved on the bronze doors and had modelled in carefully worked gold. There could be seen* suspended in the rippling breeze of heaven battalions here, battalions there,* rising up to the struggle, flying now this way, now that, to and fro, and the sky in between darkened with oncoming projectiles; now they were on the very point of joining battle with weapons at close quarters,* the battle lines were merging, and now those who lacked spear-points made hooks of their hands and entwined them in their enemies' hair, spinning them round through the air as they hung suspended by their locks. And now you could see one side gradually giving way and the other pressing down on them from above, until routed and dispersed throughout heaven the enemy turned their backs all together in flight, like a scurrying storm cloud or blustering South Winds.* For the almighty Father, his right hand armed with the thunderbolt, was driving them in confusion from the starry stronghold with pursuing flames,* and when they'd been cast out the dark dwelling of Erebus* received them.

Therefore the heavenly beings, reminded of that battle and of their ancient conquest, were burning to break down the gates of heaven and burst out. And now they would all have sallied forth, seized control of the earth, and set fire to the guilty region—and already you, wicked Judaea, would have atoned for your crimes* by the fiery immolation of your cities—had not the high-thundering Father from his perch on starry Olympus (for he was moved by so great an uproar blazing up all at once)* put a stop to their efforts and checked this unruly warfare* with reproachful words, issuing severe commands* to them all. For looking round, he saw a hundred handmaids standing by on this side and that, virginal angelic forms in human guise, ready to comply with his directions. Out of all their number gentle Clemency with her placid countenance was his choice to issue with these orders: 'Go,' he said, 'and glide down on your winged chariot through the sky. Take these words to your brothers: they are not the ones to whom the reins of heaven and the vast earth have been entrusted, so that they may contrive to instigate battles without orders and dare to throw all heaven and earth into turmoil without my authority, igniting such commotion by their passions.* Let them settle down* and come here with all speed, laying down their arms.'

He finished speaking. She speedily made her way in the winged chariot and broadcast everywhere word of the Father's monumental rage,* should they not return and calm down at once, putting aside their weapons. Piety and golden Peace joined her as companions, and with them went Hope and Faith and the supremely peaceful mother of devoted Love;* in the hands of all were branches of pale olive. And where they passed, you could see everyone immediately discarding their weapons far off and growing gentle, their fervour overcome. And now the army, their weapons laid aside, was in sight of their king, in obedience to his word. Each one took his own place in order, and as they did so they all fell silent.

Then the Father who rules the storm clouds cast his eyes around, turning his majestic head three times, and three times he produced a fearsome sound* as the universe turned on its axis. Then he began to speak: 'What madness for war is this, heavenly ones, against my prohibition?* Where are you rushing?* Is it that he can't get through it with my help, do you suppose, or that my power is finally broken? Put this frenzy from your minds, and lay aside this anxiety*—since my Son is not suffering any of this without my authorization* (you're well aware of that) in order to eradicate the collective guilt of humanity* by his death. In this way it is my fixed purpose to open up Olympus, now closed, to the human race. For that reason I willed him to perform harsh labours* and spend his life on earth enduring every extremity,* driven from all territories, suffering deprivation, and wholly destitute.

And now the end has been reached: death awaits him here today, a grievous death in spite of his innocence,* an irreversible destruction—and he himself, of his own volition, goes freely to meet his death. Yet now he shudders at the sudden sight* and fear has snatched away his disordered wits* on the very threshold of death. Indeed, as if stripped of his divinity, he has gone on as a mortal, defenceless, and his body has remained vulnerable to weapons. Under no other conditions could any human force have been effective against his divine figure; he would be impenetrable to all weapons. Not so trivial is my strength and power that I could not rescue my Son, if my intention were reversed,* even as he was caught up in the heart of death's hurricane. Let all rise up against him, every speck of humanity everywhere born and dead from the beginning of creation through all eternity. This was not how Babylon experienced me, when as giants they strove to create ways to the stars by raising a tower into the air, and were able to tear up massive mountains with their hands: even now their towers lie smoking, shattered by the thunderbolt.* And though the battalions of storm clouds and tempests were still, which could tear the mighty universe from its hinges and sweep it away, I myself could shake the earth by my hand; I could stir up all heaven* and envelop everything in a flood. Now, even now, the race of mortals could see me raging, girt with black flames and with my right hand armed with the three-pointed spear,* blowing apart this bunch of men and mowing down these ranks on all sides with my armaments. But let it be; a time will come for that city (and you won't have to wait all that long) when it will long in vain not to have touched this being, bought at a high price,* whose lineage derives from heaven on high.' So he spoke, and by a movement of his head he caused the world to tremble, shaking the celestial regions with a terrifying thunderclap.*

Straightaway the intense frenzy and rage of the angels was stilled. The whole chorus merely attended him with benevolent prayers,* and silently pitied the god from the height of Olympus. Just as when, on the empty ground of a field* closed off by fences, two young men join in contest among themselves for glory and honour, on fire for the prize, in close combat with matched weapons; from a distance all the youth, crowding round them, watches from this side and that. Then, if it happens that one increasingly fails to keep up, and his face grows pale or he falls, tripped up by the treacherous terrain, his loyal friends rise up and get behind him with their enthusiasm.* How they'd like to come to their friend's aid, if the rules didn't forbid it! And so they stand there sick at heart and curse his dismal misfortune from afar.

Just like this—defenceless, unarmed—the hero remained. They stretched him out, his shoulders bare, his whole body bare from the head down, and frenziedly attached him to the lengthy plank. Then they spread out his bare arms on the cross-beam and fastened both his hands to it with a nail on each side; his feet were pierced by a single spike, nailed together. A copious stream of blood ran down the trunk.* They pressed on with great violence. The towering timber gave a groan as the iron fastenings were driven in, while the sloping hill bellowed back all around at the dreadful din, multiplying it, and the echo of the blows reverberated.* Then above his head they inscribed on the trunk in a range of different characters* his name, his country, and the reason for his death. On his right hand and his left they had given him two companions, fixed to a pair of planks, who were deservedly paying the legal penalty of justified execution for their offences; yet it was he whom the tree lifted up far higher in the midst of them both, as if he were an inciter and perpetrator of crimes, or more abominable than all others in his misdeeds.*

Unhappy Jerusalem, unhappy stock of Judaea—readily hateful towards the righteous, and cruel even to the prophets themselves! Was this the fit reception, this the lodging, this the couch you arranged for the king of angels? Were these the companions, this the honour you provided for the one who for the mortal race came down from heaven and willingly wandered the earth in human form? He himself it was who led your race out of Pharaoh's lands, granting safe passage on foot through the waves of the salt sea and laying out a level path for you as he parted the waters. He too fed you on your way with celestial food, pitying your toils through the endless deserts. It was by his aid that you drank a sweet draught of liquid from the rock, though both springs and flowing streams were far off.* He it was who chose you alone, all other peoples set far behind,* to bring you to the stars by his services and raise you to the level of soaring Olympus by his support. Are these the gifts you heap upon him as he has deserved? Is this your worthy repayment? Do the prophets' proclamations, or any miraculous actions, not move you? Don't you feel divinity close at hand? For what perpetrator of crimes have you ever arranged such awful torments? Who else anywhere has so cruelly paid such a penalty with his body after being taken captive by an enemy?

And now, fixed to the beam at his back, he hung on high. All were turned towards him and were watching to see what signs he would give at the very moment of death, what hope or confidence remained in the one defeated.* Yet for his part he long endured everything in silence, without any movement. Not yet had all the splendour departed from his glowing face; the divine glory could still be seen in his eyes, only his cheeks and pale features were spotted and moistened with blood and with an abundance of sweat mixed with dust, and his teeth were dyed red with bleeding.* Just like Lucifer, the morning star: only just now, after being bathed in the deep-blue wave,* it was scattering its beams in starry Olympus, but if the clear appearance of the cloudless universe should be tarnished and heaven begin to grow pale with a sudden cloud, without having yet hidden its full radiance it shines on, though dulled, still beautiful in its aspect, glimmering through the dark storm cloud.

Meanwhile his mother, whom an unconfirmed rumour had recently drawn to the big city, heard a completely reliable report that her son was being led outside the walls and haled to his death, after being taken prisoner and overpowered by treachery. She grew pale, the unhappy woman, and before the messenger had finished speaking she grew stiff throughout her frame, for all that she knew these things were all happening through the definite plan of the Father and by the divine authority of her son himself. Even so, she was overwhelmed deep inside with boundless sorrow and, forgetting everything, she rushed off. The house echoed with female lamentation,* as her faithful companions tried in vain to comfort her as she wept and groaned bitterly;* and now she strayed this way and that through the city, tirelessly seeking the sorrowful spot. Now here, now there she halted, tracing every lead with her eyes and grasping at every sound with her ears,* in case she could catch any hint of a gathering or any voices anywhere. Just as when a doe, returning at evening to her familiar place of rest from feeding in the high mountains, and long mindful of her tender young, sees all the ground round about spattered with blood, but her babies she can see nowhere; at once she roams through the whole wood,* scanning it with her eyes, and groaning all the while. Then, if she sees any signs of a wolf, any signs of a marauding lion across her path, she pursues them that way, following the tracks through the entire forest, and leaves imprints with her cloven hooves* everywhere along the route. Just like this, as soon as Mary observed, on the high ridge of the olive-clad hill which broods over the city far and wide in its bulk, a vast gathering and gleaming spear-points and shields and shining cavalry, she rushed past everyone in her way* and hurried outside the city walls. Mothers came pouring out and watched her from arcades and high windows, pitying her from afar as she went.* And now she passed one lot, now another, as she rushed by at speed, despite the trampling hooves of swift horses.* Companions joined her in her tearful course: the faithful John along with his mother, unmarried Martha and her sister and Salome, and the ailing wife of Cleophas* followed her all together, all with their heads veiled in black drapery.

Look, though—as she drew close to the accursed hill, she saw the raised cross, the ladders, and the signs they had fixed up. Though still unaware as yet of what those beams were, she nonetheless shuddered with fear, and beating her worthy breast three and four times with her hand,* her breast along with her head, she said with sorrow: 'Ah, that massive frame, that strange contraption,* holds some menace or other. I know the bitter hatred of a crazed people surrounds us,* and that on all sides the race of the Jews, long hostile towards us, is calling for punishment. It was this, this, that I seemed to see all night as I lay sleepless—the sign with which the sons of Isaac once marked the outside of their doorways, each his own, once the blood of a lamb had been duly shed in the house,* when after their long exile and degrading toils they had been warned to depart in secret from the lands of the Nile.' Recounting these things, she went on her way. As she rushed forward without any restraint and forced her way through the spears and close-packed ranks, they pushed her back with the barrier of their shields and kept her at a distance. And now the evidence that her fear had not been hollow grew clearer and clearer,* and closer at hand, on the summit, could be seen the cross—rising high, rudimentary, and rough with uneven knots.

But when the unhappy woman saw close at hand that her son, punished with a hideous death and fixed to the cross, was now right in the clutches of death;* when she saw his hands—his hands and his feet—pierced through by the bronze point, and his cheeks and temples defiled by the wounding wreath; when she saw his bedraggled beard, his hair spoiled with blood,* his downcast eyes now swimming in bitter death and his face slumped on to his shoulder, and his expiring countenance, she stood fast like a rock rising on an Alpine peak, which neither the winds nor the wild violence of heaven with its forked lightning can shake, nor can the downpour, though relentless, wash it away: it stands rugged, white with frost, and immobile through the long passage of time. The very mountains, the very rivers, saw her far off and pitied the weary woman's boundless grief,* and from their sacred hilltop the soaring cedars wept. But her son, once he caught sight of his beloved mother from high on the tree, felt pity for her and immediately fixed on her his dying gaze, so far as he could, and with half-conscious eyes he returned her sweet love.*

Soon he addressed her, pale to view and overcome by her grief, for the last time as follows, dispelling her cares with his words:* 'Thus far, woman, we have stood firm. But let so great a grief not eat away at you silently in your affliction.* It is not without the Father's will* that we are enduring all this, he who regulates all things by his nod alone. This man'—for he happened to see John beside his mother, weeping and groaning abundantly—'will always be as a son to you.' Then he addressed his friend the young man: 'This woman will be your mother.* I beg you, look after her when she is left behind—you, at least—and preserve the love of our shared mother.'* At these words even his enemies, their minds struck, could not hold back their tears; those savage cohorts groaned.

Then at last his mother's voice returned to her in her distress, and she let out an enormous groan. In her sorrow, she bathed the dampened timber with a copious stream of tears as she wept uncontrollably,* and embracing the cross she uttered laments such as these: 'What sort of a return to your poor mother is this, my son,* fairest of beings? Was this the kind of death you wanted to meet? Did the thought of my love* not stop you from going to such an end, from atoning for another's fault by this death, and from dealing me a deadly wound to the heart in my despair? Ah, what sight of you meets my eyes, my son?* Is it yours, that serene countenance dearer to look upon than the light of day? Are they yours, those eyes? What depraved madness* has dared such an outrage? Ah, how changed you are from that son of mine* whom so lately the beardless throng and all the youth joyously ran to meet as you came through the jubilant city,* while along your way they strewed embroidered coverings as for a king, laying fronds from the trees and fragrant garlands on the ground beneath your feet, and universally professing your godhood. Is it with these jewels that I see you decked out, with this purple? Yet surely these were not the promises* the swift messenger sent down from Olympus once gave to a trembling girl! Is *this* how I'm uniquely fortunate above all other women, *this* how I proceed as queen of heaven?* Is this my great glory, this my high honour?* What was the point of kings proffering me sumptuous gifts after my childbirth, what was the point of celestial choirs singing songs of joy, if *that* was the fate that nonetheless awaited me, and I was dragging out my life* to witness this calamity? Happy those women, whose innocent sons the king's wicked fury took from them on the very threshold of life, while in empty fear he planned your untimely death. How I wish you had fallen beneath that deluge! This, this was the distress that the old man bade me expect,* as he terrified my trembling heart with his awful presage, and he prophesied that a time would come when a sword would pierce my breast. Now the blade has struck deep, now the wound has been driven in deep.* Yet at least cast your eyes in this direction, all you who pass this way, and restore me to the company of my beloved son, since no consolation remains to me in life, and no grief can be found greater than mine.* Join me to him too, if you have any consideration, and nail me to the tree.* Or you unfriendly mountains, you towering peaks I see spread with foliage above me, may you at least grant me mercy, I implore you. May you take thought for me, steeped as you are in my grief, and at last come to the aid of a mournful mother.* Now, now, suddenly shattered in a headlong plunge, come rushing down on me alone and put an end to such great toils.' These and other lamentations the virgin uttered in her deep dejection; and her faithful companions could not lead her away as she wept.

Even so, the armed guards continued to mock the dying man (for an enemy treats an enemy far the best amid the harshness of war), and with cruel laughter they buffeted his head. On all sides round about they abused him and merrily hollered these words to heaven: 'See, the one who boasts he's been sent from heaven and is the offspring of the supreme Father; who threatened the temple and the city and dared to lie that he's a god—that fashioner of falsehoods.* Go on, then, follow him and now reverently worship his divinity!* He who once snatched many from the jaws of death can't do himself any good when it comes to the crunch. That phoney Father of his is nowhere near him now, and can't be bothered with such things. Well, then—let him free himself now and jump down from the tree of shame, if he's got divine power, and break all his bonds.* By these signs we too will believe he's been sent from Olympus!' Such were their taunts, and in the very midst of death they heaped on him this additional pain, though he was now half-conscious. And yet he bore it all, undefeated in spirit. More mercifully than was strictly fair,* he prayed for pardon for his enemies despite their cruelty, and he asked his Father to spare them, ignorant as they were and blinded by frenzy.*

But the young men who were suffering the penalty for their offences beside him, fixed to a pair of planks in comparable punishment, were heard to contend between themselves with opposing pronouncements. One, prompted by delirium and by drawn-out agony, went so far as to bait the dying hero with insolent words, the wretch, and came out with comments such as these: 'Go now, and demolish the sanctuary of the temple, built by men's hard toil,* and raise it up again after three days. At this moment, if your lineage really derived from heaven on high and you were really the Son of God, as you yourself used to claim you were, you'd be able to save yourself—and us too—from these torments. But since you've filled all the cities with empty bluster, die with us, you sham scion of divinity.'

The other, who was hanging on Christ's right and was already near to death, could not endure this and uttered these last words: 'Unhappy man, what utter madness has settled on your mind?* We are both rightly paying the penalty for our sins;* but this man, though innocent, is betrayed by hatred. Truly, it would have been better at this point for us to confess our wrongs and plead for forgiveness and peace.' So he spoke, and then, turning his eyes to the god himself, he prayed as follows: 'You, undoubted offspring of the supreme Father (for the stars of heaven await you), look upon me from on high and be with me* then with your favour as I die!' The god assented, and honoured him with words of friendship: 'You will have a share of glory, and you will have joy along with me:* whatever realm receives me this day, that very same realm will receive you too in blessedness,' he said. 'Start picturing the stars in keen anticipation.'

Scarcely could he get these words out, for now at the very end of his departing life, until death divested his weary frame of its struggling soul, he faltered. All over his body ran a constant, copious stream of sweat,* and a dry thirst scorched his parched throat. Then, barely lifting his eyes, which were now weighed down by death,* he requested as a final favour the slightest draught of liquid, for he was thirsty. At last they just about mixed a cup of soured wine,* steeped in gall and bitter poison,* and applied the undrinkable juice, the repulsive solution, to the dying man's parched tongue on a stick. But as soon as he took just the merest sip of it,* he spat it out, and for a long time the bitter taste remained on his lips.

Meanwhile a squabble arose with great hubbub, as the servants pressed combatively to share out among themselves the tunic which his mother had once woven for her son;* it was loot they were after.* But the garment was not sewn together and therefore was not suited to being cut into pieces—so they agreed to assign it by lot. This was what in ages past the holy prophets, those far-seeing souls, had foretold would happen.*

And now the sun, ashen-faced, had almost passed the midpoint of the sphere in its course, when suddenly—look!—darkness rose up and it hid its head in the heavens, and at midday (a fearsome sight to behold) a night of unsurpassed blackness loomed up and brooded over the whole earth.* The sky was closed off and lay buried in thick cloud, stealing sight from mortal eyes* in its entirety. At this moment I could believe, were it not that sighing and grief have no place in heaven, that the eternal Father groaned in profound grief and turned away his starry eyes from the iniquitous earth. Yet he did give out signs, and bore witness to his sorrow from on high. Fires flashed out; the sky flickered in sympathy,* and the towering palace of Olympus thundered with an almighty shaking, while unseen rumblings rolled through the boundless heaven.* You would think the walls of the wrecked universe had burst apart. The earth bellowed underfoot; its sprawling surface stirred; buildings crumbled; towers toppled, shaken from top to toe. The low-lying peoples of the earth were dazed with sudden dread, as were the cities situated in the furthest parts of the world. The cause lay hidden,* but to all it seemed a mighty marvel, and in their bewilderment the nations feared everlasting darkness for the world, seeing the sky shrouded in shadow.*

Nearer at hand, however, panic struck the city of Jerusalem and laid low the trembling wits* of its people. On all sides shouting rose to heaven;* each person's mind was fully aware of their crime. To the temples they went at once, matrons of spotless character in a long line, while boys and maiden girls made their way all together;* and at all the altars they prayed for peace,* making them steam with incense in supplication. The altars smoked with their holy offerings.* But look—another sign from high heaven, more immediate this time, was given by the Father who thunders on high, as he vented his rage on the temple itself. The veil, broad and vast, which kept the eyes of the mob from the secret rites, was rent in two,* and the pillars of the temple gave an enormous crack as they fractured. And now the god, breaking out into his last words with an almighty cry, uttered a tremendous shout and said, 'There, all is finished! Take this blameless soul, Father, into your keeping'; and laying down his head, he breathed out his final breath.*

BOOK SIX

AND now evening was hurrying from darkening Olympus. The bodies still stood there unburied and unlamented on that white hill,* and even now remained fixed to the wooden beams. Joseph, who came from the region of Arimathea, could not endure such a situation; he was a man of outstanding spirit and exceptional youth, well versed in war and exceedingly wealthy in land* and in gold. He had only recently joined the company as a disciple, in admiration at Christ's momentous accomplishments, to follow wherever he instructed. And so, while the others scattered in all directions and hid themselves in the woods and deep caves in ignominious terror,* Joseph went straight up to the governor without trepidation and in the confidence of youth,* and spoke as follows: 'Best of the sons of Romulus,* word has it that in the killing of the dear master, whom our race punished with death through its cruel hatred, you kept your hands pure and went against their blind fury with all your might,* in vain. You know that he was taken prisoner by treacherous betrayal,* because he openly opposed them and rebuked their wicked crimes with his words. Do what you can: at least allow his lifeless body to be placed in earth,* as a comfort to his friends for the bitterness of his fate. I shall bury him myself in a new tomb which I prepared for myself, as is customary, when privately pondering the uncertainty of death.'

Pontius spoke these words in reply: 'How I'd now prefer to be handing his body over to you alive!* I call you to witness, powers conscious of the truth*—I tried and considered everything, to see if I could find some way to rescue this innocent man from death and let him go. We too revere piety and the sanctity of our household gods.* But ultimately we got nowhere in the face of the city's intransigence; the cruel delirium of the people proved victorious. Go, then, honour the dead man devoutly with a tomb and with the final offerings.'*

He finished speaking. Joseph hastily made his way to the rising slopes of the hill, accompanied by Nicodemus, himself also greatly stricken by the death of his dear friend.* And now they drew near, planting their footsteps with equal concern, and now the ill-starred spot could be seen from the hill.* But look—gleaming all around them they saw weapons, and the height ringed with armed soldiery:* to prevent the corpses hanging on the trunks from polluting the festive celebration of the rejoicing city on a holy day, armed lackeys had come on the injunction of the leading citizens to take down the half-dead men from the beams in the usual way and bury them on this very hill with a covering of sand. They stood there, the men who on each side were suffering the punishment they deserved, half-alive; and still breathing at the very point of death, they were longing to end their agonizing torment by extinction and were filling the whole hill with tearful cries.* At once, from this side and that, the armed men set upon them with long poles and broke the men's failing limbs, hastening those poor people's death and then taking them down from the planks. After that they tossed the corpses away and deposited them in a ditch in the hollow earth.*

But as soon as they saw lifeless the one who was paying the penalty for *our* crimes, they kept their hands off him, and did not allow further savagery against that body empty of life. They were amazed at the speed of his demise, that his frame had given way so quickly, and that his face was already miraculously pale even then.* Some people even said that they had seen the youths who roam the heavens hanging in the air around the barbaric timber, beating their wings and radiant in snow-white garments, collecting the divine essence that dripped from multiple wounds and bearing it in vessels to the upper regions of the air.* At this point only the ignoble Longinus, equipped with a lance tipped with a broad iron point, dared to defile the sacred limbs; he rushed up and struck his target's ribs with his long fir-wood shaft.* The iron grew warm as the spear drank up the holy blood* from the wound from which, they say, like a two-toned river, spouted both clear fluid and a red rush of blood. The ground was soaked, and the grass blushed with blood all around.

Into their midst the man nursed by the city of Arimathea made his way;* he climbed up the beam, took down the lifeless body of his master, and carried it far away, out of the mass of weapons, covering it with a robe* which he had just bought for such a purpose. This way, winged boys and youth of heaven, come streaming out and hasten your steps;* offer the ample tribute of eternal spring. Scatter the pale violet from full baskets, together with narcissus tresses and mourning hyacinths,* and envelop the divine body in a halo of flowers.

But see—far and wide the nearby hills bellowed back with women's wailing; the woods echoed with the voice of grief. You would think all lands were lamenting his pitiful passing. His mother herself sat sunk in sorrow on the living rock,* sick at heart, her hair dishevelled* as she cradled her bloodied son (now a pitiful corpse, alas!) over the breadth of her lap and gently kissed his eyes and the gaping wound in his breast.* No longer did she give out any further groans, no longer any further sobs, but bereft of life by the immensity of her grief she sat in silence—frozen, speechless, and barely distinguishable from the cold rock.* Around her stood other women, all beating their breasts with their hands.* Some washed his body and his wounds with warm water; some wrapped his tainted limbs in woven fabrics.* One dried his sodden knees with her unbound hair, bending over his bloodied wounds and holding them tight; another gave kisses to his hands and feet, stiff as they were. All of them gave themselves up to tears and filled the whole place with howls of sorrow. Scarcely could the menfolk tear them away from there, their own faces streaming with big tears as well.* Then, comforting the distraught women, they buried the lifeless body in the marble tomb,* and after a final address they withdrew, and her companions brought his eminent mother back to her residence.

But the people of Jerusalem, in their anxiety, were not yet completely free from every care—an acute fear still oppressed their hearts. For often they had heard that their adversary had promised his sorrowing disciples that he would one day return to the world of daylight, and that the holy prophets openly declared it. Fearing this, they promptly sent armed men to guard the mournful tomb night and day,* in case anyone should steal away by night the one buried within and fill the whole city with false rumours that the dead man had returned to the shores of light and was breathing the life-giving air and drawing sustenance from heaven.*

Come, breath,* exhaled from the mouth of the almighty Father, the breath that is a divine force with power over heaven, and the pleasure of those on high.* Whatever woes still remain for me from that awful slaughter, expel them from my mind and restore now my soul's feelings of joy, flooding my frame with the impulse of peace* by your divine power. Grant me to feel the descent of happiness on my heart, that happiness which the race of blessed Olympus enjoys, where amply on all sides in a broad torrent joy overflows,* and the spread of pleasure knows no bounds. Here the appearance of things is changed; here our joy begins. I see all things changed immeasurably for the better.

Now the god,* with a view to leading the holy prophets and the hallowed assemblies of the faithful out of the darkness and bringing them to Olympus,* had gone off as a spirit free from the shackles of the body to the shades below, the realm of silent souls. Through blind passages and sheer crags inaccessible to the sun's rays* he went, regions buried in perpetual night, the horrid halls of sightless dread. Here the brethren who roam the night had their stalls* and held their realm barred to the living, those whom the celestial Father's wrath hurled out of heaven when they ventured to devise a terrible evil,* plunging the wretched race in the caverns of Tartarus, since so great a longing for kingship* possessed them. Now they tormented with punishments the woeful spirits—though more woeful themselves—and kept them chained in the land of darkness. In the inmost area, the pit from which there is no return* to the world above, dwelt imprisoned those souls who acted cruelly while they still lived.* Now they paid the penalty they deserved, submerged in an enormous furnace* where they endured the billowing murky smoke.* There the fire was everlasting, the reborn flame forever new.

The abode of the guiltless, on the other hand, and their far-removed halls were spread around in a wide circle.* Here no conflagrations met the eye, no fires with avenging flames, but only the unmoving rest of the shades and the deep stillness of the silent world. Set apart in this region the blameless souls passed their time, those whom no sins of their own kept imprisoned here, but the fatal crime* of our first parent.* In no way did they lack our light, and they were wholly free from punishment, except that they were without that pleasing light in which the race of starry Olympus rejoices. Here were the patriarchs, a hallowed race, most ancient of their line, who first lived lives ordered by no constraint and no laws in the untended fields among their sheep, regulating themselves solely by ancestral custom, mindful of justice and cultivating righteousness of their own accord. Here too were the devout prophets* who once, filled with divine inspiration, fearlessly proclaimed things to come throughout the great cities, those who gave laws, divine institutions,* to the world, those who willingly chose to obey the laws given to them, mothers and men and those snatched away on the very threshold of life.* All were possessed by one longing—a keen desire* for heaven. And now, remembering what had been promised to them, it happened that they were enumerating* in the shadows the ages passing in their silent course, and were inferring that the end of their sufferings was close at hand.

And these were the words they exchanged joyfully in conversation:* 'There—at last, that day that was due to come around, it's nearly here: look, that day when we'll be free to look upon the light and the vault of heaven.* This day the almighty Father, clearly revealed on bright Olympus, made known to us when we were filled with divine spirit. Immediately we proclaimed it in our speech to other mortals, but we left it to a coming age as a day to be yearned for in prayers. Now, now our light will be here, the undoubted offspring of God.* He it was—he!—who was so often shown to us in the form of a raging lion, though our eyes were beset by gloom: the one who would willingly give himself up to death, one for many,* and would keep us defended by overcoming our enemy. He has conquered, yes, at last—that lion from the blood of mighty Judah,* of the lineage of David! Rejoice wherever you are, you blessed mortals; rejoice, you souls already freed from the body! Now the stars are calling you; now the door of starry Olympus, closed for so many years, is opened for us! And now it will come to pass, as promised by our voices long ago, that the mountains leap up in joy and the hills skip about,* their lovely peaks decked with vine garlands; just as frequently in the fields the ram and the young lambs gambol and frolic in the soft grass, as they follow the bleating of their mothers over the long ridges. Now let the very springs, and the very streams wandering everywhere* flow with honey; let the streams wandering everywhere flow with snow-white milk, pure milk, and the rocks drip with sweet nectar!'

Such was the constant tenor of their speech;* everything around inwardly murmured approval with surpassing joy and favourable acclamation. Just as when citizens are confined by a long siege within their city and rampart, kept safe by the barrier of the gates, while around them the enemy makes a noise and batters against the walls;* then, if they happen to see from their lofty towers an allied column approaching in the distance with reinforcements of weaponry, they rise up and lift their spirits, quickened with hope, to the stars.*

But look—entering the gates, the mightiest avenger was at hand* without delay, gleaming with divine radiance. A vast portal waited in his path, bronze with a hundred gigantic bolts: an everlasting doorway. This no violence could vanquish, neither with fire nor with the strength of hard iron.* Here the god halted and struck the grating barrier with his hand; the earth took fright and trembled far and wide with the shock, while the wandering stars of the universe trembled all together, and the palace of darkness groaned in its shadowy caverns.* At that sound, in a hideous outpouring they appeared* from the deepest chasms in a quivering throng, those brethren who shun the light, with human shape as far as the legs, and beyond that, dragons. Then they let out an unearthly roar and breathed out dreadful fire from their jaws, enveloping the whole dwelling in pitch-black smoke.* At once the gates opened wide; suddenly, look—all by themselves the doors sprang apart some way, wrenched from their hinges. Inside, seething with confusion, appeared the dwelling place and the stately halls on every side.* The darkness gradually faded and the blinding night retreated; for just so was the god seen in the murky hollows, searing the eyes and shining out with divine brilliance, as when a jewel imitating fire with its flashing gleam sparkles into the night in royal chambers and dispels the gloomy darkness, clothing the surroundings in a flood of light and bathing everything around in its glowing radiance.*

But when his enemies saw the divine being in the midst of the innermost recesses* and recognized his hated face* through the shadows, blazing with its beams and flashing with wondrous light, at once they were terrified by the sudden apparition and hurled themselves into the deepest hiding places, tucking their tails up to their bellies and smoothing them down with their tongues;* and as they lay flat they hollered fearsomely, though to no end, in the gloomy hollows. Just like the half-wild races that live in the lofty Alps and forever endure the winds and the downpours, if it happens that they have seen Roman columns approaching far off with glittering weapons, when poking their heads out of their caves,* they immediately head out and leave their smoky dwellings, and scattered along the ridges they sit on the cliff that rises most prominently into the air and marvel at the generals as they advance in the distance.

But the pure spirits nearby, cleansed instantly by the glare of light, spread out their hands and held them up to heaven, thundering with sudden joy* and shedding tears; and they could not satisfy their hearts and eyes with gazing.* Then they hailed their avenger at his side with a joyous cry,* all together as one: 'Clear light of the cloudless heaven, how gladly we look upon you, so long desired* (and we have not been cheated* in our hope)—you who bring back to the world the blessings granted to our first parent, who restore the whole human race to its former state and open unknown ways to the stars of heaven!* You have come; your face has shone forth like the lamp of heaven,* and at last the light has been returned to our eyes.

'Yet worn out with what woes, tossed by what great storms do we receive you! (For report has carried news of these things even to the land of darkness.) Who has defiled your sacred body with so unworthy a wound?* What spear, what sword has been able to bear growing warm with your blood? Has so great a crime been permitted to any mortals on earth? O you oceans that surround the globe, bounded by remote shores, what delays—what, exactly—held you back?* What barriers kept you hidden away,* when your creator was incurring so cruel a death? Then you ought to have engulfed all mortal things in your flood and completely wiped out the sinful earth! Is it *we*, surest offspring of heaven's king,* who are saved through these wounds? No, no—the reward was not worth so great a cost, our very salvation not worth it, ever! This piety of yours is enormous. Were *our* travails such a source of care to *you*, O sweet respite of humanity and pleasure of those on high?* It was *we* who roused the anger of the Father by our crime, causing him to turn away; but *you* have paid the dreadful penalty with your blood.'

Such were the words they cried out on all sides over the spectral plains. Then with joy they went out all together* from the gloom of their prison, following the avenging god to the vaults of heaven, to spend a peaceful existence among the starry dwellings. O happy souls,* race now finished with human perils, free from toils, far from sufferings! First went the father of the human race himself,* before them all, not daring to lift his face to heaven through shame at his ancient offence; then came other leading luminaries, hearts filled with true prophecy, their temples wreathed with snow-white bands.* But those others groaned, whom Tartarus swallowed into its abyss* to be consumed by fire for their crimes and tormented them in its utmost depths, that furnace spewing forth dreadful flames, from which there is no way out for wretched souls for all eternity. Most of all, the monarch of that cheerless hall, as he mourned together with his accomplices, drew out sighs from the depth of his heart, envying the blessed that heavenly seat which he himself had left, driven by boundless frenzy.

But they joyfully held their course through the yielding air towards the realms of heaven they had earned, singing of their king, those happy souls for whom peace had now been won for eternity and the door of death shut fast.* The winged breezes applauded them as they sailed through the air, the winds fell, and the storm clouds fled from the sky;* in the distance the flawless atmosphere of the shining firmament smiled upon them, and the glittering stars in the tranquillity of heaven smiled too. Up rose the dawn, greeted by the morning song of the winged beings;* and up rose the evening, from the reddening glow of the sky.

While all this was going on far away through the immensity of the void,* already the third day was hurrying from the shores of the East; and the almighty Father, beautifying the immortal limbs of his Son, breathed divine glory upon him all over—what had just now been a mortal and vulnerable body, he made immortal. Not with so radiant a light do the bright stars shine in the cloudless heaven, nor even the golden sun itself. Like a flame in the night, buried by a mound of ash, which lies low* and at no point betrays its presence by its concealed light: if someone should revive it by blowing and adding dry kindling round about,* with sudden sparks it flares up to the roof and lights up the whole house with its brightness. Like this is that one-off bird,* when the ignominy of old age has crept over it and it has heaped up for itself a tall pyre from budding branches on the top of a hill and laid aside its senility in death—all at once it rises up new, and gleaming with youth* it shines out with its crest and iridescent wings. Countless birds all around marvel at it as it goes; while it makes its way to its own people in Ethiopia and revisits the Indians.

And now on earth the wondrous sights had struck terror into the trembling spirits of humanity. When the shadows had been driven from the world and the sun had newly risen, the Magdalene, mourning intensely and pierced with longing for her lost master, made her way with her companions at daybreak, carrying in the folds of their garments the soft fragrances of their fruitful homeland—myrrh, putchuk, and the ointments of Cilicia's harvest*—as a final offering at the tomb. And as they went through the fields they talked among themselves a good deal in their sadness, on a variety of subjects:* 'Poor us, for the lamented hero did not take us with him to death!*

Who will enable us to slip past the watching guards, or who will roll away the great rock from the closed tomb, so that at least we may carry out our empty service* by fulfilling the duties that are owed at the deserted grave?' Pouring out such words, they arrived at the tomb itself, and casting about their ready eyes this way and that in close scrutiny, they noticed that the hill was empty of soldiers and watchmen, and they were amazed to see the entrance to the tomb standing open.

They went up to it. But when she saw the empty tomb, from which a great waft of perfume rolled to meet her nostrils, the lovely girl, thinking that her master had been taken away secretly by some enemy, began to weep. Tearing her unmade hair from her head, she started to fill the woods and mountains and forests with her wailing.* But suddenly a youth, shining out in white garments, of angel kind and of the race of heaven, said to her: 'What are you looking for, women? Leave off now your long mourning, and curb the tearful terror in your minds.* In certain hope now feel your happiness at hand, since he whom you mourn as dead, nailed to that fatal beam to atone for every sin and wipe out your offences freely by his death, one for all,* has come back victorious from the depths of the underworld to these shores of light after vanquishing the king of hell. Even now he draws sustenance from the air of heaven,* freed from everything in the body that is subject to death.'* So he spoke, then in winged flight he vanished into a dark cloud.*

This thing itself, which (behold!) suddenly met her eyes,* strengthened her wavering spirit and cleared away the darkness. For while the girl sat there, impatient at delay and wounded with a piercing love, marvelling at the empty tomb and the handiwork of its craftsmen,* she saw sculpted in the very marble a sandy shore and a fish stretched out on that shore, spewing out seawater and of enormous size, like those whales that swim in the depth of the ocean, terrifying ignorant sailors with their unearthly bulk. An ugly, black monster it was,* a brute of the spreading sea;* and from its wave-belching mouth the prophet,* still alive, was emerging once more restored to the air of the world above.* Then she said to herself: 'Now, oh now, may the heavenly beings lend their aid and support what I have seen. I recognize the portents of the ancients, full of true prophecy,'* she said; 'truly, just as the prophet lay hidden in the black gullet of the hideous monster for three days and three nights, enduring the jaws and the cavity of that gargantuan gulf,* so the hero, much lamented by his friends on earth above,* lay hidden enclosed in the hollow rock* and buried in earth; and just as he himself, I recall, had frequently foretold, he has returned to heaven and left the rock empty.'

As she pondered such things, suddenly, in the feigned likeness of an unknown farmer, the god himself appeared to her, standing beside the tomb. Soon, when he began to speak, the girl recognized him and lost her mind; as she turned, look!—she saw him illumined with unearthly light and dazzling with its rays.

Her legs gave way, and as she embraced his knees she could not get enough of gazing* on his glorious face; with skimming eyes she scanned his whole figure, and satisfied her mournful love with the sweet vision. At once from her sad heart all sorrow completely disappeared, and its natural beauty immediately returned to her statuesque face. But her eyes were still wet with swollen teardrops, and her unmade hair streamed over her neck. Just as when a drooping rose, dripping with rainy dew, has bowed its lovely head, its petals weighed down by the copious shower; then, if the sun should clothe the fields in glowing light* and a cloudless countenance return to the sodden sky, straightaway lifting itself up once more it rises again and reveals the heavenly beauty of its crimson breast. Such was the exquisite girl, once her grieving was set aside. In her love she burned to address her king and God in person, to hear and speak their usual words face to face;* yet while she hesitated, at a loss as to how she should open her speech, he covered himself in cloud and vanished from mortal sight.*

Report of these happenings had instantly filled the cities of Palestine. And now the priests were on edge and began to look for some way they could counter the burgeoning talk of the people,* suppress the murmurings by cunning, and snuff out the rumour. First of all they quashed the guards of the tomb, who were revealing everything, by means of bribes, compelling them to bear false witness that the corpse had been removed secretly in the dead of night. But there was no way of overcoming the truth,* and the more they strained to halt the creeping rumour, the more widely it flew and roused the whole land. There were even those who declared that they had seen tombs opening wide of their own accord and many people coming out of their graves, whose bones the earth had received long ago.*

Meanwhile the disciples, whom terror had long since scattered far and wide in panic to all quarters, without exception, were wasting away in sadness. It seemed to them all that the sun had fallen from the sky, extinguished in everlasting gloom, and that the cheering light had been completely taken* from the world. At last they assembled and returned to their previous haunts and the dwellings which had once been dear to them while their king was alive, but now seemed desolate thanks to the recent catastrophe. Their leader?—nowhere. Nowhere could those poor people gaze on that face,* or those eyes more gladdening to look upon than the clear light of day or the stars twinkling in heaven; and his sweet name sounded constantly in the ears* of them all. They grew sick with sorrow; everything around them seemed dingy with grief. Just as when a shepherd has extracted the waxy goodness from a hollow cork-tree and left the beehive empty; then too the bees, whom the black smoke dispersed far off, come crowding together from all sides and vainly approach their empty dwellings, hovering in a thick swarm all around, and sick at heart they see the honeycombs ravaged and the honey utterly plundered, piled up pointlessly for the coming winter.*

But look—as the men lay buried in such sorrow, the women, still dazed,* filled their ears with astonishing reports: they had seen, they said, winged messengers of the race of heaven; the king himself—they had seen him, shining with unearthly brilliance, and the tomb empty into the bargain, and the garments left behind. Straightaway some of them hastened to get to the steep slopes of the mountain, pressing ahead at a rapid sprint,* where the empty grave stood. To others, however, this seemed incredible and miraculous; and at first, as they wavered,* they believed that the women's eyes had been tricked in their panic by an illusion, a hallucination (just as often in dreams we think we see the faces of those who are absent, and the likenesses of those who are no longer alive),* until, late in the day, when they were gathered together in the house, he entered and revealed himself to them more clearly—the hero. By his voice and his bearing he declared himself a god,* and by his familiar form, as he emitted a divine radiance from his whole figure.

Thomas, called Didymus,* was not there, for he was wandering through the nearby towns, where fear had driven him after the recent loss of their leader. He, when he subsequently made his way back and returned to the holy city and was welcomed into the house, saw his comrades—look!—stunned by this recent occurrence and silent with blind terror. Just as when fire, bursting through the clouds, has struck a temple, or the marble mansion of a wealthy master,* and has filled the whole place with a fearsome brilliance, the citizens stand within in panic, shuddering shakes the breast of every one, and scarcely do their hearts settle down even long afterwards.* Didymus, in his ignorance, was stunned by the sight; he asked the reason,* and calmed his companions with words of friendship. But the elderly Peter embraced him, and drenching his white beard with a stream of tears he finally spoke as follows: 'We have seen him (how blessed we are now!), we have seen him in person, as we used to—our king, alive and breathing, the king of angels, who only just left us in death!' So he spoke, and as he rejoiced in his spirit he kept his gaze fixed on heaven. But Thomas, not believing his account of such things, said: 'Is it really *he* who looks again on this light of heaven that gives us breath?* Or was it rather the shadow of a likeness that appeared, and a deceptive image tricked your eyes?'

'No,' said Peter, 'it was he himself we saw, bearing those very wounds on his divine body and preserving its previous form, and we touched his genuine limbs with our hands. I saw him, I saw him myself, with my very own eyes, and I recognized his wounds! It was evening: the doors were closed, the windows closed. We lay hidden inside in fear* and tended to our bodies with food, reclining sadly at the meal set before us. Look, though: in the inmost part of the house, he himself was there unexpectedly*—the hero—and he shone out, having entered the building concealed from sight, even though the gates were closed; he was there unexpectedly, bringing us joy unforeseen. All at once the whole house seemed to be burned up at his light.* As for us, our minds were immediately thrown into panic and we shuddered at the sudden apparition,* bewildered. But he, rebuking our trepidation and empty fear, forbade us to get up from the meal in our alarm: "I am he; be at peace, one and all, and let go of your fear." And at the same time he offered all of us his limbs, for us to test them, along with the five wounds which he bore on his glorious body.* Moreover, he even reclined with us at our frugal meal, rather than fleeing, and spoke in our presence in his usual manner,* as if still mortal, those final words which recently, as he hastened to his death, he left for us to repeat. Then at length he departed and merged into thin air.' So the elderly man spoke, and his companions chimed in too along the same lines.

They had not yet finished speaking, when at once—look!—with an uproar, in rushed Cleophas, the single most faithful of the many whom the hero had added to the twelve, and he shouted out these words: 'All of you, put aside your grief! He's still alive, friends, freed from the law of death! He's still alive! I saw him with these very eyes, I saw him myself,* and with these very ears I heard the god's voice* and his familiar words! This man too heard and saw him speaking, together with me' (and he gestured and nodded towards Amaon at his side). 'For just now it happened that, while the two of us were making our way in sorrowful spirits through that region where the sloping mountains begin to rise up,* where Emmaus lifts up its soaring citadel crowned with towers, a stranger in unfamiliar costume* set out with us, wearing foreign dress and joining us unbidden as our companion. And as he relieved the monotony of our journey with varied talk, from time to time we burst into tears, drenching our cheeks, and our grief forced out groans as it burned deep within us; then he comforted us in our distress with his words and enquired into the reason* for this sorrow which resurfaced so frequently. We revealed everything from beginning to end, and told of the cruel death of our leader, at whose passing all our joy perished too,* and how by his deeds and words that towering figure roused our spirits with equally towering hopes, but subsequently let us all down by his death.*

'He could bear no more of this, and in response to our words he spoke as follows: "Aren't you ashamed, you who are always blind and void of illumination? Didn't the prophets, all of them, foretell of old the cruel death of your leader, and don't all those proclamations of the ancients declare his abominable sufferings, though you don't believe them? Of his own will he chose to meet death, one for many,* to turn aside his Father's anger, and by his own blood to mark the way to the stars. It wasn't like this that he instructed you; for often he revealed to his friends far in advance that these very things would come to pass concerning him. And indeed I remember,* only recently he proclaimed it in the middle of the city, but he kept the truth of the matter hidden beneath the riddling ambiguity of his words. Now, though, it is all clearly apparent, now everything is out in the open: the cloud has been removed, and you have not nurtured empty hopes.

'"Think of the king, who had planted his vines all set in a row,* enclosing them with a fence against the machinations of men and beasts.* He sent all his agents from the city out there to no avail: the brutish mob of rustics killed them, guiltless as they were. Finally he sent his own son to those unhappy fields. For the almighty Father himself, after so many cruel deaths* of the prophets, ordered his own Son to go down from Olympus. But look: the people of Palestine, driven by overwhelming frenzy,* put an end to even their master's Son by a pitiless death—not with impunity, though,* for any moment now the king will be there* from the city with the weapons of vengeance, and with flames he will drive out the brutish rustics and will entrust his vineyards to other tenants for their planting."

'After speaking like this, he began to explain in due order the mysterious utterances of the prophets and the deeds of our ancient forefathers, expounding how everything presaged a cruel death for Christ, so that he might bring the mortal race out of the shadow of darkness. How he demonstrated by manifest reason that all these things were foretold by ancient signs, removing the darkness from our eyes! How he charmed our senses* with a wondrous sweetness! How our hearts, now filled with resolve, burned with a new love—just as the hardness of bronze is softened in intense heat, or compacted ice melts beneath the early sun.* Yet cluelessly we failed to recognize him before we reached our destination and entered the little city.* For although he made out* that he had to continue his journey and asserted that he was making for a quite different destination, we both entreated him to enter the same lodging with us graciously as a guest.* That was the course of action suggested also by the rapid approach of evening, which was already shrouding the earth in the pitch-black mantle of night. He gave in, and consented to share the meagre meal of his companions. As soon as he laid hands on the baked bread, the loaves of wheat, and broke it in the usual manner, all at once our night departed, and at long last the light came to our eyes. I recognized him, and humbly worshipped his revealed divinity.* But suddenly he departed like smoke into the wafting breezes,* as he spurned human sight and shunned our senses.'

Such was Cleophas' tale, and though everyone else believed it, Thomas denied the truth of his story and held fast to that position: 'I'll say it again: no one will ever convince me of these things, unless I gaze on the sight of him in person with these very eyes in clear daylight, and unless I touch his wounds with these very hands.'

So he spoke. At that moment—look!—the god, in ample radiance, was there unexpectedly once again, returning to his disciples.* And yet the doors remained closed, as did the windows; just as the golden sun penetrates with its light the gleaming roundels of a glass panel which keeps the breeze out of the building, casting its searching beams into the dark corners of the house,* and yet no traces of its passage are visible as the light is transmitted, but it repeatedly goes to and fro without damage to the metal framework. They all threw themselves to the ground and hailed him on their knees; and when Didymus saw him in plain daylight displaying his wounds and calling on him by name,* he shuddered and immediately collapsed face downwards, filled with self-reproach.* Finally he spoke as follows: 'It's true—your appearance, I can see that; you're the true God; I know it all. I could not believe—I confess it—that you were alive after your death and were again breathing this light of heaven that gives us breath,* this air. Those words of yours, the last you gave us, had completely vanished from my faltering heart.* Mad I was, not to believe that you could return to us after incurring death, when only lately you recalled others who had been buried for three full days to the world above—and I remember it and was present. But a perverse spirit* had taken possession of me. Yet even so, perhaps this great madness did not come without your divine will* (so I believe, anyway): maybe one day* our distant descendants will derive some benefit from the fact that one man hesitated at this point and wanted to touch your body with his hands first, so that an apparition or empty shadow should not deceive his eyes.'

As he entreated him with such words, the god and the light itself moved on from him, going up now to this group and now to another, and strengthening their hearts. Nor did he leave the mortal regions of the world until the rising sun returned on the fortieth day. As it happened, Peter and his companions were skimming through the salt sea,* propelling their craft with the oars as they earned their livelihood by their usual work, catching fish in the deep. And now, tired out by the labour they had spent in vain through the whole course of the night, they were uselessly drawing in their dripping nets, when they saw a remarkable young man gazing out from the wave-beaten shore at the watery expanse. At first they did not recognize the god and his divine figure,* since he had concealed himself in mortal form. But then he himself called to them with words like these as they floated on the sea, saying 'Make for the right, men; drive your boat this way. This way you won't have poured out your toil in vain.' Without delay they obeyed his instructions and turned their course eagerly to the right through the waves, and cast their knotted nets.

The deep-blue stretch of the sea sounded with splashing as its surface was disturbed.

And now the elderly Peter nodded wordlessly to his companions, calling them to help in silence by a signal from his head and hand, denoting a vast haul. Scarcely could all of them heave in the full nets; the trapped fish were leaping through the meshwork. At this point John sensed divine intervention, and was the first to speak: 'Hey,* friends—I'm not wrong on this: a god is here, that teacher* of ours—it's him! I recognize the divine glory of his face. How he radiates joy from his features and his noble eyes!' As soon as Peter heard this, he had no hesitation: he leapt right out of the boat and flung himself into the waves of the sea, to be the first to get to his king through the salt surge—even though he was much afraid at the winds swelling over the sea. Then the rest of the crew turned towards land, and they all eagerly made their way to dry ground in their oar-impelled vessel.* Then, to restore their strength with food, they heaped up bread* on tables as they were instructed, and they got ready to roast the live fish on the shore all together, piling glowing charcoal underneath them all around. A pungent reek rose up to heaven.

Once their hunger was checked, the best of kings himself got up, and revealing his divine nature* he finally spoke to his companions as follows: 'Let peace be your wish, men; praise peace* as you live your lives in tranquillity. Hail forever, my friends, and forever farewell.* Keep me in remembrance; I am summoned by bright Olympus.* And now ready your spirits for hardship by enduring everything, and have no fear at entering the presence of cruel despots and speaking to rulers and teaching the truth. Let the majesty of thrones and kings' proud sceptres* not strike you with terror, you who have no need of this daylight. At that point you won't need to look long and hard for the right moment to speak, nor for the correct manner.* I shall be there in person for all of you, directing your speech. The resources of rhetoric will be given to each one of you, and power and reassurance from heaven on high will not fail you. When the golden sun raises its light at its tenth rising, the Father will breathe upon you with the breath of heaven, and with superhuman power will fill your spirits with an infusion of divinity. Relying on this protection, you will broadcast my name everywhere without fear of kings and the powerful.* Then a holy race will lift itself up to the golden stars, just like a thick vine-shoot raises itself unrestrained and runs riot in its growth, bending under the weight of leaves and produce. And at last, when the final day dawns upon the earth, I shall rouse all bones from the opened tombs, and those whom the earth covered will emerge once more into the light. Their packed throngs will fill a valley here and hills there: mothers and men,* and those who passed on after scarcely tasting the light of life. I myself will give laws, sitting as assessor in the middle of the valley, weighing the lives and the offences of the peoples.* And you too will be with me, raised high on twelve seats, judging the race of mortals alongside me; and the twelve tribes of the race will be subject to your judgement, and the world will wonder at the honour bestowed on you.

'Meanwhile, Peter (for I have found you second to none in your devotion), I set you at the head of all these who willingly follow my commands, to hold first place and keep the key. With this particular distinction I mark you out;* do you remember to rule and give laws to the peoples with leniency. Supreme power is now granted to you over the nations: now protect the faithful with peace, and recall to your banners those who have rebelled.* Whomsoever you have condemned with righteous anger on earth, loathing their mortal sin,* after admonishing them in vain and removing them from human interaction and the company of the faithful, the same will be hated by heaven. Let them not hope for the abode of the blessed, unless you mercifully deign to grant them pardon and restore them, improved, to their former condition. Now it is granted to you to close and to open the gates of starry heaven to afflicted mortals.'

Such was his commission as he left the earth and the human race. Like this does a shepherd on the point of death, when entrusting his sheep and sheepfolds to his dear sons, instruct them on the thieving and trickery of wolves and indicate the pastures harmful to the flock. Like this, too, does a sailor, now worn out with age, commit his ship to the keeping of his companions and teach the inexperienced the different districts of the sea, the shallows, sandbanks, and shipwrecking Sirens.*

When all this had been seen to, a glowing cloud covered the steep heights of the whole of the palm-clad hill all around, and the curving shores shone with heavenly flames. Meanwhile new joy stirred all heaven into action: the company of celestial angels, the sacred creatures of the air, offered applause with their hands and many-hued wings, and renewed their dances;* the halls of heaven thrilled with their thronging. Some hung suspended from the watchtowers, joyfully clinging to the topmost battlements of heaven and crowning its lofty walls. Others, coming towards them, prepared to pass through the open portals, each entrusting themselves to the breeze and darkening the sky* with their wings. Some took up the plectrum and the lyre; for others it was the double pipe that supplied their song;* still others blew into hollow horns and raucous trumpets or clashed bronze cymbals. And when they had performed their dances three times before the Father's throne in swift formation, they passed three times through the shining realms in play and dived down from the height of heaven.* Just so did they succeed each other in their winged array, with assorted harmony and multifarious music, as, when the towering city of Remus* was not yet fallen and laid low, and the Tarpeian citadel still stood, and Rome, supreme in her beauty,* gave laws to the peoples* it had subdued far and wide, the victorious consul, in celebration of wars fought all over the world, entered the city on his return and went up on to the lofty Capitol.*

Like this did the true offspring of God* make his way to heaven in his cloud-borne course. But in order to sway his Father's heart whenever he was preparing to inflict deserved punishment on the human race in anger at their offences, he carried with him all the tokens of his monstrous execution,* in particular the twofold beam and the abominable pillar to which he had been tied by the arms and had suffered cruel lashes, along with the pitiless bundles of rods and the cords stained with blood, the spear, and the cup suspended on a smooth reed. Also visible were three great spikes with sharpened points, with which his hands and feet had been pierced, and the rough chaplet fashioned from interwoven thorns. There too were the insignia of the Roman Senate, hung from a long spear; a lantern concealed in a hollow horn, which a pinewood pole raised on high; and the cane which he had borne in his hand as king in place of a sceptre. All these things the heavenly pages carried before him, each with a different item, as they made for the celestial stronghold through the void. The disciples gazed upwards in bewilderment, following with their eyes the swarm of winged beings. Through the air they saw their king, raising his hands aloft and cleaving the calm expanse of heaven, when suddenly this pronouncement issued from the glowing atmosphere: 'Don't be afraid.* Why do you stand there gazing at the heights of heaven? Together with his Father, the god has received Olympus for his rule.'

Instantly the towering abode of heaven was heard resounding far off with singing and with tuneful melodies among the stars. In response the men on earth applauded and sang these joyful strains, reaching for heaven with their eyes and hearts: 'All you peoples, join with us in celebration and song,* and sing of God taking possession of the heights of heaven by his ascent! Let the race of beasts and birds and the mute swimmers* rejoice, and the stretches of the earth spreading far and wide! Let the very mountains, the very rivers give voice in gladness, the springs that unfurl the streams from their spouts, and the sea that encircles the lands in its endless windings.* Let them all know their creator and sing his praises, how in his vastness he has ruled, always the same, without beginning, God in company with God the Father, filling all things with his spirit; how in time he created all things without elements or seed*—the heaven, the earth, the sea, and all living beings everywhere beneath the wandering heaven; how he separated the earth from the sea, the sky from the earth, and lit up the halls of heaven with illuminating fires, stippled the lap of earth* with assorted greenery, and supplied crops to the fields and refreshing juice to the vines. You set all things in motion; you are the one the boundless sky* and the showers that mass in the sky above obey. The clouds and the winds fear you; you are the one the evening and the sunrise look to, and it's at your nod that they fulfil their functions. To you, too, the deep blue expanse of the sea, bearer of marvels, submits. You it is who balance the weight of the earth in your powerful hands and suspend its heavy mass in the empty air, positioning the constituents of the universe in an eternal compact,* so that all things make for the centre, striving in concordant motion. You pass through the void on rippling ways, conveyed by clouds, and you ride seated on the swift wings of the breezes.

'Not for you does irrevocable time flee,* its horses at full tilt; before your eyes it remains ever the same and ever present—that which is, that which has been, and that which will come hereafter. Even the sun itself, fixed at the peak of heaven, stood fast in obedience to you; even the moon itself, growing into its horns, and the stars brought their course to a complete standstill.* At your bidding fire has often forgotten its usual power and been made harmless: the youths stood in the heart of the furnace unscathed, and cried your praises to the stars.* You divide the ship-bearing sea, setting the waves hard, and enable peoples to go through the midst of the surge unharmed.* You bend the course of rushing rivers as the banks look on in wonder. You bring forth plentiful water from the rocks by touching them,* just as you stay the flow of gushing springs and rivers. The very earth trembles in terror at the sight of you, and the mountains you touch from afar send up smoke to the stars.* Kings get to their feet in fear and lay down their sceptres and their arms for you, and they stand quaking far off and worship your divinity.

'You give ears to the deaf, and eyes to those without sight; you give voice to the mute and strength to the afflicted. You recall to life those who have met their death and been buried, and you can rekindle their lost senses. The awful power of untimely death did not fill you with terror, nor the dismal dwelling of Erebus, a place fertile with fear.* At you the spirits shuddered. The ruler of the domain of darkness* could not endure you plundering the pitiless realm of the shades on every side, and hid himself in trepidation in the deepest caverns;* the Furies, grovelling with fear, skulked far apart until you were borne up to the stronghold of heaven with your prodigious spoils. Now you reign there victorious and govern the blessed council of the angels, and setting in order the times you see in advance far off, you restore the world's fleeting ages and do not allow the rolling passage of the sun* to rest. Hail, creator of all things and healer of the boundless universe! Look favourably upon us,* look favourably upon our race, for whom by your death the door of heavenly Olympus stands open, and the Father finally forgets his age-old anger.'

Such things as these they sang joyfully below the cliff on the shore, the eleven leaders and the entire youthful throng.* Yet even so, amid this outpouring of joy, they had not discarded their empty fear, having not yet had their spirits reinforced by the breath of divinity from heaven; still they sought out hiding places and hollow caves. Just as when a hawk, swooping from his lofty seat, has caught and carried off a dove to disembowel with his hooked beak, the other doves scatter in all directions and swiftly take refuge in the nooks of towers, with a feeble medley of moaning;* just so did they, in bewilderment after the death of their king, remain cooped up indoors, awaiting the divine power that would come from heaven on high, as their master had promised them.

And now the promised day was at hand.* For the tenth time the rising sun had put the darkness to flight from the earth with its flaming torch. The almighty Father, in the cloudless expanse of heaven,* where a purer air nurtures the stars with glowing brightness,* sat at the heart of his stronghold in the midst of the denizens of heaven, allocating times and obscure processes to the universe. Before him appeared his Son, having now shed his mortal figure, gleaming with rays and sparkling with wondrous light, who addressed him with profound love:* 'O Father,' said he, 'it is finally time to bring aid* to my disciples. After the loss of their leader, intense fear has promptly driven them all this way and that, and everything frightens these unheroic people, born as they are of mortal body.* Cast this terror from their souls and strengthen their hearts, lest they prove unable to race eagerly into all eventualities. For them, on my account, Jerusalem and every part of Judaea is devising snares, loathing them with cruel hatred. But you promised, Father, that one day it would be these men who would declare our indestructible name among the nations by acts of unparalleled daring, wherever the world is bounded by Ocean, and would call converted peoples to new rites; nor does your purpose waver.* These men (since you don't indeed refuse the fortress of heaven) I have often heartened myself as they teetered, relying on your faithfulness,* and I filled them with courage; for I promised them that help and protection from the stronghold of Olympus would instantly be with them, and relying on that they could despise kings and their threatening commands and rush eagerly into death of their own accord for the love of true religion.'

With these words, he displayed his hands and feet, pierced with sharp iron, and the gaping wound in his chest, and the wreath of barbed thorns which he had worn as a sacrificial victim.* The Father, bound to him in undying love, agreed to his prayer, and lightly kissing him he gave his Son the following answer:* 'You ask for things already granted. What you desire will be given to you,* my Son. With the breath I promised—no need for entreaty—I shall breathe upon those you refer to, and shall inflame the men with our own fire, so that for your sake they will cast aside their love of the alluring light and not fear sword or flames or the bite of wild beasts* or those tables of torture with their mangling wheels. And those who now shrink in dread from every motion of the breeze* will hurl themselves eagerly into guaranteed dangers of their own accord, and by their struggle they will set their souls free from their body and make them glorious, triumphant in their scorn for death and in their true valour. Not heat nor cold will stop them, either when the devastating star splits the parched fields* or when winter sets fast the greenish-blue rivers with ice; rather, they will be heard beyond the Ganges, past furthest Bactra, and with their words they will reach Ismara and the regions of Thrace, the Chinese far sundered from Cadiz, and the Britons dyed in their warpaint.* They shall fill the earth with their teachings, and making all things new they will raise the greatest temples to you after wandering throughout the world.* The nations, converted, shall hasten to your name, nations completely divided from the whole world* over the seas, and with all things transformed the Golden Age will go forth. These things I have often promised to you, and you share my universal knowledge.

'Nor is it just for the virtuous ones that these wounds of yours have now earned the opening up of Olympus, my Son—those guiltless souls whom the fatal fault of their first father* burdened with the blackness of night. Rather, they will soon make others worthy of heaven, and still others over the centuries, whose transgressions* once kept them far from their seat among the stars: so great is the reward, such the power and generosity, of your sacrifice. And whatever the human race has done from the beginning of the universe, whatever sins they will commit in years to come—even if all of this should be gathered into one, that small portion of your blood is enough and more to wash it all away and eliminate it altogether. Furthermore, the time will soon come when the heavenly sun will have completed nearly three hundred spans of five years* and true poets, forgetting the falsehoods of the Greeks, will tell of your death in altered song among the peoples.* All cities will resound with your praises, and in particular those by the bountiful shore of prosperous Italy, home of the wandering Adda and the Serio with its mossy stream, clearer than amber and like nothing so much as a coiling snake; and where the king of rivers, the Po, advances in its swirling course,* scouring the precarious walls of turreted Cremona, so that its wave barely keeps back from the tumbledown buildings. There on every bank, like snow-white swans among the clouds, boys and unmarried girls will then sing virtuous songs, and joining together on the soft grass* they will begin to accustom themselves to our praises in competition, and youthful choruses will sing of you with their fresh voices. These things remain fixed for you;* no power can move them from their order.' And speaking thus, he breathed sweet love into his Son.

Meanwhile, with much cursing of the abominable crime of the traitor Judas, the disciples were preparing themselves for the commissions they had been assigned, being allocated by lot different regions to make their way to and teach new customs and new rites. But so that the rest of their youthful band might follow the instructions of twelve elders, as before, they completed their number and sacred senate* with what remained to be supplied, and alone of all the companions you, Matthias, rejoice at having been elevated by lot to so great an honour, despite your obscure background and undistinguished lineage. Then they all prayed among themselves in sorrow like this: 'Oh if only, if only Olympus might be unsealed and the almighty breath of the nurturing spirit now breathe upon us from heaven,* since the god promised us all so often that it would come to our aid! Surely he foretold everything truly; this one thing alone is still missing from that truth.' Such words as these they exchanged with each other* in their anxiety, sick at heart.

Look, though—all at once the heights of heaven seemed to come rushing down, and the lofty dwelling of those on high thundered with an enormous crash. They looked up:* a new radiance shone in their eyes,* and a vast cloud seemed to be descending from the pinnacle of the sky, glowing with specks of light, and through the entire building its scattered beams burst forth. Then a harmless fire, of imposing dimensions, immediately stood over the head of all of them,* and the surrounding air smouldered with glowing ashes, just as sometimes a shower of sparks leaps from the hissing iron while the Chalybes strike mighty blows in turn on their anvils, raising their sturdy arms as they turn the glowing mass with curved tongs.* For the almighty Father and his coeval Son breathed down upon them from their stronghold on high with all-powerful breath, and infused the men with divine power. 'It's God—look, all at once! Look—it's God!'* Without exception their frozen hearts began to warm with the breath of supernatural inspiration, as the men were touched and filled with the presence of divinity.* They were possessed by a sacred delirium, and drank deeply the draught of God in their inmost marrow.

There was no delay, no breathing space.* Engulfed three times in the glittering rays of the fire with its awesome gleam, three times in the whirlwind of winged air,* they were set aflame with enchanting love and their spirits caught fire; for each and every one of them intense emotions whipped their leaping hearts into action. The feelings of terror dispersed from their minds.* Wondrous things they spoke, wondrous songs they sang. The same pronouncement was received and clearly understood (amazing to relate) by a great range of different peoples, and each person seemed to themselves to be hearing their native speech. For at that time many had come here from different parts of the globe in their enthusiasm for religious observance and desire to see the city, which on that day was celebrating a sacred ritual, fifty days having passed since the first rites—those rites in which we set a lamb upon the table for the feast.* Here the man born in the land of Libya heard his own words; here the Gauls heard theirs, as did the Romans and the Parthians and the Scythians, as well as the Thracians who live beneath a freezing star, and Africans, Cretans, and those who had come from the race of the Phrygians; also the Indians and Arabs and sand-roaming Garamantes.* All those around marvelled, and the speakers themselves marvelled too. For as though stripped of their human form and mortal limbs, they ranged with their minds the halls of heaven and the open sky, fully engrossed, and silently enjoyed the talk of the angels.*

And now they prophesied things to come. From their spirits God expelled the dark cloud, purifying their hearts within—that cloud which fogs the enfolding frame and damply dulls human minds.* And those lately terrified by everything with base dread* of a cruel death as they sat shut up in dark caves now dared to go about freely and confidently in full daylight, released from their terrors. No longer did they care about mortal things. They did not fear sword or flames or the bite of wild beasts,* but bore witness among the people that their king, carried off by a death he had not deserved,* derived his lineage from heavenly Olympus. And now they all felt ashamed at having been afraid, and a spirited hope for death blossomed more and more as they drank in the fervent inspiration: just as when the earth gapes with abundant cracks when every field is parched, then, if a dark shower of rain comes from the sky, the grasses which droop in death straightaway raise their heads once again, the fields put aside their shabby appearance, and the whole countryside regains its true splendour.*

And so they went their different ways far and wide through the various regions, singing praises and telling of the glorious deeds of their leader; and now (as the prophets of old had declared would come to pass)* their proclamation went out into every land. They heard it, even those whom an impassable zone blazing with the direct heat of the merciless sun keeps divided from the rest of the world in the realms of the desert, and the ocean which thunders around the globe at its furthest edge.* At once they laid down laws and an established system of holy rites* for the cities. With purifying water the ingrained wickedness and the contagion of ancient fault was washed away* for the people, and the new religion raised up new altars everywhere. From this time on they called the people Christians after the name of Christ.* Throughout the world the golden race arose, and by far the loveliest sequence of ages came into being.*

[in prose:]
If there is anything here done or said contrary to the ordinances of the Holy Fathers, let it be undone or unsaid. Whoever you are, the author wishes you to be advised that he did not take on such a perilous work avidly for the sake of praise, but you should know that it was commissioned from him with the promise of respectable rewards by two supreme pontiffs, first Leo X and then Clement VII, both from the most illustrious family of the Medici of Tuscany, to the generosity and industry of which this age owes the awakening and revival of literature and the civilized arts, which had been altogether snuffed out.* I want you to be aware of this: it is prohibited, as in other cases, for anyone to venture to print this poem hereafter without the knowledge or agreement of the author, or to put it on sale without penalty anywhere.

EXPLANATORY NOTES

For biblical sources see Summary and Biblical Correspondences. It is not possible to record here every instance of Vida's engagement with classical and other models; readers are encouraged to consult items listed in the Select Bibliography. Full details of the editions by Hankins/Gardner and von Contzen et al. referred to in these notes are given in the Select Bibliography. The notes below are ordered by line numbers within each book and cross-references are to book and line numbers within Vida's original Latin poem; line numbers are given in the running heads at the top of each page of the translation.

BOOK ONE

3 *you who fill . . . nurturing Spirit*: classical epics regularly begin with an invocation to the Muse, goddess of poetry; Vida replaces this with an invocation to the Holy Spirit. These opening lines recall the address to the goddess Venus as the generative force in nature at the start of Lucretius' philosophical poem *De rerum natura* (*On the Nature of the Universe*). The description of the universal permeation of the Spirit also echoes Virgil, *Eclogues* 4.51 (= *Georgics* 4.222) and *Aeneid* 6.724–6, both parts of the Virgilian corpus which had been read as prefiguring Christian doctrine. Other models include Lucretius 1.277–9 and 5.92; Virgil, *Aeneid* 1.236 and 1.280; Lucan, *Civil War* 1.110; and Prudentius, *Apotheosis* 153.

the king twice-born: Christ, born in divine form from God the Father and in human form from the Virgin Mary. For readers familiar with classical mythology, the expression suggests the god Bacchus, born from his human mother Semele and then later from the thigh of Jupiter. Ovid uses the epithet 'twice-born' of Bacchus at *Metamorphoses* 3.317, and parallels between Christ and Bacchus are frequent in Christian literature.

bring the spirits of the righteous to heaven: Vida's seven-line opening sentence is modelled on the seven-line opening sentence of the *Aeneid*. Virgil's sentence ends with Rome, Vida's with heaven, in both instances signalling the goal towards which the action of the poem is leading. '[T]he cruel prison' (line 6) refers to the underworld, from which the souls of the righteous will be freed by Christ's Harrowing of Hell (see 5.125–235).

pine-clad Monte Viso: the first simile of Vida's epic evokes the topography of northern Italy. The local colour points to Vida's own origins, since his native city of Cremona lies on the River Po.

4 *We have come to the end*: quotes Virgil, *Aeneid* 12.803 (Jupiter forbids further opposition from Juno).

the sweet fruit: the fruit in the Garden of Eden, eaten by Eve and then Adam as a result of temptation by the serpent (see Genesis 3:1–24). This act, the original instance of human sin, led to the expulsion of Adam and Eve from paradise.

4 *this is not your true abode*: compare the prophecy of the Penates to Aeneas at Virgil, *Aeneid* 3.161–8, and 4.889–94 below.

rest from your labours: echoes Virgil, *Aeneid* 3.393.

There is your home, there your country: recalls Virgil, *Aeneid* 7.122 (Aeneas hails Italy).

who moves the stars: modelled on Virgil, *Aeneid* 9.93 (of Jupiter).

discard . . . this intention: echoes Virgil, *Aeneid* 4.319 (Dido appeals to Aeneas).

5 *This is not the time . . . for such guidance*: closely modelled on Virgil, *Aeneid* 2.521–2 (Hecuba to Priam).

endure in your heart like men your harsh toils: an exact quotation of Homer, *Iliad* 2.299, as translated into Latin at Cicero, *De divinatione* 2.30.

assured rewards await you: echoes Virgil, *Aeneid* 5.348–9 (Aeneas resolves a dispute over prizes).

struck their ears: echoes Virgil, *Aeneid* 12.618 (Turnus hears the city being attacked).

his home was freely open to all, night and day: the clear recollection of Virgil, *Aeneid* 6.127 (on the underworld) implicitly anticipates the news of Lazarus' death.

6 *the ruler of the world of gloom*: Satan.

the mightiest avenger: Christ. The expression is used of Hercules at Virgil, *Aeneid* 8.201 (for parallels between the Hercules and Cacus episode in the *Aeneid* and Christ's Harrowing of Hell, see Introduction).

turned his thoughts in every direction: like Dido contemplating her suicide at Virgil, *Aeneid* 4.630.

a trumpet gave the mighty signal: modelled on Virgil, *Aeneid* 7.519–20 and 11.474–5.

As far as the groin their appearance is human: compare Virgil, *Aeneid* 3.426–7 (the monster Scylla).

with a tail coiling in vast spirals: see *Aeneid* 2.208.

forms conjured up by the human imagination: for this list of infernal horrors, compare Virgil, *Aeneid* 6.285–9, which also includes the hundred-handed Briareus (whose attribute is here given to Satan in line 147). Centaurs, Scyllas, and Cerberus are listed by Lucretius (4.732–48) as figments of the imagination (see also Lucretius 3.1011–13, echoed by Vida in line 149).

in place of hair, hung twisting snakes: see Tibullus, *Elegies* 1.3.69, on the infernal Fury Tisiphone.

7 *with eager spirits and equipped with resources*: like Aeneas' companions gathered for the flight from Troy at Virgil, *Aeneid* 2.799.

wastelands rough with decay: compare Virgil, *Aeneid* 6.462 (also of the underworld).

And now he will be here: like the impious, homicidal Pyrrhus at Virgil, *Aeneid* 2.662.

8 *the resolution . . . rising within me*: echoes Virgil, *Aeneid* 1.582 (Achates to Aeneas).

Cast off delay . . . your strength: compare Vulcan's exhortation to the Cyclopes at Virgil, *Aeneid* 8.441–3.

9 *the true offspring of God*: the first of Vida's many variations on Virgil, *Eclogues* 4.49.

the ruler of shining Olympus: one of the numerous classicizing expressions adopted by Vida to denote God.

with friendly words in their sadness: as Aeneas consoles the Trojan women and men at Virgil, *Aeneid* 5.770.

10 *drew in the air of heaven*: compare Virgil, *Aeneid* 1.546–7 and 3.339, both passages concerning the survival of a character who is indeed still alive.

the punishments for sins and the joyful rewards of the righteous: the language here recalls the scenes of posthumous punishment and reward on the shield of Aeneas at Virgil, *Aeneid* 8.666–70.

11 *treasure of the Ganges*: the great Indian river, suggesting oriental exoticism.

appearances and reputation made no difference to her: strongly recalls the degradation of Dido following the start of her sexual involvement with Aeneas at Virgil, *Aeneid* 4.170–1.

12 *began to kiss his bare feet*: literally 'began to lick', reinforcing the canine comparison.

a Fury drove out of their mind: a classicizing expression used here to denote demonic possession. In classical mythology, the Furies (Erinyes) are hellish goddesses of vengeance.

Father Noah, sower of the vine: for Noah and his vineyard, see Genesis 9:20–7 (and for the expression, compare Virgil, *Aeneid* 7.178–9). Melchizedek, traditionally identified with Shem, is mentioned as king of Salem (Jerusalem) at Genesis 14:18.

once the rains were over . . . ocean had been checked: i.e. after the Flood (Genesis 6:5–8:22).

the Jebusites: held Jerusalem until their defeat by King David.

with barbarian wealth: compare the description of the forces of Antony and Cleopatra at Virgil, *Aeneid* 8.685. For Solomon's building of the temple, see 1 Kings 6.

robes steeped in purple dye and stiff with gold: compare Virgil, *Aeneid* 11.72 (offerings at the funeral of Pallas). The bronze cauldrons (line 391) come from *Aeneid* 5.266.

13 *the sacred wooden chest*: the Ark of the Covenant (Exodus 25:10–22), containing the tablets of stone inscribed with the Ten Commandments (Exodus 34.1–28).

the race of Isaac's descendants: the Jews (a suitably epic patronymic: see also 1.951, 2.493, 2.611, 3.715, 4.373, 5.805).

as the prophets had once foretold: a repeated phrase in Vida's poem, emphasizing Christ's fulfilment of ancient prophecies (see also 2.10, 2.169–70, 2.892–4, 3.131, 3.436, 6.975–6).

holding out the rods: literally *thyrsi*, the ivy-wreathed wands brandished by devotees of Bacchus (see note on 1.2–3 above).

14 *boys and unmarried girls*: a recurring Virgilian expression (see *Georgics* 4.476; *Aeneid* 2.238–9 (perhaps the main model here), 6.307).

marking his path far and wide as he came down: like the portentous shooting star at Virgil, *Aeneid* 2.693–8, anticipating the simile immediately following this line.

15 *they all rouse their spirits*: compare Virgil, *Aeneid* 12.251, where the Italians react to an omen. For this and the following lines, compare also *Aeneid* 5.136–8 (tense anticipation before a boat race).

Jethro: St John, Vida's source for this episode, does not name the man healed at the Pool of Bethesda.

to dip me in the curative pool: like sheep being dipped at Virgil, *Georgics* 1.272 (entirely suitable in the context of the Sheep Pool!).

flickers with its forked tongue: compare the Virgilian snake simile at *Aeneid* 2.471–5; also the viper at *Georgics* 3.416–39, and the snakes of Cerberus at Horace, *Odes* 3.11.17–20.

16 *sweeping through the plains of the air with a whirring whirlwind*: compare the description of the elemental force of the wind at Lucretius 1.271–94 (already echoed in lines 1–2 above: see note), especially 1.273.

blood of livestock and of birds, and the smoking entrails: for the end of blood sacrifice following Christ's own self-immolation, see Hebrews 9:7–10:12.

Only learn justice: quotes Virgil, *Aeneid* 6.620 (the tormented sinner Phlegyas in the underworld). See also 4.193 below.

and these your atonements: Christ echoes the words of Virgil's Sibyl at *Aeneid* 6.153.

there blazed up an overwhelming resentment: this time it is the priests who resemble the Virgilian Hercules (see *Aeneid* 8.219–20); but they are also like Amata, enraged at the arrival of the Trojans in Italy and the loss of Turnus as her son-in-law (see following note).

the flames of anger scorched them within: compare *Aeneid* 7.345.

The age-old motives for their anger . . . remained firmly lodged there: like the inveterate anger of Juno, the divine opponent of Roman destiny, at Virgil, *Aeneid* 1.25–8.

17 *marvelling at each individual feature*: like Aeneas gazing at the temple of Juno at Carthage (Virgil, *Aeneid* 1.453–6).

bronze doors creaking on brazen hinges: compare once again the temple of Juno at Carthage (Virgil, *Aeneid* 1.449), and the gates of Tartarus at *Aeneid* 6.573–4.

gleaming ivory: points to the ivory gate of Virgil's underworld (*Aeneid* 6.895).

Don't you . . . see: a formula of didactic poetry, borrowed by Virgil (*Georgics* 3.103) from Lucretius (2.196, 2.207, etc.). At this stage, however, Jesus maintains, Jerusalem is beyond such teaching.

in a far different city: i.e. in Rome, under the popes.

a mighty subject: compare Virgil, *Aeneid* 7.791, part of the ekphrasis of Turnus' shield. Vida's subject, the creation of the universe, is rather more 'mighty' (*ingens*) than that of the myth of Io in the Virgilian passage.

the massive structure of the vast universe: Lucretian language (see Lucretius 5.96), wholly suitable for such cosmic meditations.

18 *a work impossible to describe in human words*: compare Virgil, *Aeneid* 8.625, introducing the ekphrasis of the shield of Aeneas (see Introduction).

the unordered deep: compare Ovid, *Metamorphoses* 1.7, from Ovid's account of the creation of the world.

the first beginnings of things: Lucretius uses the phrase of atoms at 2.333 and 3.31; see also Lucretius 2.1062.

the constituents of creation: another Lucretian expression for atoms (see Lucretius 1.59, 1.176, etc.), used also by Ovid in a sense nearer to that here in his creation narrative at *Metamorphoses* 1.9.

the globe of sevenfold heaven: an allusion to the seven heavenly spheres thought to surround the earth. For the expression, see Virgil, *Aeneid* 12.925, and 4.66 below.

it was possible to see: compare Virgil, *Aeneid* 8.676, emphasizing the vivid visual impact of the work of art, as here (see also 1.369 above, and 1.655, 2.631, 3.424, 4.845, 5.601, and 6.718 below). See also 'you could see' at lines 619, 638, 650, 674, and 701 below.

Not yet . . . the watery plane of the sea: for this theme, see Tibullus, *Elegies* 1.3.37–40; Ovid, *Metamorphoses* 1.94–6 (in both instances as part of descriptions of the Golden Age).

the resourceful earth . . . grew bright with flowers: modelled on Lucretius 1.7–8, describing the natural fertility inspired by Venus.

the two lights: the sun and moon.

19 *were sweeping . . . with their two-pronged tails*: like the dolphins on the shield of Aeneas at Virgil, *Aeneid* 8.673–4.

Not far from here: another marker of ekphrastic description (compare Virgil, *Aeneid* 8.635, and see also *Aeneid* 6.440); see also line 674 below.

19 *bounded over the luxuriant pastures*: see Lucretius 1.14.

propagate your race . . . each after your own kind: yet another reminder of the prologue to Lucretius, 1.20.

he might hold the earth in his sway: Adam's intended destiny is here described in similar terms to the destiny of the Romans at Virgil, *Aeneid* 1.236.

a field nearby: the Garden of Eden.

a fountain, silvery with its translucent waters: like the spring in the story of Narcissus at Ovid, *Metamorphoses* 3.407.

four streams: the rivers Pishon, Gihon, Hiddekel, and Euphrates.

all those . . . into the light of day: a further parallel with Roman destiny, this time echoing Virgil, *Aeneid* 6.790.

20 *encircling . . . in gigantic spirals*: compare the serpents which attack Laocoon at Virgil, *Aeneid* 2.216–19.

with their grudging sunlight: compare Virgil, *Aeneid* 6.270, part of a simile comparing Aeneas' journey through the underworld to a nocturnal journey in the woods.

On my side there is no delay: compare Virgil, *Aeneid* 2.701 and 12.11, and see 5.358 below.

carrying out his cheerless orders: God had ordered Abraham to sacrifice his son Isaac as a test of his faith.

21 *a mother bird . . . from her wound*: the pelican, feeding its offspring on its own blood, was commonly used as a symbol for Christ, sacrificing himself for the redemption of humanity. A thirteenth-century hymn (*Adoro devote*) sometimes attributed to St Thomas Aquinas addresses Christ as 'pious Pelican', and in Dante's *Paradise* Beatrice refers to Christ as 'our Pelican' (25.113).

rummaged for food in her opened breast: recalls Virgil's description of the vulture which devours the flesh of Tityos in the underworld (*Aeneid* 6.597–600).

the wife of aged Manasseh, Susanna: St John does not supply a name for the woman taken in adultery. In providing her with the name Susanna, Vida may be thinking of the story of Susanna, unjustly accused of adultery by two elders in Daniel 13. The name Manasseh means 'he who makes to forget' (see Genesis 41:51), perhaps suggesting that this is the effect the elderly husband has had on his errant wife.

her father had united her . . . marriage: the phrasing recalls the account of Dido's marriage to Sychaeus (to whose memory she will be unfaithful) as related by Venus to Aeneas at Virgil, *Aeneid* 1.345–6.

22 *swelled inordinately with empty satisfaction*: the expression is taken from Propertius, *Elegies* 3.6.3, of a lover deceived by a false report of his beloved.

keeping his eyes fixed on the ground: like King Latinus at Virgil, *Aeneid* 7.249–50.

Will anyone come forward . . . the first wounds: echoing Turnus' challenge at Virgil, *Aeneid* 9.51.

23 *the hard-hearted race*: here the Jews; at Virgil, *Georgics* 1.63 and Ovid, *Metamorphoses* 1.414, the human race.

nothing untried, nothing at all undared: compare Juno at Virgil, *Aeneid* 7.308–9 and Cacus at *Aeneid* 8.205–6.

contributions of silver to the emperor per head: i.e. taxes mandated by Rome, a reference to the 'Render unto Caesar' controversy (Matthew 22:15–22; Mark 12:13–17; Luke 20:20–6).

terrible desire: a Lucretian and Virgilian phrase (see Lucretius 4.1090; Virgil, *Georgics* 1.73 and *Aeneid* 6.373, 6.721, 9.185).

24 *evil delights*: also Virgilian: see *Aeneid* 6.278–9.

They were standing in prayer . . . directing their outspread hands: compare Virgil, *Aeneid* 6.313–14 (souls on the banks of the River Styx).

through all manner of misfortunes: like Aeneas and his followers (Virgil, *Aeneid* 1.204).

put an end to such great toil: see Virgil, *Aeneid* 2.619. The additional echo of *Aeneid* 1.241 points to the modelling of the scene as a whole on the beseeching and prophetic exchange of Venus and Jupiter in *Aeneid* Book 1 (compare also 'put aside your fear' at line 874 below with *Aeneid* 1.257, and 'as the years gradually slip by' at line 919 with *Aeneid* 1.283).

if it is so overwhelming . . . the human race to heaven: a close echo of Virgil, *Aeneid* 1.33, suggesting a parallel between Christ's mission to save humanity and Aeneas' mission to found the Roman race.

25 *there will be one*: Judas Iscariot.

a mighty augment for the uninhabited sky: the expression is modelled on Virgil, *Eclogues* 4.49, referring to the miraculous child of the Golden Age.

What descendants . . . this religion!: compare Virgil, *Aeneid* 3.409.

26 *simply go on*: echoes Venus' exhortation to Aeneas at Virgil, *Aeneid* 1.389 and 1.401.

will restore . . . to a better condition: the language recalls Virgil, *Aeneid* 1.281, where Jupiter foretells that Juno will 'change her plans for the better' to enable the fulfilment of Rome's destiny.

supreme in her beauty: Vida here borrows Virgil's praise of Rome from *Georgics* 2.534. See also 6.705 below.

a priest . . . place of highest honour on earth: the pope. God here foretells the supremacy of the papacy over the Christian world.

cut down by the onslaughts of invading peoples: referring to all assaults on Rome throughout her history, but with a particular contemporary resonance following the Sack of Rome in 1527 (see Introduction).

So it has been decided: an exact quotation from the Virgilian prophecy of Jupiter, *Aeneid* 1.283 (see note on line 854 above).

26 *suddenly, hurled from the ruddy sky, there flashed out a thunderbolt*: Vida's language recalls Virgil, *Aeneid* 8.524–6, describing the thunder and lightning from heaven which confirm Aeneas' divine calling.

Everywhere around glowed far and wide: see previous note; a similar Virgilian divine omen may be suggested here: compare *Aeneid* 2.697–8.

27 *shone brightly . . . a divine fragrance*: compare Virgil, *Aeneid* 1.402–5, where Venus' divinity is revealed to her son Aeneas, as Christ's divine nature is revealed here in the Transfiguration.

in the midst of two prophets: Elijah (carried to heaven by a fiery chariot: 2 Kings 2:11) and Moses (who led the exodus from Egypt).

gave them laws and the custom of sacred rites: like Jupiter giving customs to the race of Trojans and Latins at Virgil, *Aeneid* 12.836–7 (see 4.116 and 4.795 below).

kissed his Son: like Jupiter kissing his daughter Venus before his prophecy at Virgil, *Aeneid* 1.256, or Aeneas kissing Ascanius at *Aeneid* 12.434.

BOOK TWO

28 *anxious at the turn of events*: anticipates the bee simile of lines 17–21 by recalling Virgil, *Aeneid* 12.589, itself part of a bee simile.

they saw his renown increasing far and wide: compare Virgil, *Aeneid* 8.14, reporting the news of Aeneas' increasing fame in Latium.

Rumour took flight: see *Aeneid* 3.121, 7.392, and 8.554 (Fama).

when winter unleashes its fury . . . and watery Orion holds sway: a close adaptation of Virgil, *Aeneid* 4.52 (Aeneas detained at Carthage by poor sailing weather).

buzz around the doorways and in the entrance: like the bees at Virgil, *Georgics* 4.188.

It was that time . . . worries set aside: modelled on descriptions of night at Virgil, *Aeneid* 2.268–9 and 3.511.

legion: Vida's use of this term for the devils may recall the story of the healing of the demoniac, who when asked his name replies 'My name is Legion; for we are many' (Mark 5:9; Luke 8:30)—see 4.464 below.

Just so the birds . . . fill the curving shores: Gardner links this simile to the return of the quails to Nettuno, described by Biondo Flavio in his *Italia Illustrata* (1451).

29 *reciting things both done and not done*: compare the activities of Rumour (Fama) at Virgil, *Aeneid* 4.190.

had gained the upper hand in the half-razed temple: as in the doomed city of Troy at Virgil, *Aeneid* 2.327.

grating on their hinges of sounding bronze: compare the gates of Tartarus at Virgil, *Aeneid* 6.573–4 (and see note on 1.556–7 above).

without any reason to guide their movements: recalls Aeneas' mental state during the fall of Troy at Virgil, *Aeneid* 2.314.

terrible apparitions: compare *Aeneid* 2.622 (again from the fall of Troy).

30 *transformed himself into every guise*: like the versatile shape-shifter Proteus at Virgil, *Georgics* 4.441.

dedicated to unutterable iniquity: compare Dido 'doomed to the bane to come' at Virgil, *Aeneid* 1.712.

he planned now this way out, now that: like a boxer trying different approaches at Virgil, *Aeneid* 5.441, and Arruns hunting Camilla at *Aeneid* 11.766. The further reverse echo of *Aeneid* 8.365 in line 86 implies that Judas, by failing to reconcile himself to poverty, has not made himself 'worthy of a god'.

a Gaetulian lion: from Gaetulia, the Roman name for a part of Libya (for Gaetulian lions, see Virgil, *Aeneid* 5.351 and Horace, *Odes* 1.23.10).

Jora the Galilean: an invention by Vida. The biblical sources say only that Satan entered into Judas.

Do you wander . . . at the bidding of someone else: the language recalls the actions of the besotted lover in Roman poetry (see Lucretius 4.1122; Virgil, *Eclogues* 6.52; Ovid, *Amores* 1.9.15–16, 2.19.21–2).

half-male hangers-on: used with equal scorn of the Trojans by Aeneas' rival Iarbas at Virgil, *Aeneid* 4.215.

31 *mingling into the blackness of night*: like Mercury departing from Aeneas at Virgil, *Aeneid* 4.570 (see also 10.664), having delivered the same command 'End this delay!' (*Aeneid* 4.569).

entwined a terrible fire in . . . his bones: like Cupid inspiring Dido with love at Virgil, *Aeneid* 1.660, and the serpent thrust into Amata by the fury Allecto at *Aeneid* 7.355.

What are you devising?: for the form of the question, see Virgil, *Aeneid* 4.271 and 12.796.

so deadly a desire: see note on 1.818 above.

swollen with empty euphoria: see note on 1.754 above.

all these the winds . . . whirl through the air: modelled on Virgil, *Aeneid* 9.312–13.

There was no delay, no rest: like the relentless blows in the boxing match at Virgil, *Aeneid* 5.458, or the unremitting battle at *Aeneid* 12.553. See also 4.519, 5.391, and 6.933 below.

they began . . . in varied discussion: closely modelled on Virgil, *Aeneid* 6.160 (Aeneas and Achates discuss the words of the Sibyl).

the young man: Lazarus (see 1.100–20, 1.236–99).

32 *his mind possessed far better judgement*: like those Trojans who remained suspicious of the wooden horse (Virgil, *Aeneid* 2.35).

what was at issue was Christ's life and blood: Vida's language recalls the climactic struggle between Aeneas and Turnus at Virgil, *Aeneid* 12.765.

32 *It is not unclear . . . nor does it require elucidation*: the opening of Nicodemus' speech echoes that of Drances in the council of the Latins at Virgil, *Aeneid* 11.343–4.

that this man is guided by a manifest divinity: closely echoes *Aeneid* 11.232 (Aeneas' destiny recognized by Latinus).

the true offspring of God . . . dismal wickedness: see note on 1.409 above. For 'the true offspring of God' (line 168), see note on 1.237 above. For 'so that he might atone for our dismal wickedness' (line 170), compare *Aeneid* 2.184.

Ah, the errant minds, the unseeing hearts, of men!: a close echo of Lucretius 2.14.

33 *a violent fury surged up in them all*: like Turnus at Virgil, *Aeneid* 12.9.

The pestilence lurked: compare Virgil, *Aeneid* 7.505, of the Fury Allecto.

the wrath that had been simmering in them all: see note on 1.538–9 above.

in the hollow of a bronze cannon . . . a path has been made through the enemy: for Vida's celebrated cannon simile, compare the simile of the boiling cauldron at Virgil, *Aeneid* 7.462–6, and the comparison involving a Roman siege engine at *Aeneid* 12.921–3, both of which are echoed in these lines. In line 213 'a path has been made through the enemy' quotes Virgil, *Aeneid* 9.356 (the expedition of Nisus and Euryalus).

34 *at the cost of so much toil*: the futility of this effort is hinted at by the echo of Virgil, *Aeneid* 11.227–8, where the Latin ambassadors report the failure of their mission.

that he has left no form of wickedness unattempted: see note on 1.795 above.

he grants pardon: compare Virgil, *Aeneid* 11.107 (Aeneas grants a truce for the burial of the dead).

triumphant in his sedition: like Drances at Virgil, *Aeneid* 11.340.

the descendants of Romulus: the Romans, whose city was founded by Romulus.

Let one life be given in exchange for many: closely echoes Virgil, *Aeneid* 5.815 (Palinurus is to be sacrificed for the safety of the Trojans).

He's had it: often said to be the cry raised at the defeat of a gladiator: compare *Aeneid* 12.296, with commentators' notes.

this better resolution: see note on 2.153 above.

Their attitude was unanimous: like that of the Trojans in resolving to leave Thrace at Virgil, *Aeneid* 3.60.

as he breathed fury: like the herdsman Tyrrheus at Virgil, *Aeneid* 7.510. The same passage is echoed in Vida's preceding line: for 'appearing unexpectedly', compare *Aeneid* 7.506.

35 *swivelling his blazing eyes this way and that*: like the Fury Allecto at Virgil, *Aeneid* 7.448–9.

a memorable price for that extraordinary deed: the tone is sarcastic, as at Virgil, *Aeneid* 4.93–5, echoed here.

the feast day: the Jewish festival of Passover.

prompted by signs from heaven: compare Virgil, *Aeneid* 6.379.

through the salt waves of the sea: for the crossing of the Red Sea, see Exodus 14:15–31.

defended by a daunting force of fighting men: quotes Lucretius 1.728 (on Sicily).

36 *lofty Rome had crushed*: compare Virgil, *Aeneid* 1.263–4, where Jupiter prophesies Aeneas' conquests in Italy. For 'lofty Rome', see *Aeneid* 1.7.

was trampling in slavery: indicates the fulfilment of Jupiter's prophecy at *Aeneid* 1.284–5.

some were toppled . . . by the invincible power of time: compare Lucretius 3.451, on human decrepitude.

time . . . through the forgetfulness of the ages: quotes Catullus 68.43.

who tread great Olympus with light footfalls: modelled on a line of the Roman epic poet Ennius' *Annales*, addressing the Muses (see the Loeb edn., fragment (fr.) 1); the position of Vida's line at the head of a catalogue also recalls Homer, *Iliad* 2.484.

love whirls me onwards: quotes Virgil, *Georgics* 3.292, also in a discussion of poetic composition.

in bearing through long ages the names of the race: may recall a line from Angelo Poliziano's *Elegies* (1.7), though may derive from Virgil, *Georgics* 3.47.

borne aloft . . . sights of mortals: the language evokes Horace's poetic transformation into a swan at *Odes* 2.20.1–5.

the trackless places . . . new kind of garland: modelled on Lucretius 1.926–30 and 4.1–5. In line 328, 'lull the . . . stars with . . . song' quotes Petrarch, *Bucolicum Carmen* 1.70.

all the peoples who were making for the temple: the catalogue which begins here and ends at line 529 ('and a bloody one at that') is a standard feature of epic poetry. Notable classical examples include the catalogue of ships in Homer (*Iliad* 2.484–759) and the catalogues of Italian forces at Virgil, *Aeneid* 7.641–817 and 10.163–214. Each of these is preceded by an invocation, as here.

37 *jutting cliffs and rocks that menace the ocean*: for the language, see Virgil, *Aeneid* 1.162–3.

the bride: Lot's wife, who was turned into a pillar of salt for looking back at Sodom (see Genesis 19:17–26).

sends up great spurts to heaven: modelled on Lucretius 6.816–17.

overgrown with thorns: compare Virgil, *Georgics* 2.411 (weeds assail the vineyard).

37 *This is your doing, corrupting passion*: compare Virgil, *Aeneid* 10.188.

unspeakable violence upon the boyish angels: see Genesis 19:1–16.

the oarage of their swift wings: like Mercury at Virgil, *Aeneid* 1.301, and Daedalus at *Aeneid* 6.19.

38 *young men and girls long to pluck . . . ever desired*: modelled on Catullus 62.42–4 and Ovid, *Metamorphoses* 3.353–5. In both cases the subject is sexual desirability and the loss of virginity, appropriate to the context of the destruction of Sodom.

hills once lavish in palms: compare Ovid, *Metamorphoses* 15.710 on Sorrento.

a race comfortable in their living: recalls Virgil, *Aeneid* 1.445, on the Carthaginians.

producer of horses: used of Agrigento at Virgil, *Aeneid* 3.704.

the prophet . . . on a fiery chariot: Elijah (see note on 1.948 above).

winter has not yet shaken from the branches their glory: compare Virgil, *Georgics* 2.404, and Horace, *Epodes* 11.5–6.

a leader . . . beneath the false image of Christ: Antichrist, said by early Church Fathers such as Irenaeus (*Against Heresies* 5.25.3) to be from the tribe of Dan.

39 *invert right and wrong*: compare Virgil, *Georgics* 1.505 (on the Roman civil wars).

would appear . . . an avenger: Christ, again like Hercules (Virgil, *Aeneid* 8.201–3, and see note on 1.123 above).

the true offspring of God: see note on 1.237 above.

That foe . . . he would snatch up in a whirlwind: like Ajax the son of Oileus, punished by Pallas Athena at Virgil, *Aeneid* 1.44–5.

There followed a cloud of young men: closely modelled on Virgil, *Aeneid* 7.793 (part of the Virgilian catalogue).

Cana . . . dark wine: see 3.980–1002 below.

a boy come back . . . after experiencing death: for the raising of the son of the widow of Nain, see 4.315–42 below.

39 *Greek Sebaste, which lost its ancient name*: Samaria, given the name Sebaste by King Herod in honour of the emperor Augustus (Sebastos in Greek).

the leader who brought the laws: Moses. See Numbers 8:5–26.

40 *Manasseh*: the oldest son of Joseph (Joshua 17:1–12), not the character mentioned at 1.729.

silvery with its clear waves: see note on 1.652 above.

spring is never-ending: compare Virgil, *Georgics* 2.149, in praise of Italy.

fields once ruled by indigenous giants: modelled on Virgil, *Aeneid* 6.793–4 (Latium ruled by Saturn in the Golden Age).

These were their names . . . another name: compare Virgil, *Aeneid* 6.776, similarly following a breathless list of resonant place names.

eked their living from the rough ground: see *Aeneid* 11.319.

the shepherds once saw . . . the Jordan slow down and stop: see Joshua 3:7–17. For the shepherds wondering from a high place (Vida's addition to the biblical story), compare Virgil, *Aeneid* 2.307–8.

41 *two-named Luz*: originally named Luz, then Beth-el (see Genesis 28:19, 35:6).

its king: Lazarus (see 1.100–20, 1.236–99).

they wearied the woods: used of hunting also at Virgil, *Aeneid* 9.605.

which it was . . . tireless hunting: modelled on *Aeneid* 7.748–9.

held their celebrations amongst themselves: modelled on Virgil, *Georgics* 1.301.

Rachel's cries of mourning: see Jeremiah 31:15; Matthew 2:18.

saw the sun halt . . . at the leader's command: see Joshua 10:12–14.

a boy of notable appearance: Saul of Tarsus, who after his initial persecution of Christians would go on to be St Paul, author of biblical epistles. Paul was thought to have been beheaded at Rome in the reign of Nero.

will instil himself . . . cast out his fury: for the conversion of Saul, see Acts 9:1–22.

in order to present . . . so joyous a day: modelled on Virgil, *Aeneid* 5.651–2.

Will one of you . . . in advance: see note on 1.769–70 above.

42 *I'll be there . . . that same door*: perhaps recalls Venus' promise of support for Aeneas at Virgil, *Aeneid* 2.620.

which he tilled with a hundred ploughs: modelled on Virgil, *Aeneid* 7.539.

beside a pleasant spring: compare Lucretius 4.1024.

he would sing . . . clear sky and rain: an account of the content of a singer's recital is a traditional feature of ancient epic (see especially the song of Iopas at Virgil, *Aeneid* 1.740–6). This summary of Simon's favoured themes strongly recalls Virgil's *Georgics*, especially the section on weather signs in the first book, which it echoes (for 'what . . . the monthly phases of the moon had in store' in line 567, compare *Georgics* 1.353).

now with light fingers, now with an ivory plectrum: like Orpheus at Virgil, *Aeneid* 6.647.

43 *this traditional feast and these annual ceremonies*: modelled on Evander's account of the rites of Hercules at Virgil, *Aeneid* 8.185–6.

We have a king . . . justice or piety: compare Ilioneus' report of Aeneas to Dido at Virgil, *Aeneid* 1.544–5.

sends us to your door in entreaty: echoes Aeneas to Evander at *Aeneid* 8.145.

fabrics of glowing purple: echoes Lucretius 2.35.

gleamed . . . with gold: evokes the same passage as in the previous note, Lucretius 2.27.

You would think . . . woven figures: Simon's song is presented as a kind of ekphrasis (on inset songs in epic, see note on 2.566–8 above), an impression reinforced by 'you could have seen' in line 625 and 'you'd think you could see' in line 631 (see note on 1.609 above).

43 *the leader of the exiles*: Moses, who led the Jews out of Egypt.

44 *thirst had parched . . . built up over a long period*: like the wolf in a simile at Virgil, *Aeneid* 9.63–4.

the first founder of Jerusalem's stronghold: Melchizedek (see Genesis 14:18–20).

who knew very well what was going on: like Vulcan, the divine creator of the shield, at Virgil, *Aeneid* 8.627, but unlike Aeneas, its human recipient, at *Aeneid* 8.730.

in royal opulence and with the banquet laid out: compare Virgil, *Aeneid* 1.637–8 (feast prepared in Dido's palace) and 6.604–5 (sinners tormented by lavish unattainable banquets in the underworld).

45 *consecrated . . . to his companions*: Vida's description of the institution of the Eucharist echoes Dido's post-banquet libation and circulation of the wine-bowl at Virgil, *Aeneid* 1.736–40, as well as the words of consecration from the Mass (in lines 656–62).

Ever since then . . . in commemoration: compare Virgil, *Aeneid* 8.268–9, and see Introduction.

He himself . . . enters into the bread: a reference to the doctrine of Transubstantiation (which holds that the bread and wine are transformed into the body and blood of Christ at the words of consecration), a key theological difference between Catholics and Protestants.

a cauldron boiling on the fire: compare Virgil, *Aeneid* 6.218–19 (funeral of Misenus) and 8.463 (cauldron simile).

an example for imitation: the ritual of foot-washing on Maundy Thursday was practised in the Catholic Church in Vida's time and continues to this day.

drawing a groan from the depth of his breast: like the ghost of Hector announcing the fall of Troy at Virgil, *Aeneid* 2.288.

the final day: echoes Panthus' lament at *Aeneid* 2.324, again evoking the fall of Troy.

46 *the dismal powers of Erebus*: a classical term for hell.

Preserve yourselves, men: perhaps recalls Aeneas' exhortation to his comrades at Virgil, *Aeneid* 1.207. The rest of the line is taken from *Aeneid* 1.683.

The oldest of them: Peter.

I shall bring it about . . . get away with it: like Aeneas vowing desperate vengeance on the Greeks at Virgil, *Aeneid* 2.670.

such a flood of eloquence: suggests the empty rhetoric of which Turnus accuses Drances at Virgil, *Aeneid* 11.378. In the same Virgilian speech, compare also 'sprightly spirit' (line 708; *Aeneid* 11.386) and 'the flight of your feet' (line 721; *Aeneid* 11.390).

the damp night . . . in its course: modelled on Virgil, *Aeneid* 5.835–6.

47 *his mind remained unshaken*: recalls a crucial moment in the *Aeneid*, where Aeneas' resolve remains firm against Dido's entreaties (Virgil, *Aeneid* 4.449).

I shall cancel the shared sin of humanity: modelled on Virgil, *Aeneid* 12.16 (Turnus accepts the challenge to single combat with Aeneas).

checked . . . deep in his heart: like Aeneas confronted by Dido at Virgil, *Aeneid* 4.332.

He soothed him . . . his anxiety: echoes Virgil, *Aeneid* 7.755, on the hypnotic powers of the priest Umbro.

the backer and deviser of the crime: a combination of two hostile descriptions of Ulysses from Virgil's *Aeneid* (2.164, 6.529).

as arranged: see note above, this likewise evokes the first of these Virgilian episodes: compare *Aeneid* 2.129.

there they were unexpectedly: see note on 2.259 above.

Now their shields . . . grated: closely modelled on a line from Ennius' *Annales* (Loeb edn., fr. 355).

their oily torches dispersed the night: echoes Virgil, *Aeneid* 1.727 (torches at Dido's banquet).

48 *Hey, stop now . . . you're looking for*: combines wording from Virgil, *Aeneid* 9.376 with *Aeneid* 1.595 (Aeneas reveals his presence to Dido and the Trojans).

Why the swords: for the phrasing, see *Aeneid* 11.735.

weighed down by sleep and wine: compare Virgil, *Aeneid* 2.265, 6.520, 9.316–17.

masking that crime . . . devoted affection: perhaps modelled on Virgil, *Aeneid* 4.172, where Dido disguises her irregular liaison with Aeneas under the name of marriage.

a gang of young men . . . around him: modelled on Virgil, *Aeneid* 2.63–4. The rest of line 802 echoes a description of hunting at *Aeneid* 4.121, setting up the hunting simile that follows.

cast ropes of hemp around his neck: like the Trojans hauling the wooden horse into their city at Virgil, *Aeneid* 2.236–7.

uncontrolled in his advance: modelled on Virgil, *Aeneid* 11.742.

He was unaccustomed to fighting: echoes and reverses Virgil, *Aeneid* 5.402–3.

49 *his windy tongue*: compare Turnus' reproach to Drances at Virgil, *Aeneid* 11.390.

an ignominious wound: like the disfigurement of Deiphobus at Virgil, *Aeneid* 6.497, whose wounds include the loss of his ears.

with a healing hand: like that of the physician Iapyx at Virgil, *Aeneid* 12.402.

would have driven . . . through the ribs: modelled on Virgil, *Aeneid* 10.682.

a Molossian hound . . . a stag tamed to follow its master's orders: 'a Molossian hound' from Epirus in north-western Greece, but seemingly used in classical literature to denote any large dog. The 'stag tamed to follow its master's orders' is like the tame stag of Silvia at Virgil, *Aeneid* 7.487.

50 *Now let creation's law . . . crashing down*: evokes Lucan 1.79–81 (cosmic dissolution) and Virgil, *Georgics* 1.324 (an autumn deluge). See also 3.728 below.

the golden race, distinguished for its devotion: for 'the golden race', see Virgil, *Eclogues* 4.9 (and note on 6.985–6 below). For 'distinguished for . . . devotion', compare Virgil, *Aeneid* 1.10 (of Aeneas).

Christ's companions . . . hollows in the rocks: compare Virgil, *Aeneid* 5.676–8, and for line 867 ('at the approach of a foaming boar or a fierce lion'), see Lucretius 5.985. The episode of a disciple escaping by slipping out of his clothing comes from Mark 14:51–2.

There was no breathing space, no chance for rest: see note on 2.140 above.

the trackless groves . . . endless clamour: compare Virgil, *Aeneid* 5.150 and 8.305.

were there demanding punishment, all of them hostile: modelled on Virgil, *Aeneid* 2.72 (the Greeks demand punishment for Sinon).

This monstrous scoundrel: compare Virgil, *Aeneid* 4.613 (Dido curses Aeneas).

grant me your silence and attention: an appropriate utterance for a priest, who might normally use such a formula to signal the beginning of a ceremony (see Horace, *Odes* 3.1.2).

51 *Are you he, then . . . from the height of heaven?*: the opening of the question is modelled on Virgil, *Aeneid* 1.617 (Dido to Aeneas). For 'the true offspring of the supreme god', see note on 1.237 above, and for 'whom prophets . . . foretold', see note on 1.409 above.

standing weary and weaponless with all eyes upon him: another echo of the Sinon episode—see Virgil, *Aeneid* 2.67–8.

with a thousand . . . following me: like Diana accompanied by her nymphs in a simile at Virgil, *Aeneid* 1.499.

stricken by this cruel calamity . . . from afar: like Aeneas reacting to his encounter with Dido, whom he abandoned, in the underworld at Virgil, *Aeneid* 6.475–6.

52 *why did he have so great a craving for life?*: modelled on Lucretius 3.1077 (humans refuse to accept their mortality).

in his confusion at the sudden turn of events: like Turnus at Virgil, *Aeneid* 12.665.

crested fowl: refers to cockerels crowing in the morning.

that midnight had now passed: echoes Virgil, *Aeneid* 8.407–8.

the pain of remorse . . . deep in his brittle bones: modelled on Virgil, *Aeneid* 5.172 (a ship's captain loses his temper) and 8.219–20 (Hercules). See also 1.538–9 above, and 5.101–2 and 5.510 below.

they say . . . no solace: a number of details in this account of Peter's remorse recall the inconsolable grief of Orpheus for Eurydice in Virgil, *Georgics* 4.464–6, 4.507–20.

Aurora: goddess of the dawn.

53 *they were dragging . . . behind his back:* like the Trojan shepherds dragging the captured Sinon at Virgil, *Aeneid* 2.57–9.

surging forward . . . in a packed crowd: like the Trojan and allied forces at Virgil, *Aeneid* 12.280.

kept his eyes . . . ever so intently: modelled on Virgil, *Aeneid* 2.1 (the Carthaginians await Aeneas' narration).

could not get enough of looking at him: the echo of Dido's fixation on Aeneas at Virgil, *Aeneid* 1.713, together with the focus on Christ's physical beauty, may imply a homoerotic element in Pilate's admiration of his captive. See note on 5.3–4 below.

he pitied the cruel fortune: modelled on Virgil, *Aeneid* 6.332 and 12.243.

From where . . . upon you?: a metaphorical adaptation of Virgil, *Aeneid* 9.19–20.

What home . . . sprung from: combines elements from Virgil, *Aeneid* 8.114 and 4.191.

addressed him now on this topic, now on that: once again, Pilate's reaction to Christ recalls Dido's behaviour towards Aeneas—see Virgil, *Aeneid* 1.748–52 and note on 2.980 above.

assailed . . . by a cruel tide of cares: like Aeneas at Virgil, *Aeneid* 8.19.

BOOK THREE

54 *winged Rumour . . . author unknown*: the opening lines of Book 3 present a combination of Virgilian descriptions of the activity of Rumour (Fama: see *Aeneid* 11.139–41, 3.121, 7.392, 8.554, 7.549, 4.173, 7.104, 10.510–11, 2.17). On Rumour in the *Christiad*, see P. Hardie, *Rumour and Renown: Representations of* Fama *in Western Literature* (Cambridge, 2012), 418–29; and for line 1, compare 6.392 below.

fearsome forecasts of the prophets: modelled on Virgil, *Aeneid* 8.335–6.

to secure the deliverance: (*pro libertate*), compare *Aeneid* 6.821 and 8.648 (moments of Roman sacrifice).

the elderly Joseph: Joseph plays no part in the narrative of Christ's final days in any of the gospels. His introduction here appears to be an innovation by Vida.

through the shadows . . . of night: modelled on Virgil, *Aeneid* 9.373.

But look—slipping out of the hands and weapons: like Panthus at Virgil, *Aeneid* 2.318, and Polites at *Aeneid* 2.526.

54 *he barely recognized his friend, flustered as he was*: like Aeneas barely recognizing Deiphobus in the underworld at Virgil, *Aeneid* 6.498.

stop there: echoes Virgil, *Aeneid* 6.465.

Where do our fortunes stand?: compare Aeneas' question to Panthus as Troy falls at Virgil, *Aeneid* 2.322.

just poured out tears and emitted groans: probably modelled on Virgil, *Aeneid* 3.344.

At last he managed a brief answer: compare Virgil, *Aeneid* 4.333.

our salvation wiped out: see Virgil, *Aeneid* 1.555.

demanding severe punishment and bloodshed: see note on 2.877–8 above.

might perhaps bring himself to feel pity: perhaps echoes Virgil, *Aeneid* 2.145 (the Trojans pity the captive Sinon).

55 *beg . . . for pardon*: see *Aeneid* 3.144.

At this . . . roused their spirits: like Aeneas and Achates at Virgil, *Aeneid* 1.579.

hope for some kind of salvation: echoes and reverses (perhaps ironically) Virgil, *Aeneid* 2.354.

come up with reasons for your entreaty: modelled on Virgil, *Aeneid* 4.51.

Worthiest of the Romans . . . by your justice: the opening of Joseph's appeal recalls the first words of Aeneas' speech to Evander at Virgil, *Aeneid* 8.127–8.

the one man . . . in his wrongdoing: echoes Venus' description of Dido's brother Pygmalion at Virgil, *Aeneid* 1.347.

pay an undeserved penalty by his blood: see Virgil, *Aeneid* 7.595.

have plunged him in these troubles: like Deiphobus at Virgil, *Aeneid* 6.512. The 'savage race' is the Jews; Vida's treatment of Christ's antagonists (and relatively positive presentation of Pilate) reflects medieval and Renaissance anti-Semitic attitudes.

56 *tears soaked . . . in a generous shower*: modelled on Virgil, *Aeneid* 6.699 and 9.251.

comforted . . . with words of friendship: see *Aeneid* 5.770.

he himself sat . . . down in a comfortable seat: like Evander entertaining the Trojans at Virgil, *Aeneid* 8.176.

It's completely right . . . unjust race: compare Virgil, *Aeneid* 5.800–4 (Neptune to Venus). For line 81 ('I call as my witnesses . . . stars') compare similar oaths at *Aeneid* 3.599–600 and 9.429.

what is this man's fortune . . . is he sprung?: for the first question, compare Virgil, *Aeneid* 1.517, and for the others, see note on 2.989 above.

if my intuition is correct: echoes *Aeneid* 7.273.

no mortal sound . . . he is either a god: compare Aeneas' address to Venus at Virgil, *Aeneid* 1.327–8.

a spirit that scorns . . . the light of day: echoes Virgil, *Aeneid* 9.205 (Euryalus agrees to join Nisus' expedition).

found worthy of glorious marriage: like Anchises, 'found worthy of glorious marriage to Venus', at Virgil, *Aeneid* 3.475.

I can see that all is safe: compare Achates' words to Aeneas at Virgil, *Aeneid* 1.583.

Indeed I shall speak, nor . . . in silence: compare especially Anchises' words to Aeneas at Virgil, *Aeneid* 6.722, clearly evoked again in line 108 (' . . . and won't keep you in doubt and perplexity'). Here Anchises is about to explain the mystery of divine immanence and the transmigration of souls, relevant to Joseph's narrative of the Incarnation. Like Anchises', Joseph's exposition begins with 'First of all' (line 112; cf. *Aeneid* 6.724).

57 *he called . . . after his own name*: for this aetiological detail (see Introduction), compare Virgil, *Aeneid* 1.277 (Romans named after Romulus).

a very long sequence: recalls Virgil, *Aeneid* 1.641.

whom . . . obey: see note on 1.1–2 above. For 'the sail-strewn sea', see Virgil, *Aeneid* 1.224.

a woman never joined . . . of daylight: modelled on Virgil, *Aeneid* 7.659–61 (Aventinus, the son of Hercules).

as in past times prophets foretold would come to pass: see note on 1.409 above.

to share the worries of her soul: modelled on Virgil, *Aeneid* 11.822 (Acca, confidante of the virgin Camilla).

her eternal love of maidenhood: like the warrior maiden Camilla at Virgil, *Aeneid* 11.583–4.

well aware of the prophets . . . of the future: like the divine craftsman Vulcan at Virgil, *Aeneid* 8.627.

destined to hold . . . beneath his powerful sway: see note on 1.647 above.

58 *already she was . . . marriageable*: like Lavinia at Virgil, *Aeneid* 7.53.

when look!—again . . . "Make haste . . . delay!": the mysterious voice may also owe something to the instructions given to Latinus concerning his daughter's marriage at Virgil, *Aeneid* 7.95–101; see also 3.231–2 below.

At once . . . through the small city: see note on 3.1–4 above.

each one longed for the lot to favour him: compare Livy 21.42.2.

While their hopes . . . would turn out: modelled on Virgil, *Aeneid* 8.580.

There was an age-old altar: echoes Virgil, *Aeneid* 2.512–14 (altar in Priam's palace).

indicating his choice: perhaps evokes Virgil, *Aeneid* 2.121.

A blush . . . mixing lilies with red roses: compare the blush of the maiden Lavinia at Virgil, *Aeneid* 12.64–9.

thronged by a circle of young men: like Queen Dido at Virgil, *Aeneid* 1.497 (see also 5.87 below, and *Aeneid* 1.503 for 'so was . . . ').

kissing her: see note on 1.956 above.

59 *began to dance wildly*: like the divinely possessed Sibyl at Virgil, *Aeneid* 6.77–8, or the frenzied Dido at *Aeneid* 4.300–1.

no one out of the whole assembly: modelled on Virgil, *Aeneid* 5.378–9 (no one dares to challenge the boxer Dares).

I was won over and gave way: Joseph's capitulation, like parts of his refusal, recalls that of the elderly Anchises at Virgil, *Aeneid* 2.699–704.

drawing long sighs from the depth of her heart: like Aeneas addressing Venus at Virgil, *Aeneid* 1.371.

superstition induced me: compare Lucretius 1.101.

an eternal love of maidenhood: see note on 3.144 above.

I too have my own opposing orders: echoes Virgil, *Aeneid* 9.136–7.

not to give in . . . to any marriage: may evoke Dido's rejection of marriage at Virgil, *Aeneid* 4.18–19.

the Jordan reverse its flow . . . halt their course: for these impossibilities, compare Virgil, *Aeneid* 4.489.

60 *Three times I tried . . . words did not follow*: for the frustrated triple effort, see Virgil, *Aeneid* 2.792–3 and 6.700–1 (based on Homer, *Odyssey* 11.206–8). For the failure to speak, compare *Aeneid* 12.911–12.

after fixing my eyes . . . on the formidable girl: echoes Virgil, *Aeneid* 11.507 (Turnus gazes at the warrior maiden Camilla).

he prophesied . . . that I would surely be famous: recalls the prophecy concerning Lavinia at Virgil, *Aeneid* 7.79–80.

the resolve that is rising in my mind: compare Virgil, *Aeneid* 9.191.

I now take you into my embrace, come what may: modelled on Virgil, *Aeneid* 9.277 (Ascanius to Euryalus).

I roused myself from bed . . . to my bride: a combination of elements from Virgil, *Aeneid* 3.176 and 2.760.

an intense light suddenly filled my eyes: echoes Virgil, *Aeneid* 9.110–11.

The panels of the ceiling above: see Virgil, *Aeneid* 8.25.

She was wholly unaffected by my speech: like Dido unmoved by Aeneas in the underworld at Virgil, *Aeneid* 6.470 (the previous line in Virgil is echoed in the following line in Vida, 'fixed her eyes on . . . and held out . . . ').

how changed she was from her usual form: like the dream vision of Hector at Virgil, *Aeneid* 2.274. For the following simile, see *Aeneid* 1.592–3, though here with the added piquancy that the Virgin Mary herself was often the subject of the kind of gilded statue described by Vida.

61 *the luminous cloud . . . blazing with the sun's rays*: modelled on Virgil, *Aeneid* 8.622–3.

to be grazing around the golden temples of her head: echoes Virgil, *Aeneid* 2.684 (portentous flames encircle Ascanius).

struck senseless . . . appearance of things: modelled on Virgil, *Aeneid* 12.665.

The heavenly ones . . . without your divine will: echoes Virgil, *Aeneid* 2.777–8 (the image of Creusa reassures Aeneas) and 5.56 (Aeneas to his comrades).

bathed her breast in welling tears: like Dido at Virgil, *Aeneid* 4.30.

that love of hers . . . which alone she cherished: see note on 3.144 above.

shining eyes downcast: like Lavinia at Virgil, *Aeneid* 11.480.

Indeed I shall tell you: see note on 3.106 above.

how shall I begin: compare Virgil, *Aeneid* 4.284.

By these tears: echoes Virgil, *Aeneid* 4.314 (Dido to Aeneas).

the sun . . . the pale earth: modelled on Virgil, *Aeneid* 4.6 and 7.148.

pondering the utterances of past prophets: like Anchises interpreting an oracle at Virgil, *Aeneid* 3.102.

I don't think it was without a definite design: echoes Virgil, *Aeneid* 5.56–7 (and for 'motionless or fixed', see *Aeneid* 4.15).

62 *a royal virgin, without intercourse . . . daylight*: the prophecy evokes Isaiah 7:14.

at whose coming . . . through the whole world: a double evocation of Virgil's messianic fourth Eclogue—see *Eclogues* 4.52 and 4.9, and 6.985 below. For 'at whose coming', see the prophecy of Augustus at *Aeneid* 6.798.

An unfamiliar light suddenly met my eyes: see Virgil, *Aeneid* 9.731 (also 9.110) and note on 3.258 above, and compare 6.349 and 6.916 below.

I saw heaven parting down the middle: a near-quotation of Virgil, *Aeneid* 9.20.

beyond all other: echoes Virgil, *Aeneid* 3.321, as does line 333.

he strengthened . . . with a divine assurance: modelled on Virgil, *Aeneid* 3.611 (Anchises reassures Achaemenides).

Put away your fear: at several points the angel's speech recalls Jupiter's reassurance to Venus of the certainty of Roman destiny in Virgil, *Aeneid* 1.257–96. This relationship is established from the very beginning by this exact quotation of the opening words of Jupiter's speech.

to make you the mother of his child: evokes Juno's promise of offspring to Aeolus at Virgil, *Aeneid* 1.75.

You will see him . . . the very heaven-dwellers: like the Romans at Virgil, *Aeneid* 12.839.

will restore him to the . . . rule: echoes Venus' question to Jupiter at Virgil, *Aeneid* 1.253.

He will receive no limits . . . he will reign for ever: a clear evocation of Jupiter's prophecy of the boundless rule of Rome at Virgil, *Aeneid* 1.278–9 (see note on 3.337 above), while also recalling Luke 1:33. See also *Aeneid* 1.285 and 3.97.

63 *my purpose remains . . . unmoved*: echoes Virgil, *Aeneid* 4.449 and 7.314.

63 *The heavenly Father . . . with divine breath*: see 3.132–3 above, and 3.433 and 6.644 below.

So you do not think . . . empty: echoes the River Tiber's prophecy to Aeneas at Virgil, *Aeneid* 8.42.

worn-out old age . . . from long years: like Evander at Virgil, *Aeneid* 8.508.

will bear a child: John the Baptist.

a cloud . . . embraced me in its yellow wings: compare Virgil, *Aeneid* 4.700 (Iris, anticipating the rainbow simile in lines 378–80) and 8.369 (night embraces the earth).

such tints as the misty rainbow . . . its colourful garment: I have translated the reading *imitatur* in line 378, shared by all printed editions, rather than Hankins's/Gardner's *imitantur*. For the expression in these lines see Virgil, *Aeneid* 4.701 (Iris) and 5.87–9 (another rainbow simile, already echoed in lines 373–7).

was spread through all my limbs . . . my whole body: line 386 is modelled on Lucretius 3.707 and 4.629. For 'permeated my whole body', see Virgil, *Aeneid* 6.727 (immanence of the divine spirit).

64 *just as the earth . . . its fertile warmth*: modelled on Virgil, *Georgics* 2.325–7.

At this . . . their applause: compare 1.959–60 above.

Then the heights . . . flickered out: echoes the divine union of Venus and Vulcan at *Aeneid* 8.391–2.

as she did so . . . with tears: like Aeneas at Virgil, *Aeneid* 6.699 (and see note on 3.73–4 above).

I could not believe her: compare Virgil, *Aeneid* 6.463.

so wayward were my senses: echoes Virgil, *Aeneid* 2.54 (the Trojans are deceived by the wooden horse) and *Eclogues* 1.16.

a polished . . . with close-set ornaments: for lines 409–10, compare Ovid, *Metamorphoses* 8.318 and Virgil, *Aeneid* 12.273–4, and for line 411 *Aeneid* 12.942.

he wore . . . otherwise bare: echoes Virgil, *Aeneid* 11.488–9 and 12.430 (heroes arming for battle).

Below ran . . . with a double meander: modelled on Virgil, *Aeneid* 5.250–1 (a cloak embroidered with the story of the boy Ganymede).

embroidered boys: echoes Virgil, *Aeneid* 5.252 (see previous note). The boys are Shadrach, Meshach, and Abednego, sentenced by Nebuchadnezzar to be thrown into a furnace for refusing to worship an idol—see Daniel 3 (and 6.770–2 below).

to the king of the heaven-dwellers: see Virgil, *Aeneid* 3.21.

could be seen: see note on 1.609 above.

Scion of the bloodline of kings: modelled on Virgil, *Aeneid* 6.125 (the Sibyl to Aeneas).

what crime . . . without a definite design?: evokes Virgil, *Aeneid* 2.776–8 (Creusa to Aeneas: see note on 3.279 above).

Do not be in doubt: echoes Virgil, *Aeneid* 3.316.

65 *the almighty Father . . . from the celestial stronghold*: see note on 3.356–7 above.

your prophets once proclaimed would happen: see note on 1.409 above.

she indeed is that mighty portal . . . impassable for any human being: Vida alludes here to the Marian antiphon *Alma Redemptoris Mater* ('Kindly Mother of the Redeemer, you who remain the permeable gate of heaven . . .').

passes and repasses by that way: used of travel to the underworld and back at Virgil, *Aeneid* 6.122.

joining you in stable wedlock: echoes Virgil, *Aeneid* 1.73 (Juno promises a wife to Aeolus; for line 444, see *Aeneid* 1.74–5, but also 10.53) and 4.126 (Juno plots the marriage of Dido and Aeneas).

vanished into the insubstantial breeze: like Mercury at Virgil, *Aeneid* 4.278, or Apollo at *Aeneid* 9.658.

struck enchanting love into my breast: modelled on Lucretius 1.19 and 1.924.

reproaching myself . . . returned to my mind: combines elements from Virgil, *Aeneid* 2.745 and 12.669.

wrapping the truth in riddles: echoes Virgil, *Aeneid* 6.100 (the riddles of the Sibyl).

burning with a crackling fire: modelled on Virgil, *Aeneid* 7.74 (the omen of Lavinia). The 'horned seer' is Moses, who through an error in the Vulgate text of the Bible was frequently represented with horns. For the story of the burning bush, see Exodus 3:2–4.

the harmless flame . . . touching it: compare Virgil, *Aeneid* 2.683–4 (omen of Ascanius).

the fleece of snow-white wool: see Judges 6:36–40. Gideon's fleece was traditionally interpreted as a prefiguration of Christ's Incarnation through the Virgin Mary (see e.g. Jacopo Sannazaro, *De partu Virginis* 2.84–92).

the truth of the matter was established: modelled on Lucretius 5.104.

66 *for whom . . . since the start of her pregnancy*: see 3.365–6 above (the internal echo is signalled by Mary's 'I remember everything' in line 472).

amazing to tell: a common expression in Virgil.

gave . . . the embraces she desired: echoes Venus and Vulcan at Virgil, *Aeneid* 8.405 (Vida's engagement with the Virgilian passage continues in the following lines: compare *Aeneid* 8.388–90).

Uniquely blessed . . . above other mothers: see note on 3.331 above. All these passages recall the words of the Hail Mary.

What has caused . . . my late old age?: modelled on Virgil, *Aeneid* 9.19–20.

66 *queen of heaven*: echoes the opening words of another Marian antiphon, *Regina Caeli* (see note on 3.438–40 above).

pitying the toils: compare Virgil, *Aeneid* 1.597 and 6.56.

to the king of heaven: see note on 3.422–3 above.

in his goodness... ancient ancestors: these lines paraphrase the Magnificat, the hymn uttered by Mary at Luke 1:46–55.

Already at that time the Caspian realms . . . and all Egypt trembled: closely modelled on the reaction of eastern realms to prophecies of Augustus at Virgil, *Aeneid* 6.798–800.

67 *Even your own people . . . to Olympus on high*: Vida seems to be referring specifically to Virgil's fourth Eclogue, known to the Romans ('your own people') by the time of these words. This interpretation is reinforced by echoes of *Eclogues* 4.17 (especially 'by his father's powers') in lines 513–14; see also note on 3.530–1 below. Line 515 ('would bring . . . to Olympus') echoes 1.7 above.

I often saw him . . . in clear daylight: closely modelled on Aeneas' report of his visit from Mercury at Virgil, *Aeneid* 4.358–9.

If only . . . was true: modelled on Virgil, *Aeneid* 6.187–9 (Aeneas longs to see the Golden Bough).

Cull shining flowers and bring gleaming white lilies in handfuls: echoes Virgil, *Aeneid* 6.883–4 (Anchises offers funeral tributes to Marcellus, perhaps injecting an anticipatory note of mourning here in Vida).

Ah, if only . . . on every side: lines 530–1 closely recall Virgil, *Eclogues* 4.53–4, preparing the way for the announcement of a new Golden Age in line 538, modelled on the same poem (see *Eclogues* 4.12). Further echoes of the so-called messianic eclogue in these lines include 'all dread removed' (line 532: compare *Eclogues* 4.14) and 'bring peace to the world . . . and reign as a god in your Father's Olympus' (lines 532–3: compare *Eclogues* 4.17).

Then the savage sword . . . make its entrance in the world: line 537 strongly echoes Virgil, *Georgics* 1.508, while restoring the positive vision conveyed by the same imagery at Isaiah 2:4. The language of line 538 evokes Virgil, *Eclogues* 4.8–12 (the return of the Golden Age: see previous note). See also 4.198 below.

Augustus Caesar . . . was holding a census: evokes the image of Augustus reviewing the gifts of subject peoples at Virgil, *Aeneid* 8.720–1. In line 542, 'who held supreme power in the world' echoes *Aeneid* 10.100 (of Jupiter).

setting out from our home: echoes Virgil. *Aeneid* 7.209 (of Dardanus, now received into heaven—as Mary will be in due course).

walls and scattered dwellings: modelled on Virgil, *Aeneid* 8.98–9 (Evander's humble settlement). For the description of night in line 548, see *Aeneid* 3.198–9.

a most welcome lodging: modelled on Virgil, *Aeneid* 5.128.

68 *Here then . . . made our way together, exhausted*: modelled on Virgil, *Aeneid* 3.276.

as I rather think, and consider it fitting to believe so: modelled on *Aeneid* 12.188.

all the most serious hardships: echoes Virgil, *Aeneid* 3.315 (the tribulations of Aeneas).

to experience . . . misfortunes: echoes Virgil, *Aeneid* 1.9 (also of Aeneas).

and lightened our load: echoes Virgil, *Aeneid* 3.709 (of Aeneas' father Anchises).

so he could get through life . . . from his small children: evokes Virgil, *Aeneid* 8.408–13 (simile of poor woman's relentless work).

deep slumber held . . . fast: echoes Virgil, *Aeneid* 8.27 (description of night).

an intense light . . . gleam: see note on 3.258 above.

kneeling on both knees: modelled on Virgil, *Aeneid* 12.492.

Just like . . . storms the heaven: compare the weather simile at Virgil, *Aeneid* 9.668–71.

69 *decorated the doorway . . . with flowers and assorted garlands*: like the offerings of Iarbas at Virgil, *Aeneid* 4.202.

they bent and . . . knelt on the ground: modelled on Virgil, *Aeneid* 3.93 (the Trojans react to divine omens).

a voice like this . . . 'Do not be afraid, men[']: echoes Virgil, *Aeneid* 9.112–14 (a voice from heaven announcing the transformation of the Trojan ships).

new-found joy: see Virgil, *Aeneid* 10.325.

and return it to its original condition: echoes Virgil, *Aeneid* 12.424 (divine healing of Aeneas' wound).

three times they had moved . . . and threefold dance: modelled on Virgil, *Aeneid* 11.188–90 (cavalry display at funeral rites).

they contemplated him . . . intently with their whole heart: like Dido fixated by Cupid disguised as the boy Ascanius/Iulus at Virgil, *Aeneid* 1.717–18.

70 *trimming a small section . . . a fragment of Samian pottery*: referring to the circumcision, eight days after his birth, when Jesus received his name in accordance with Jewish custom (see Luke 2:21). In his *Natural History* (35.46), Pliny the Elder records that the priests of Cybele castrated themselves with shards of Samian pottery.

by the Greek name Christ: meaning 'the anointed one', or Messiah.

until she observed forty sunrises: for the forty-day period of purification following childbirth, see Leviticus 12.

At the altars themselves . . . bearing ritual objects: a combination of elements from Virgil, *Aeneid* 2.550 and 6.809/8.85.

the unsleeping flame in the sanctuary: echoes especially Virgil, *Aeneid* 2.297 (the ghost of Hector passes on the eternal flame to Aeneas).

70 *were pouring from bowls the blood*: echoes ritual offerings at Virgil, *Aeneid* 5.98 and 6.248–9.

the seven lights in a row: the seven-branched candelabrum (menorah), described in Exodus 25:31–40.

71 *the blazing altar exhaled eastern fragrance*: closely modelled on Lucretius 2.417, where the incense of the mythical island of Panchaea is given as an example of pleasant scents.

who bore the name of his ancestor: echoes Virgil, *Aeneid* 5.564.

more devoted to the cause of righteousness: modelled on Virgil, *Aeneid* 2.427 (Ripheus, most righteous of the Trojans).

he had foreknowledge of what would happen: see Virgil, *Aeneid* 6.66 (the prophetic Sibyl).

he longed to put an end . . . by death: see 6.45 (and 5.56) below.

accompanying his master's step: like Evander's dogs at Virgil, *Aeneid* 8.462.

by his power of smell: see *Aeneid* 4.132 (hunting hounds). In general Vida's hunting hound simile recalls that at *Aeneid* 12.749–57.

directs his course now this way, now that: modelled on Virgil, *Aeneid* 5.441 (siege simile).

As tears welled up . . . as follows: modelled on Virgil, *Aeneid* 11.41 (Aeneas mourns for the young Pallas).

Hail to your goodness: echoes Virgil, *Aeneid* 9.641 (Apollo applauds Ascanius).

Much desired you come: echoes Silius Italicus, *Punica* 1.483, but may also suggest the biblical idea of the Desire of Nations (see Haggai 2:7).

Now . . . you are letting me go off: Vida alludes to the opening words of Simeon's prayer in the Vulgate Bible, *nunc dimittis* (Luke 2:29), under which title it had long been a part of the Christian evening liturgy.

an end . . . promised: 'an end of my labour' may recall Virgil, *Aeneid* 1.241 and 7.117–18, with 'as . . . you promised' picking up *Aeneid* 1.237.

a light in the darkness: perhaps an allusion to the Vulgate text of John 1:5.

72 *To whom can I match you in glory?*: echoes Virgil, *Aeneid* 11.125 (Drances to Aeneas).

What thanks can I give you: possibly draws on Virgil, *Aeneid* 11.508–9 (Turnus to Camilla).

your maiden's dowry will be great grief: modelled on Virgil, *Aeneid* 7.318 (Juno prophesies the unhappy consequences of Lavinia's betrothal).

breaking its compact: see note on 2.856–7 above.

on the spot . . . by a peaceful death: closely modelled on Virgil, *Aeneid* 9.445 (death of Nisus).

The others were astonished . . . would compass: loosely based on Virgil, *Aeneid* 2.120–1 (the Greeks wonder whom Calchas will choose for sacrifice). For 'whose destruction . . . would compass', see *Aeneid* 9.315–16.

not for long did the matter remain in doubt: modelled on Virgil, *Aeneid* 9.395.

the outcome . . . perplexity: for 'the outcome fully enlightened us' and 'freed us from our perplexity', see Virgil, *Aeneid* 5.523 and 6.29 respectively.

blows remain for us: echoes Virgil, *Aeneid* 10.29.

A star trailing its . . . ample radiance: clearly evokes Virgil, *Aeneid* 2.693–8 (omen of a comet).

just as of old . . . a wondrous light: a reference to the pillar of fire which guided the Israelites on their flight from Egypt (see Exodus 13:21–2).

73 *immense in his fame . . . in his glorious deeds*: like Aeneas at Virgil, *Aeneid* 1.379.

tossed on a surging tide of worries . . . afflicted with vain terror: for line 765, see especially Virgil, *Aeneid* 8.19 (also *Aeneid* 4.532; Catullus 64.62). Line 766 is an almost exact quotation of Lucretius 3.1049.

brings you to our lands: echoes Virgil, *Aeneid* 1.616 (Dido questions Aeneas).

Not far from here . . . inhabited by our people: closely modelled on Virgil, *Aeneid* 8.478–9 (the city of Mezentius).

feigned new-found joy with his deceptive countenance: a more sinister adaptation of Aeneas' dissimulation at Virgil, *Aeneid* 1.209.

whom the stars obey: echoes Virgil, *Aeneid* 10.176 (a soothsayer; see also 5.117 below).

with a great throng pressing round them: modelled on Virgil, *Aeneid* 1.497 and 4.136.

comets . . . ominously glow mournfully red: echoes Virgil, *Aeneid* 10.272–3 (comet simile).

I, a poor man . . . a lowly roof: closely recalls Virgil, *Aeneid* 8.365–6 (Evander's humble hospitality).

dyed in Tyrian purple: like the luxurious attire of Aeneas in Carthage at Virgil, *Aeneid* 4.262 (and for the horse, see *Aeneid* 4.134–5).

the star that appeared: echoes Virgil, *Aeneid* 8.681 (the 'Julian star' appears over the head of Augustus).

74 *flared up with rage*: like Aeneas about to kill Turnus at Virgil, *Aeneid* 12.946.

seizing . . . from their mothers' breast: like the prematurely dead infants at Virgil, *Aeneid* 6.428.

Come on—get up, break off delay: echoes Mercury's exhortation to Aeneas to leave Carthage at Virgil, *Aeneid* 4.569.

the sevenfold Nile: see Virgil, *Aeneid* 6.800.

drained of colour: like the Trojans fleeing at the sight of the serpents sent to kill Laocoon at Virgil, *Aeneid* 2.212.

trusting . . . in the darkness of night: echoes Virgil, *Aeneid* 9.378 (Nisus and Euryalus flee from their enemies).

74 *the first land to recognize . . . the paths of the sun*: the science of astronomy originated in ancient Egypt. For the language, see Lucretius 1.128, 5.69, 5.76, and 5.774.

Every breeze struck terror . . . so precious a being: closely modelled on Virgil, *Aeneid* 2.728–9 (Aeneas' anxious flight from Troy). For 'so precious a being', see Horace, *Odes* 1.24.2.

the light breath of the breezes: quotes Lucretius 5.236.

the talkative pools: echoes Virgil, *Aeneid* 11.458 (the noise of swans).

75 *over rocks damp and green with gleaming moss*: clearly echoes Lucretius 5.949–51 (the life of early humans in nature).

the birds . . . with their fluid warbling: closely modelled on Virgil, *Aeneid* 7.33–4.

the marjoram tree . . . its soft shade: recalls Virgil, *Aeneid* 1.693–4 (Venus transports the sleeping Ascanius to Idalia).

as the god made his arrival: echoes the arrival of Hecate (accompanied by omens) at Virgil, *Aeneid* 6.258.

diversions known to him: echoes Virgil, *Aeneid* 9.379.

the sound of the sistrum: the sistrum was a rattle which was used in the worship of the goddess Isis. Joseph is essentially saying that he had arrived in Egypt, the home of the worship of Isis.

I feared everything . . . all was safe: like Dido at Virgil, *Aeneid* 4.298.

a report, spread abroad . . . broadcast on all sides the news: compare Virgil, *Aeneid* 8.554, and see note on 3.1–4 above.

the Palestinian king . . . the thriving city: Herod, and Bethlehem.

bawling they left the sweet light of life: evokes the lamentation of the souls of infants in the underworld at Virgil, *Aeneid* 6.426–9.

76 *the vision . . . frayed her spirit*: modelled on Virgil, *Aeneid* 9.294.

So it turned out . . . destruction for many: see 3.720–1 above (the prophecy of Simeon: 'I foretell that this birth will bring death to many').

noting and retracing the steps I had taken: echoes Virgil, *Aeneid* 2.753–4 and 9.392–3.

Perhaps you are also keen to know: modelled on Aeneas' narration at Virgil, *Aeneid* 2.506.

in its first flower: echoes Virgil, *Aeneid* 7.162 (the youth of the Latins).

night would close up the sky and bury the day: modelled on Virgil, *Aeneid* 1.374 (day would end before Aeneas could give a full account of his toils).

we were scared witless at the sacred fires: compare the reaction to the miraculous flames on Ascanius/Iulus' head at Virgil, *Aeneid* 2.685–6.

terrifying flashes of lightning: see Virgil, *Aeneid* 8.431 (the forge of Vulcan), and 6.934 below.

as she wove fine thread . . . with shrill shuttle: closely modelled on Virgil, *Aeneid* 7.14 (Circe's loom).

77 *he fulfilled the love of his true Father*: an echo with inversion of Virgil, *Aeneid* 1.716, where Cupid disguised as Ascanius fulfils the love of his *false* father Aeneas.

vigorous energy . . . came to his limbs: echoes Virgil, *Georgics* 4.418.

the marvellous boy followed, holding her hand: like the boy Ascanius leaving Troy, holding the hand of his father Aeneas, at Virgil, *Aeneid* 2.723–4.

was gone . . . from his mother and me: another echo of the flight from Troy, this time of the disappearance of Creusa at Virgil, *Aeneid* 2.743–4. This continues in the following lines with 'I . . . filled the way with my shouting' (see *Aeneid* 2.769) and 'blaming only herself' (see *Aeneid* 2.745).

presents its face to heaven . . . its former glory: a combination of elements from Virgil, *Aeneid* 8.591 and 8.339.

For three days we wandered in bewilderment: modelled on Virgil, *Aeneid* 3.203–4 (the wanderings of Aeneas and the Trojans).

no teacher's art: echoes Virgil, *Aeneid* 12.427 (the surgeon Iapyx acknowledges the supernatural nature of Aeneas' cure; see also 8.442 (divine skill of the Cyclopes)). See 4.246 below.

78 *they could not get enough . . . features of the god*: modelled on Virgil, *Aeneid* 1.709–14 (Dido and the Trojans admire Cupid disguised as Ascanius/Iulus) and 8.265 (Cacus).

from every inch . . . he cast sweet love: closely modelled on Lucretius 4.1054. See also 4.809 below.

or as the warm glow . . . silver or gold: compare Lucretius 4.1126–7. The simile also evokes those describing Ascanius at Virgil, *Aeneid* 10.133–8 (perhaps also suggested by 'his noble head' at line 960 above).

From here came . . . our suffering: echoes Virgil, *Aeneid* 4.169–70 (the beginning of Dido's tragedy).

From this kindling was a . . . fire then lit: echoes Virgil, *Aeneid* 1.176 (Achates lights a fire).

sooner would fortresses lurk unseen by day on the mountains: compare Matthew 5:14 ('A city that is set on an hill cannot be hid').

could lie . . . without recognition: like the body of Priam at Virgil, *Aeneid* 2.557–8.

Bacchus' dark liquor: wine.

79 *the liquid was seen to . . . grow dark*: a more positive version of the omen at Virgil, *Aeneid* 4.453–5 (wine turns into blood).

if pleasure prompts you in your heart: echoes Virgil, *Aeneid* 6.675.

bringing his speech to an end here he . . . fell quiet: closely modelled on the end of Aeneas' narrative at Virgil, *Aeneid* 3.718.

79 *the strength in this man's body is failing him*: may echo Virgil, *Aeneid* 5.396 (the old boxer Entellus laments his lost strength).

everyone kept their eyes fixed intently: clearly echoes Virgil, *Aeneid* 2.1 (Aeneas' audience waits for him to begin his narration).

BOOK FOUR

80 *This young man, unsurpassed in his good looks*: John. The expression is modelled on Virgil, *Aeneid* 1.544–5 and 7.649–50.

enjoying the blessed sight of the celestial beings: may evoke Virgil, *Aeneid* 7.90–1 (a priest communes with the divine).

the queen of birds: the eagle, the traditional symbol of St John the Evangelist. The words 'soars aloft' (*alta petens*) in line 10 echo the same phrase in an eagle simile at Virgil, *Aeneid* 9.564.

fixing her eyes . . . in a piercing stare: compare Virgil, *Aeneid* 7.249–51 (Latinus) and 1.717–18 (Dido).

heavy with sleep: like Deiphobus, actually asleep, at Virgil, *Aeneid* 6.520.

In the beginning: Vida's poetic treatment of the opening of St John's gospel begins with the second word of the Vulgate text, but also the first word of Anchises' disquisition on divine immanence in creation at Virgil, *Aeneid* 6.724 (see note on 3.106 above).

Not yet had he forged . . . the dusky firmament: for the 'not yet' theme, see note on 1.612 above. For 'the starry orbs' and 'lights shone in the . . . firmament', see Statius, *Silvae* 2.1.42.

the eternal Father . . . miraculous to say: Vida strikingly uses three different forms of the adjective *aeternus* ('eternal') in the space of two lines. The aside 'miraculous to say' is characteristically Virgilian.

earthly limbs or mortal parts: a further distinct echo of Anchises' exposition on the nature of existence—see Virgil, *Aeneid* 6.732 and note on 4.20 above.

the sea, the earth, and the boundless sky: see note on 1.1–2 above, and 4.921 below. The line combines elements from Ovid, *Metamorphoses* 1.257 and Lucretius 5.473.

81 *from each comes a shared mutual devotion*: a remarkable adaptation of a line from Lucretius describing human sexual union (4.1216).

the seas and the lands and the deepest recesses of heaven: modelled on Virgil, *Aeneid* 1.54 and *Eclogues* 4.51/*Georgics* 4.222 (see note on 1.1–2 above, and 4.1002 below).

directing all things . . . divine will: like Virgil's Jupiter at *Aeneid* 4.269.

to undertake such great labours: evokes the suffering hero Aeneas at Virgil, *Aeneid* 1.10–11.

these things I shall tell . . . from the very beginning: compare Jacopo Sannazaro, *De partu Virginis* 1.6–7, and Virgil, *Aeneid* 7.37–40.

the lands that lie below: see Virgil, *Aeneid* 1.224.

the universal craftsman: for this description of the Creator, see Ovid, *Metamorphoses* 1.79, and 6.797 below.

had hammered out: compare 1.605 above.

enflamed with eternal love . . . spheres of the sevenfold heaven: for 'spheres of the sevenfold heaven', see note on 1.605 above; for 'enflamed with . . . love', see especially Virgil, *Aeneid* 7.496 (Ascanius' love of glory).

no small part: echoes Virgil, *Aeneid* 10.128 (a mighty rock).

ungrateful . . . blinded by delirium: modelled on Virgil, *Aeneid* 2.244 (the Trojans take the wooden horse into Troy: see also 5.30, 5.251, and 5.912 below).

82 *every race . . . roam the mountains*: the language of these lines is heavily Lucretian, recalling in particular Lucretius 1.4, 1.161–3, 1.404, 2.78, 2.597, and 2.1081. See also Virgil, *Georgics* 4.223.

his wife: Eve (the 'man' here is Adam). See also 1.644–73 above.

all the line descended . . . light of day: modelled on Virgil, *Aeneid* 6.789–90 (the Roman descendants of Iulus).

gruelling labour was added: evokes Virgil, *Georgics* 1.150 (end of the Golden Age), and more generally *Georgics* 1.145–6.

together with . . . shameful destitution: clearly echoes Virgil, *Aeneid* 6.273–7 (hellish personifications at the entrance to the underworld).

outlasted many ages in its life on earth: modelled on Virgil, *Georgics* 2.295, *Aeneid* 11.160, and (especially) Lucretius 3.948.

uneducated, ignorant, and empty of reason: 'ignorant' like Aeneas viewing his prophetic shield at Virgil, *Aeneid* 8.730 (see also 10.666). For 'empty of reason', see Michael Marullus, *Hymns to Nature* 1.1.33 and 3.1.155.

83 *gave them laws and observances and sacred practices*: see note on 1.952 above (and 4.795 below).

circumcise with a sharpened potsherd: see note on 3.641–2 above.

they were reckoning up the times: like Anchises in Elysium at Virgil, *Aeneid* 6.691 (an episode recalled also by the 'vale' (*Aeneid* 6.679) and outstretched hands (*Aeneid* 6.685)).

the one cry of them all: echoes Virgil, *Aeneid* 5.616 (unanimous exhaustion of the Trojan women).

we are far sundered: like the Trojans kept from Italy at Virgil, *Aeneid* 1.252.

If . . . any traces of ancient fault survive: modelled on Virgil, *Eclogues* 4.13/31 (last traces of wrongdoing at the start of the new Golden Age).

And you, for whom . . . waiting: echoes Virgil, *Georgics* 1.24 (deification of Augustus) and *Eclogues* 4.11.

83 *true offspring of the highest Father*: see 2.892–3 and note on 1.237 above.

break off delay: see notes on 2.112 and 3.808 above.

took pity . . . from the citadel of heaven: modelled on Virgil, *Aeneid* 5.727 (Jupiter's pity for the Trojans).

84 *keeping him away from their territories*: modelled on Virgil, *Aeneid* 1.299–300 (Dido and the Trojans).

in spreading . . . tidings: echoes Virgil, *Aeneid* 2.98 (rumours spread by Ulysses).

make its way to the surrounding cities: modelled on Virgil, *Aeneid* 9.10 (Aeneas' movements in Italy).

as once so many truth-telling Sibyls sang: the Sibyls were prophetesses believed to have foretold the birth of Christ. They included the Cumaean Sibyl, to whom Virgil attributed the prophecy in his fourth Eclogue (echoed in 'sent down from heaven', line 175: see *Eclogues* 4.7).

in a great throng . . . went up to him: echoes Virgil, *Aeneid* 1.509 (the Trojan embassy approaches Dido).

where he came from: see note on 2.989 above.

the god will be here—look, God is here: recalls Virgil, *Aeneid* 6.46 (the divinely possessed Sibyl). See also 4.232, 6.171, 6.534, and 6.565 below (and 1.187 above).

learn justice: see note on 1.533 above.

wash off the stain of sin: echoes Virgil, *Aeneid* 6.741–2 (purification of souls in the underworld: also picked up in 'wash away' in line 196).

the infection of ancient fault, and the Golden Age will come into being: two echoes of Virgil's fourth Eclogue—see notes on 4.133 and 3.537–8 above, and 6.981–6 below.

85 *he might leave nothing unexperienced*: like Dido leaving nothing untried at Virgil, *Aeneid* 4.415.

refused and shrank from his touch: modelled on Virgil, *Aeneid* 7.618 (Latinus refuses to declare war on the Trojans).

held out both palms in supplication: see Virgil, *Aeneid* 6.685 (Anchises welcomes Aeneas).

thundered with a deafening crash: echoes Virgil, *Aeneid* 2.692–3 (omen confirming the destiny of Ascanius/Iulus: see Introduction). The allusions to this passage continue in the following lines, with 'descended from . . . heaven' (line 216) and 'marking its passage far and wide' (line 219: see *Aeneid* 2.697–8).

were bearing linen garments and white robes: combines elements from Virgil, *Aeneid* 11.775–6 and 1.702.

as Jesus departed John called after him: like Aeneas recognizing and addressing his divine mother at Virgil, *Aeneid* 1.406.

so often promised . . . our God! Behold the god: for 'so often promised', see Virgil, *Aeneid* 6.791 (prophecy of Augustus), and for 'our God! Behold the god', see note on 4.190–1 above. Vida here reworks the Baptist's proclamation 'Behold the Lamb of God' (John 1:36).

will atone . . . to his heavenly Father: combines elements from Virgil, *Aeneid* 11.849 and 1.334.

Choose him as your leader: see Virgil, *Aeneid* 8.503.

86 *The matter was believed . . . among them*: a combination of elements from Virgil, *Aeneid* 2.196 and 6.716.

he could share with them his concerns: see note on 3.136–7 above.

into all eventualities: see Virgil, *Aeneid* 9.277 (Ascanius and Euryalus; also 9.292).

masterful skill: see note on 3.953 above.

our art was . . . where fish abound: recalls Virgil, *Aeneid* 12.518–19 (a young fisherman).

the salty shallows in a small vessel: clearly echoes Virgil, *Aeneid* 5.158 (boat race).

There joined us as companions: quotes Virgil, *Aeneid* 2.339 (Trojans join Aeneas' band).

the mute swimmers: fish—see Lucretius 2.342–3, and 6.738 below.

coarse with their uncombed beards: echoes Virgil, *Georgics* 3.366 (Scythians).

the deviser of evil himself: modelled on Virgil, *Aeneid* 2.264 (Epeos, inventor of the wooden horse).

I heard . . . with these very ears: recalls Aeneas' report of his encounter with the god Mercury at Virgil, *Aeneid* 4.359.

But a few out of many . . . I shall set them out: modelled on Virgil, *Aeneid* 3.377–9 and 12.25.

87 *the enduring achievements . . . that he . . . left behind*: see Virgil, *Aeneid* 6.512.

the king of Bethany rich in palm trees: Lazarus (see 1.100–20, 1.236–99 above).

Many were blind: like sightless moles at Virgil, *Georgics* 1.183.

fluid in their infected bodies: quotes Lucretius 3.503.

as it permeated their . . . frame: likewise taken from Lucretius 3.492.

after their death: echoes Virgil, *Aeneid* 10.641 (ghost simile).

with a long line of flaming torches: echoes Virgil, *Aeneid* 11.143–4 (funeral of Pallas).

88 *the pitiable body . . . in an untimely death*: the lines contain two reminiscences of the dead youth Pallas, from Virgil, *Aeneid* 11.59 and 11.28 (repeated from *Aeneid* 6.429).

had . . . reached adolescence in . . . his age: echoes Virgil, *Aeneid* 3.491.

88 *He was like a hyacinth . . . with her delicate fingers*: the two similes here recall in particular the flower simile describing the dead Pallas at Virgil, *Aeneid* 11.67–71 (see also *Aeneid* 9.435–7, on the death of the boy Euryalus).

frenziedly all through the city: like the raving Dido at Virgil, *Aeneid* 4.68–9.

the pallor . . . with soft down: the youthful pallor echoes Virgil, *Aeneid* 12.221 (Turnus), while the downy cheeks recall *Aeneid* 10.324 (the youth Clytius).

all warmth . . . drifting away: recalls the death of Dido at Virgil, *Aeneid* 4.704–5.

a man generous with his fortune: echoes Virgil, *Aeneid* 11.338 (Drances).

in popular favour: see Virgil, *Aeneid* 6.816 (excessive populism of Ancus Marcius).

Why should I speak again: see Virgil, *Aeneid* 10.36.

when he turned fresh water . . . into wine: a reference to the wedding at Cana, narrated at 3.980–1002 above.

mothers and men: the first two groups among the crowd of souls in the underworld at Virgil, *Aeneid* 6.306. See also 4.845, 4.961, and 6.655 below.

89 *consoled them benevolently with friendly words*: see note on 1.256 above.

"No one . . . will depart this day unsatisfied": modelled on Virgil, *Aeneid* 5.305 (Aeneas promises prizes to competitors).

the race of Isaac's children: see note on 1.398 above.

divine sustenance: manna (see Exodus 16; also Psalms 78:24, John 6:31).

loathsome hunger: echoes Virgil, *Aeneid* 3.367 (report of the prophecy of Celaeno).

he cut the loaves of bread . . . among all the people: echoes Virgil, *Aeneid* 1.212 and 1.194 (preparations for a feast).

I have seen . . . with its blasts: the claim to autopsy recalls Aeneas' eyewitness account of the ravages of Neoptolemus at Virgil, *Aeneid* 2.499–500. The roughening of the waves echoes *Aeneid* 3.285 (winter storms).

90 *We were trembling with fear*: modelled on Virgil, *Aeneid* 2.685 (omen of Ascanius/Iulus).

almost on the point of death: see *Aeneid* 3.685 and 9.143.

We shuddered at the sudden vision: like Aeneas in the underworld at Virgil, *Aeneid* 6.710.

Where has your confidence in me disappeared to: echoes Virgil, *Aeneid* 8.395–6 (Vulcan to Venus).

Let all fear be gone: quotes *Aeneid* 11.14 (Aeneas reassures his men).

he calmed the swollen seas: like Neptune at Virgil, *Aeneid* 1.142.

skimming over the surface of the water: again like Neptune stilling a storm, this time at Virgil, *Aeneid* 5.819.

yet more amazing to say and see: see note on 3.480 above.

he called Peter to him . . . in his trusty ear: "Go . . . king": modelled on Virgil, *Aeneid* 5.546–8 (Aeneas gives instructions to a companion of Ascanius/ Iulus).

in a forbidden union: echoes Ovid, *Metamorphoses* 10.353 (incestuous love of Myrrha).

at a time when . . . mournful displays: apparently a reference to the Ten Days of Repentance culminating in Yom Kippur, the Day of Atonement, though von Contzen et al. see the phrase translated here as 'mournful displays' as alluding to the Feast of Tabernacles (Sukkot), with its 'shady booths'.

91 *with scant space in between*: see 4.410 above, with note on 'almost on the point of death'.

The woman . . . flames of fire from heaven: perhaps recalls the punishment of the Locrian Ajax at Virgil, *Aeneid* 1.44–5, also for a sexual offence.

he had the power neither . . . to give out speech: echoes Virgil, *Aeneid* 1.408–9 (Aeneas laments the inadequacy of his communication with his mother Venus; see also *Aeneid* 6.688–9).

a legion issuing from the lairs of Erebus: see note on 2.28 above. On Erebus, see note on 2.694 above.

fearsome bellowings: echoes Virgil, *Aeneid* 12.103–4 (a bull prepares for battle).

as he . . . roared inhumanly: like the monster Cacus at Virgil, *Aeneid* 8.248.

monstrously burst his . . . chains: again, recalls the action of Cacus at Virgil, *Aeneid* 8.225 (though 'monstrous' there refers to a rock).

like a wild beast he spent his life: echoes Virgil, *Aeneid* 4.551 (Dido laments that she could not live her life in this manner).

wherever there were hollow rocks: see Virgil, *Aeneid* 5.677–8.

his hands tied behind his back . . . were dragging him: like the captive Sinon at Virgil, *Aeneid* 2.57–8.

The captive strained . . . with its curved horn: both narrative and simile clearly evoke the struggles of Laocoon, who is compared to a wounded sacrificial bull, at Virgil, *Aeneid* 2.220–4.

92 *he called on . . . a miracle!*: the endings of both lines occur repeatedly in Virgil's *Aeneid*.

Not so monstrous a sound . . . an enormous cascade of waters: a third occurrence of 'monstrous(ly)', after lines 469 and 488 above. The repetition reinforces the link between simile and narrative. The simile refers to the Cascata delle Marmore, a series of man-made waterfalls near Terni in Umbria constructed in Roman times and fed by the River Velino. For 'an enormous cascade of waters', see Lucretius 5.263 and 6.609.

the whole region became a sea: recalls Virgil, *Eclogues* 8.58 (Damon invokes a cataclysm).

the whole heaven . . . bellow back: echoes Virgil, *Aeneid* 9.504 (and 12.722).

92 *they started to panic within*: like Trojans trapped inside a burning tower at Virgil, *Aeneid* 9.538.

to enter the hidden places of the lower world: modelled on Virgil, *Aeneid* 6.140 (the underworld).

by the ungentle goads: echoes Virgil, *Aeneid* 11.452 (the Latins in turmoil at the approach of the Trojan forces).

There was no delay, no respite: see note on 2.140 above.

as he panted . . . from his lungs: the line is taken from Lucilius, *Satires* 3.134 (Loeb edn.), quoted by the grammarian Nonius Marcellus.

93 *A cry went up to the glittering stars*: evokes several Virgilian expressions, especially *Aeneid* 2.488 and 11.832–3.

to relieve . . . with help: echoes Virgil, *Aeneid* 2.452 (Trojan resistance to the invading Greeks).

not by . . . any particular skill: the line adapts Virgil, *Aeneid* 12.427 (see note on 3.953 above).

bring meandering rivers . . . their course: the language here recalls Jacopo Sannazaro, *De partu Virginis* 2.22 (nature rejoices as the Virgin sets out to visit Elizabeth).

You are the light of humanity: see Matthew 5:14.

he chose seventy: see Luke 10:1–2, where harvest imagery is also prominent, as in the following simile here.

turns the soil with a hundred ploughs: recalls Virgil, *Aeneid* 7.539 (Galaesus, richest of the Italians).

which surely . . . without some divine power: see note on 3.279 above.

94 *she crept up*: like the wooden horse entering Troy at Virgil, *Aeneid* 2.240.

I myself . . . saw . . . before my very eyes: quotes Virgil, *Aeneid* 12.638.

which I saw in abundance: modelled on Virgil, *Aeneid* 2.5 (Aeneas' eyewitness account of the fall of Troy).

he was revealed . . . as God: see *Aeneid* 1.405 (Venus reveals her divinity).

flung a hollow cloud around him: like the hollow clouds in which Aeneas is concealed at Virgil, *Aeneid* 1.516 and 5.810.

Indeed, I remember: quotes Virgil, *Aeneid* 7.205 (Latinus; see also *Aeneid* 1.619 (Dido), and 4.858, 6.520 below).

the recent killing: see *Aeneid* 2.718.

the king, warned . . . his brother: Herod Antipas, who had married his (half-) brother's wife Herodias.

the very king of Erebus: Satan (see note on 2.694 above).

did not give up or let . . . be: see Virgil, *Aeneid* 2.534 (tenacity of Priam).

95 *time for inflicting harm*: echoes Virgil, *Aeneid* 7.511 (the Fury Allecto).

to turn . . . into as many spelt loaves: echoes Virgil, *Aeneid* 10.83 (transformation of the Trojan ships into nymphs) and 7.109 (Trojan picnic).

But his tricks did not escape . . . the deity: recalls Virgil, *Aeneid* 1.130 (Neptune perceives Juno's trickery).

lead his . . . mind astray with empty longing: echoes Virgil, *Aeneid* 1.721 (the disguised Cupid surreptitiously manipulates Dido's emotions).

the troubled sea: see Virgil, *Georgics* 4.262.

is dashed against the rocks and is turned back: compare Virgil, *Aeneid* 7.590 (another simile of storm-beaten rocks).

a hope—an empty one: may recall Virgil, *Aeneid* 10.648 (Turnus is led astray by a phantom Aeneas).

thought he had won: echoes Virgil, *Aeneid* 11.712 (the overconfidence of a treacherous warrior).

96 *like a horse . . . a vast stretch of terrain*: the simile is modelled on Virgil, *Aeneid* 11.492–7, which it echoes in a number of details. For 'a vast stretch of terrain' (line 651), see Virgil, *Georgics* 3.202–3.

no one . . . superior to him in holiness: see note on 2.579–80 above.

Enemy and countryman . . . with no distinction: echoes Virgil, *Aeneid* 1.574 (Dido offers the Trojans a share in her kingdom) and 10.108 (impartiality of Jupiter).

things both deserved and undeserved: compare Virgil, *Aeneid* 12.811 (tribulations of Juno; see also *Aeneid* 9.595, and 4.786 below).

and evil ways: echoes Virgil, *Aeneid* 11.347 (Drances on Turnus).

Matthew . . . Zacchaeus himself: two tax-collectors, of whom the former would go on to write the gospel of Matthew. For Zacchaeus, see 1.94–9 above.

oppressed by mental darkness: echoes Aeneas' reaction to learning of the fate of Polydorus at Virgil, *Aeneid* 3.47.

97 *perpetrator of wrong*: see note on 2.765 above.

to leave for home . . . late at night: modelled on Virgil, *Georgics* 3.467 (signs of sickness in sheep).

his sweet children run up to snatch kisses: clearly evokes Lucretius 3.895–6 (see also Virgil, *Georgics* 2.523).

the sonorous streams: echoes Virgil, *Aeneid* 12.139 (Juturna the river nymph).

at whose command . . . for the thirsty peoples: for Moses' striking of water from the rock, see Exodus 17:1–7 (and 2.634–8 above).

their hair . . . tied back with soft leafage: a combination of elements from Virgil, *Aeneid* 4.147–8, 4.459, and 5.556.

a love of fair virtue: see Statius, *Thebaid* 4.128.

98 *a host of elm trees . . . shielded with their bending branches*: recalls Virgil's description of the elm tree at the entrance to the underworld at *Aeneid* 6.282–3.

98 *we wasted much time pursuing empty questions*: echoes Virgil, *Aeneid* 2.287 (the ghost of Hector ignores Aeneas' empty questions).

pre-eminent among the whole number: see Ovid, *Metamorphoses* 11.525.

and glared: echoes Virgil, *Aeneid* 9.794 (lion simile).

Sooner could clouds . . . in the fields: closely modelled on Lucretius 5.128–9 (see also Lucretius 3.784–5).

clasping his right hand . . . clinging to his left: echoes Pallas' reception of Aeneas at Virgil, *Aeneid* 8.124.

desire for . . . commendation: compare Virgil, *Aeneid* 5.138 (competitors in boat race) and 6.823 (Brutus).

99 *how many peoples, how many cities . . . as king*: recalls Virgil, *Aeneid* 7.236–8 (Trojan embassy to Latinus).

the sceptre, and the holy diadem: see Virgil, *Aeneid* 7.248.

it would result . . . with its winding rim: modelled on Virgil, *Aeneid* 8.147–9 (Aeneas warns Evander of the ambitions of his opponents).

to suffer all kinds of things: literally 'things deserved and undeserved'—see note on 4.663 above.

he freely offered himself: see Virgil, *Aeneid* 8.611.

he could have protected himself . . . the darkness of night: echoes Virgil, *Aeneid* 8.658 (the Gauls attack the Capitol under cover of darkness).

sacrificial entrails: echoes Virgil, *Aeneid* 8.183 (sacrificial banquet).

rites and sacred practices: see note on 1.952 (and 4.116) above.

the law-giving teacher: Moses.

they know—and they admit they know: evokes Virgil, *Aeneid* 12.794 (Jupiter to Juno; see also *Aeneid* 11.344).

the only one who: echoes Virgil, *Aeneid* 6.846 (Fabius Maximus, the unique saviour of Rome).

100 *thirst in the very midst . . . river's flow*: the suggestion of the infernal punishment of Tantalus perhaps points to the inevitable posthumous destination of these latter-day sinners.

the man's supreme virtue . . . completely unreceptive: echoes Virgil, *Aeneid* 4.3–4 (Dido's fixation with Aeneas) and 12.647 (divine disfavour).

radiated sweet love from his whole figure: see note on 3.963 above.

so much my love . . . with each passing hour: modelled on Virgil, *Eclogues* 10.73 (the poet's love for Gallus).

are bound to him by mighty bonds: compare Lucretius 4.1113 and 4.1204/1205 (on sexual union!), followed by Manilius 4.828.

wandering about everywhere: echoes Tibullus, *Elegies* 1.3.59 (birds in Elysium).

a crowded forest . . . in constant succession: closely modelled on Virgil, *Georgics* 2.17 (botanical profusion).

Just one man's head . . . one man (whoever he is): St John himself, according to tradition. The parenthetical expression of uncertainty injects a note of dramatic irony.

he bids us despise our possessions, share out our wealth: like Evander exhorting his guest Aeneas to despise wealth at Virgil, *Aeneid* 8.364. Vida alludes to the same passage in 'get used to deprivation' (line 829), which echoes *Aeneid* 8.365 (and for 'to endure poverty' in the same line, see Horace, *Odes* 3.2.1).

Not if a hundred tongues . . . in an iron breast: this treatment of a traditional epic motif is closely modelled on Virgil, *Aeneid* 6.625–7 (the Sibyl on the punishments of sinners in Tartarus).

the scarcity of food pressed upon us: echoes Virgil, *Aeneid* 7.113 (the Trojans hungrily consume their 'tables').

we constantly judged . . . equal to the wealth of kings: recalls Virgil, *Georgics* 4.132 (contentment of the old Corycian gardener).

101 *matrons and men . . . set on following him*: for 'matrons and men', see Virgil, *Aeneid* 2.797, note on 4.354 above, and 4.961 below. Line 846 combines elements from *Aeneid* 3.60 and 10.182.

a terrible yearning for possessions: echoes Virgil, *Aeneid* 8.327 (the decline of the Golden Age; see also Virgil, *Georgics* 4.177).

follow the camp: see Lucan 4.676 and (especially) 10.407.

And indeed I remember: see note on 4.598 above.

within a spear's throw: echoes Virgil, *Aeneid* 11.608 (battle manoeuvres).

whipped up . . . by the breath of the gusty winds: quotes Lucretius 6.428 (waterspouts).

had offered . . . to his tender lips: modelled on Virgil, *Aeneid* 11.572 (the infant Camilla is fed on mare's milk).

For he used to instruct the mortal race . . . trapped in darkness as they were: Vida polemically evokes Lucretius' condemnation of religion at 1.62–79, repurposing the Roman poet's praise of Epicurus' victory over religion to assert the superiority of the Christian religion to earth-bound materialism.

102 *cast aside puffed-up conceit*: recalls Virgil, *Aeneid* 11.346 (Drances on Turnus).

with no craving for . . . praise: see Virgil, *Aeneid* 5.751.

scorn mortal riches: see note on 4.826–7 above.

blessed with a little: see Virgil, *Aeneid* 9.607.

Your home here is not your true home . . . limbs from your soul: see note on 1.54–5 above. Lines 890–1 echo Virgil, *Aeneid* 4.385 (Dido threatens vengeance on Aeneas).

untroubled rest: evokes Virgil, *Georgics* 2.467 (praise of country life).

changeable chatter: an echo of Virgil, *Aeneid* 12.228 (Juturna spreads rumours).

102 *seek a beautiful death through their wounds*: compare Virgil, *Georgics* 4.218 (war among the bees) and *Aeneid* 11.647.

earthly limbs and mortal bodies: a clear allusion to Anchises' disquisition on the human condition at Virgil, *Aeneid* 6.732 (see note on 4.31 above).

the one whom the sea . . . its spreading plains: see notes on 1.1–2 and 4.36 above.

the clear expanse of the . . . heaven: see Statius, *Thebaid* 1.25, and 5.204 below.

103 *the race of spotted panthers*: modelled on Ovid, *Metamorphoses* 3.669. Christ is here instructing his followers not to fear being exposed to wild beasts in the arena.

lick your wounds with their tongues: a more reassuring modification of Virgil, *Aeneid* 10.560, where hungry fish are pictured devouring the dead.

put from your minds . . . anxieties: echoes Virgil, *Aeneid* 1.562 (Dido welcomes the Trojans).

leaves to the trees: a reminiscence of Horace, *Odes* 4.7.2 (the return of spring).

the varieties of wrongdoing: echoes Virgil, *Georgics* 1.506 (evils of civil war) and *Aeneid* 6.560 (sinners in the underworld).

don't allow your hearts to become accustomed: recalls Anchises' plea against civil war at Virgil, *Aeneid* 6.832.

If any traces of ancient fault remain: see note on 4.133 above.

mothers and men: see notes on 4.354 and 4.845–6 above.

104 *this is the way to the stars*: there may be a suggestion here of Virgil, *Aeneid* 9.641 (Apollo congratulates Ascanius/Iulus).

"Almighty Father . . . keep all dangers from us": a verse paraphrase of the Lord's Prayer ('Our Father . . . '). For 'your name and your praises' (line 973), see Virgil, *Aeneid* 1.609; and for 'the ages . . . begin to go forth' (line 974), see Virgil, *Eclogues* 4.12 ('promised to the world' may point towards the Christian interpretation of this Virgilian prophecy).

prophesying things to come: John goes on to foretell the events of the Last Judgement, which he himself was traditionally thought to have described in the Book of Revelation. The passage also recalls the picture of the Last Judgement in the medieval poem *Dies irae*, familiar from its liturgical use.

shrouded in a dense glow . . . extinguished in the starry night: these lines are closely based on two verses from Cicero's poem on his own consulship, quoted at Cicero, *De divinatione* 1.18.

upon the renewal . . . their bodies: echoes Lucretius 5.907 (polemically), and Virgil, *Aeneid* 6.306 (souls in the underworld).

the deepest recesses of heaven: see note on 4.43 above.

105 *the trumpet's curved bronze*: the line-ending echoes Lucan 1.431.

he will set apart the righteous: as in the underworld depicted on the shield of Aeneas at Virgil, *Aeneid* 8.670.

will be pressed down by . . . night everlasting: compare Virgil, *Aeneid* 6.827 (souls in the underworld).

envelop the truth in obscuring riddles: like the enigmatic oracles of the Sibyl at Virgil, *Aeneid* 6.98–100.

stood around . . . in great numbers: like the bees crowding round their 'king' at Virgil, *Georgics* 4.216.

the beginning and end of all things: an allusion to Christ's description of himself as 'Alpha and Omega, the beginning and the end' (Revelation 1:8, 21:6, 22:13).

the fount of truth and the light and the way for all people: see John 14:6, 'I am the way, the truth, and the life'.

an age will come . . . as the years glide past: closely modelled on Virgil, *Aeneid* 1.283 (prophecy of Jupiter).

106 *Such things . . . persevered in saying*: echoes Virgil, *Aeneid* 2.650 (obstinacy of Anchises).

BOOK FIVE

107 *the Roman . . . to spare him*: the juxtaposition of 'Roman' and 'to spare' may recall Anchises' formulation of the mission of Rome at Virgil, *Aeneid* 6.851–3 as 'to spare the conquered, and war down the proud'.

casting his mind around in all directions: see Virgil, *Aeneid* 4.285 and 8.20.

The man's renown . . . from the gods: the clear echoes of Dido's infatuation with Aeneas at Virgil, *Aeneid* 4.3–4 (note the line numbers within the book) and 4.12, and the emphatic repetition of the element *vir-* (man) in *viri virtusque*, imply a homoerotic motive for Pilate's interest. See note on 2.980 above.

filling . . . with their uproar: modelled on Virgil, *Aeneid* 2.679 (complaint of Creusa; see also *Aeneid* 7.502).

No rest came to his mind: echoes Valerius Flaccus, *Argonautica* 7.244 (Medea).

avenging Furies: see Virgil, *Aeneid* 4.610 (Dido's curse).

for his valuable service: the expression is modelled on Virgil, *Aeneid* 5.537.

the deadly reward for my crimes: the similarly treacherous wooden horse is described as 'the deadly gift' of Minerva at Virgil, *Aeneid* 2.31.

Oh, what was I after: compare Corydon's lament at Virgil, *Eclogues* 2.58.

the true offspring . . . the true God: see note on 1.237 above.

The darkness is scattered . . . restored to me: see Virgil, *Aeneid* 12.669.

blinded by frenzy: like the doomed Trojans at Virgil, *Aeneid* 2.244 (see note on 4.75 above).

107 *his mental torment . . . vault of heaven*: evokes Dido's frenzy at Virgil, *Aeneid* 4.531–2 and 4.451.

108 *turning . . . this way and that*: like the Fury Allecto at Virgil, *Aeneid* 7.448–9. See also Virgil, *Georgics* 3.433, and 2.262 above.

Ah, what shall I do: see Virgil, *Aeneid* 4.534 (Dido: the following line in Virgil is echoed in line 36, 'Shall I go back again as a suppliant').

terrifies . . . with his thunderbolt: like Jupiter at Virgil, *Aeneid* 1.230.

mighty earth . . . receive me: recalls Virgil, *Aeneid* 4.24 (Dido), 10.675–6 (Turnus), and 12.883–4 (Juturna), though the wording quotes an unattributed phrase cited by Quintilian, *Institutio oratoria* 9.2.26.

Now your sinful crimes . . . were fitting: a clear reminiscence of the suicidal Dido's regrets at Virgil, *Aeneid* 4.596–7.

to break the thread of his loathsome life: modelled on Dido's resolve to end her life at Virgil, *Aeneid* 4.631.

bring his cruel pain to an end: see Juturna at Virgil, *Aeneid* 12.880.

thick night . . . in shadow: echoes Virgil, *Aeneid* 2.360 (the fall of Troy) and 6.866 (the doomed Marcellus).

Everything . . . blackening gloom: closely resembles a line of Furius Antias preserved in Aulus Gellius, *Noctes Atticae* 18.11.4. See also Virgil, *Aeneid* 11.824.

the king of angels is swayed by prayers: an implied riposte to the Sibyl's declaration of divine implacability at Virgil, *Aeneid* 6.376.

persisting in . . . that same position: like the obstinate Anchises at Virgil, *Aeneid* 2.654.

109 *the hiding place of his soul*: for the expression, see Virgil, *Aeneid* 10.601.

tying a horrid loop . . . to a bending tree: echoes Virgil, *Aeneid* 12.603 (suicide of Amata).

he shut off the airways of his breath: the deliberately harsh line recalls Virgil, *Aeneid* 9.580, where a warrior is killed by an arrow.

it was not permitted . . . a tainted doorstep: modelled on Virgil, *Aeneid* 6.563 (Tartarus).

with a crowd . . . close round him: see notes on 3.184 and 3.780 above (another parallel between Pilate and Dido: see note on 5.3–4 above).

The moment I saw . . . I was astounded: the parallel with Virgil, *Eclogues* 8.41 again suggests that Pilate's reaction to Christ goes beyond disinterested respect (see note on 5.3–4 above).

emit no mortal utterance . . . surely a god: see Virgil, *Aeneid* 1.328.

the surest offspring of a god: an adaptation of Virgil, *Aeneid* 6.322 to monotheistic sensibilities (already effected by Juvencus, as Gardner notes).

resentment flared up . . . beyond all measure: modelled on Virgil, *Aeneid* 5.172 (see also 9.66, and note on 2.952 above).

Then the elderly Annas: a high priest, father-in-law of Caiaphas. The phrasing recalls the introduction to Drances' speech at Virgil, *Aeneid* 11.336, and the beginning of that Virgilian speech (11.343–4) is recalled in the opening lines of Annas' speech here.

110 *Don't you see . . . this new religion*: Annas adopts a characteristically Lucretian phrase (*nonne vides*) to cast suspicion on Christ's new religion, just as the Epicurean poet had attacked the evils of religion—but paradoxically Annas' complaint is that Christ frees people from the fear of death, a major aim also of Lucretius.

Gaining influence through sedition: echoes Virgil, *Aeneid* 11.340 (of Drances).

whom the very stars obey: see note on 3.777 above.

has established . . . feigned divinity: combines elements from Virgil, *Aeneid* 6.622 (corrupt legislator) and 7.385 (feigned divinity).

he threatens . . . to the flames: closely modelled on Virgil, *Aeneid* 12.654–5 (hostile advance of Aeneas). For the alleged threat, see 2.229–31 above.

draw down the stars by his words: an allegation of sorcery (see e.g. Propertius 1.1.19–24 and Horace, *Epodes* 5.45–6).

are enthralled by sumptuous banquets: echoes a line of the satirist Lucilius (20.604 in Loeb edn.) preserved by the grammarian Nonius.

and defile everything with their touch: like the Harpies at Virgil, *Aeneid* 3.227.

Obviously . . . change his mind!: recalls Dido's sarcasm at Virgil, *Aeneid* 4.379–80 (and for 'change his mind', see *Aeneid* 1.237 and 1.260).

111 *Keep . . . the holy altars*: a clear echo of Virgil, *Aeneid* 1.525 (the Trojans appeal to Dido). The reader's knowledge of the later destruction of the temple of Jerusalem by the Romans lends the appeal an ironic undertone.

while Christ's glory . . . with bitter goads: echoes Drances' envy of Turnus at Virgil, *Aeneid* 11.336–7.

as you are fully aware: perhaps points to the echo of 2.225–8 above.

the violence flared up among them all: like Turnus' mounting fury at Virgil, *Aeneid* 12.9.

the Adige or the Po: rivers in northern Italy, mentioned together at Virgil, *Aeneid* 9.680. The Po flows through Vida's native Cremona: see note on 1.25 above. This river simile recalls *Aeneid* 2.496–9.

the king and scion of kings, Herod: Herod Antipas, the tetrarch, son of Herod the Great.

112 *possessed as he was . . . at close quarters*: echoes Evander's youthful enthusiasm to meet Anchises at Virgil, *Aeneid* 8.163–4.

kept his eyes resolutely fixed: like Dido at Virgil, *Aeneid* 6.469, and Pallas Athena at *Aeneid* 1.482.

I shudder to recall: may recall the narrator Aeneas' report of the snakes sent to attack Laocoon at Virgil, *Aeneid* 2.204.

112 *the sea, the land, and . . . boundless heaven*: see notes on 1.1–2 and 4.921–2 above.

everything starts to grow dark: see note on 5.64 above.

the sun hide . . . in pitch-black gloom: compare Virgil, *Georgics* 1.467, on the reaction of the sun to the death of Julius Caesar.

true offspring of God and true God: see 5.25–6 and note on 1.237 above.

It was we: i.e. humanity, represented by Adam and Eve. The tree of life in Eden was traditionally connected with the wood of the cross in typological exegesis.

you who pitied . . . too much: see Prudentius, *Psychomachia* 1, itself modelled on Virgil, *Aeneid* 6.56.

113 *was beaten and battered . . . waves of care*: for the striking onomatopoeia, compare Catullus 11.4 and Tibullus, *Elegies* 2.4.10.

The more . . . their inflamed hearts: modelled on Virgil, *Aeneid* 7.787–8.

empty superstition: echoes and reverses Virgil, *Aeneid* 8.187 (Evander's rites for Hercules).

broke him off mid-speech: modelled on Virgil, *Aeneid* 4.388 (Dido terminates her exchange with Aeneas).

unsurpassed by any in . . . his wickedness: an echo with reversal of Virgil, *Aeneid* 1.544–5 (Aeneas unsurpassed in justice and righteousness).

no hope at all of escape: compare Virgil, *Aeneid* 9.131, and Lucan 10.538–9.

blinded by frenzy: see notes on 4.75 and 5.30 above.

with all the force they could muster: modelled on Virgil, *Aeneid* 9.532 and 12.552.

his . . . enemy will pity him: echoes Virgil, *Aeneid* 2.645 (Anchises).

114 *for a linen garment . . . with its white fabric*: recalls the description of the clothing of the river god Tiberinus at Virgil, *Aeneid* 8.33–4.

its horns blunted: compare Virgil, *Georgics* 1.433 (weather signs).

satisfy with his blood the penalty: echoes Virgil, *Aeneid* 7.766 (Hippolytus).

their hearts were fuelled more and more: see note on 5.231–3 above.

in their bitter hatred . . . the ultimate punishment: like the Trojans calling for punishment for Sinon at Virgil, *Aeneid* 2.71–2.

All vied . . . to rage: like the Rutulians at Virgil, *Aeneid* 7.472.

insubstantial souls . . . without a body: echoes Virgil, *Aeneid* 6.292 (apparitions in the underworld). See 5.540 below.

that white lamb: for Christ as the Lamb of God, see note on 4.232 above.

seemed . . . to come rushing down on all sides: compare Virgil, *Aeneid* 8.525 (portentous thunderbolt signalling Aeneas' destiny).

rough hail: see Virgil, *Georgics* 1.449.

Spare the god, Roman: once again, the combination of 'spare' (repeated in the following lines) and 'Roman' recalls the statement of Rome's mission at Virgil, *Aeneid* 6.851–3—see note on 5.1–2 above.

I really believe . . . from the gods: closely modelled on Virgil, *Aeneid* 4.12 (Dido's admiration for Aeneas); see also 5.4 above.

Refrain from staining . . . refrain from: see Virgil, *Aeneid* 3.41–2.

the descendant of Romulus: Pilate, the Roman—see note on 2.246 above.

to resist their . . . frenzy: see Virgil, *Aeneid* 4.91 (Dido's capitulation to love).

115 *the awful ruler of the shades*: Satan. On Erebus, see note on 2.694 above.

as he nursed . . . in his fixated heart: like the resentful Juno at Virgil, *Aeneid* 1.36.

a dark, hulking, inescapable monster: compare the Virgilian monsters Polyphemus (*Aeneid* 3.658) and Rumour (Fama) (*Aeneid* 4.181). Vida's Fear has more in common, however, with the Dira sent by Jupiter at *Aeneid* 12.845–68 to disorientate Turnus.

fitting itself out . . . a dark body: echoes Ovid, *Metamorphoses* 8.209 (Daedalus fits out Icarus with wings; see also 5.544 below), and Virgil, *Aeneid* 12.862 (Dira: see note on 5.310 above).

this revolting fowl . . . made a noise: these lines strongly evoke Virgil's description of the Dira (see note on 5.310 above) at *Aeneid* 12.876 and 12.866.

his hair stood on end . . . stuck in his throat: combines a number of Virgilian passages describing reactions of horror. See *Aeneid* 2.774 and 4.280 (Aeneas), 12.868 and 12.905 (Turnus).

they seized the moment: like Turnus at Virgil, *Aeneid* 11.459.

gaining influence through sedition: see note on 5.115 above.

116 *Such was their persistent roar*: see note on 4.1042–3 above.

an intractable race: echoes Virgil, *Aeneid* 1.339 (the Libyans).

the hidden contagion . . . his heart: compare the snake thrust into Amata by Allecto at Virgil, *Aeneid* 7.347.

a beaked trireme: an ancient warship with three banks of oars.

he changes course . . . fortune calls: modelled on Virgil, *Aeneid* 5.22–3, in an identical context of sailing in a storm.

did not . . . spare his voice: a clear echo of Virgil, *Aeneid* 2.534 (indignation of Priam).

your rage . . . a step back: echoes Virgil, *Aeneid* 11.413 (of Fortune).

There's no delay on my part: see note on 1.689 above.

condemned on a false charge: see Virgil, *Aeneid* 6.430.

A sorry punishment . . . impious blood: closely modelled on Latinus' rueful prediction to Turnus and his supporters at Virgil, *Aeneid* 7.595–7, when similarly overpowered.

116 *no wrongdoing . . . in this bloodshed*: echoes Virgil, *Aeneid* 10.901 (Mezentius).

in front of the entrance: echoes Virgil, *Aeneid* 2.469 (Priam's palace) and 6.556 (underworld).

mocked the prisoner: like the Trojans taunting the captive Sinon at Virgil, *Aeneid* 2.64.

In place of a golden band: modelled on Virgil, *Aeneid* 11.576 (Camilla's wild clothing).

his fair temples: this detail is perhaps unexpected; it may serve to suggest Christ's heroic character (see e.g. Homer, *Iliad* 1.197).

a reed from the river: compare Virgil, *Georgics* 2.414.

at the open gates: echoes Virgil, *Aeneid* 2.330 (the Greeks enter Troy).

117 *shouting goes up to heaven*: modelled on Virgil, *Aeneid* 12.409 (the clamour of battle).

they covered . . . with a blindfold of cloth: an adaptation of Virgil, *Aeneid* 11.66 (bier of Pallas).

his beard, stiffened with blood: compare Virgil, *Aeneid* 2.277 (the ghost of Hector), and Ovid, *Metamorphoses* 12.270 and 14.201.

defiled his . . . body with dirt: like Mezentius' self-disfigurement at Virgil, *Aeneid* 10.844.

There was no pause, no respite: see note on 2.140 above.

The woods do not lack . . . exhausted in death: Vida here elaborates on Matthew 8:20 and Luke 9:58.

the axe resounded . . . into the wood: compare Virgilian descriptions of tree-felling at *Aeneid* 6.180 and 11.135–6.

a form of torture: echoes Virgil, *Aeneid* 8.487 (tortures employed by the tyrant Mezentius).

a harrowing death . . . protracted agony: recalls the death of Dido at Virgil, *Aeneid* 4.693–4.

At that time . . . no honour or glory: modelled on Virgil, *Aeneid* 12.135 (the Alban hill).

venerable wood: echoes Virgil, *Aeneid* 12.767.

We who were born . . . with joy: a clear reminiscence of Virgil, *Aeneid* 8.268–9 (rites at the Ara Maxima); see also *Aeneid* 1.49.

and illuminate the whole world with its light: adapts a line from Cicero's poem on his own consulship, quoted in *De divinatione* 1.17.

when a single day gives . . . to destruction: modelled on Lucretius 5.95, later evoked by Ovid at *Amores* 1.15.24.

118 *from all sides . . . to witness the spectacle*: closely recalls the Trojans' reaction to the captive Sinon at Virgil, *Aeneid* 2.63–4.

every spot was seething: may evoke Virgil, *Aeneid* 4.407 (bustling preparations for Aeneas' departure).

with his hands bound . . . with an uproar: another echo of the Sinon episode—see Virgil, *Aeneid* 2.57–8, and note on 5.420–1 above. The same lines had already been adapted by Juvencus (4.588–9).

ranks fitted with shields . . . beside him: echoes Virgil, *Aeneid* 7.793–4 (Turnus' forces).

bronze bugles blared with answering blasts: this alliterative line is a close adaptation of Virgil, *Aeneid* 7.615.

Some followed on foot: see Virgil, *Aeneid* 7.624.

hills rang with their rumpus: like the clamour of spectators at the boat race at Virgil, *Aeneid* 5.150.

whose judgement was better: see note on 2.153 above.

the remuneration due: the expression has something of the bitterness of Priam's words to Pyrrhus at Virgil, *Aeneid* 2.537–8.

with faltering steps: echoes Ascanius/Iulus following Aeneas 'with unequal steps' at Virgil, *Aeneid* 2.724.

at so crucial a moment: recalls Virgil, *Aeneid* 1.672 (the pivotal moment of Aeneas' arrival in Carthage).

to see . . . the cruel death of: see Virgil, *Aeneid* 12.636.

a spectator of his own self: because Father and Son are united in the same Trinitarian being.

rising . . . in nine tiers: the language recalls Dido's temple of Juno at Virgil, *Aeneid* 1.448. The nine tiers correspond to the nine celestial orders: Seraphim, Cherubim, Thrones, Dominions, Virtues, Powers, Principalities, Archangels, and Angels.

119 *circling . . . with a ring*: modelled on Virgil, *Aeneid* 10.122 and 11.475.

his whole being resplendent with light: echoes Virgil, *Aeneid* 10.539 (a priest).

he fixed his eyes . . . lands of Judaea: like Jupiter looking down on Carthage at Virgil, *Aeneid* 1.226.

white with human bones: like the rocks of the Sirens at Virgil, *Aeneid* 5.865, and the plains of Latium at *Aeneid* 12.36. The description probably alludes to the name of the hill, Golgotha (the place of the skull).

dead bodies . . . with sun-baked corruption: compare Virgil, *Aeneid* 8.197 (remains of Mezentius' victims).

surveying everything: quotes Virgil, *Aeneid* 3.651 (Achaemenides looks for rescue).

A loyal supporter . . . gleam of weapons: see Virgil, *Aeneid* 1.184 (Aeneas looks for the remainder of his fleet) and 11.602 (plains ablaze with weapons).

119 *the sheep are dispersed . . . in every direction*: see Matthew 26:31 and Mark 14:27, quoting Zechariah 13:7. Vida's simile signals the fulfilment of Christ's prophecy.

divided his wavering thoughts: see note on 5.1–2 above.

he recalled . . . looking up to the sky: echoes Virgil, *Aeneid* 10.781–2 (a dying warrior recalls his homeland).

120 *Oh why . . . care for your son*: combines elements from Virgil, *Aeneid* 3.710–11 and 2.595 to elaborate on one of the Seven Last Words of Christ (Matthew 27:46, Mark 15:34).

That supreme Father . . . heard them, too: modelled on the reaction to Allecto's infernal trumpet-call at Virgil, *Aeneid* 7.516–17.

But no force could hold back: closely recalls the grief of Evander at Virgil, *Aeneid* 11.148.

anguish flared up in all of them: see note on 2.952 above.

War is what they incited . . . arms!: echoes Virgil, *Aeneid* 1.541 (see also *Aeneid* 11.453).

unsurpassed in his skill . . . the trumpet: like the trumpeter Misenus at Virgil, *Aeneid* 6.164–5.

rose . . . in . . . flight: see Virgil, *Aeneid* 2.303.

just like doves . . . hollow towers: Vida's simile recalls the short dove simile at Virgil, *Aeneid* 2.516. For the description of the storm in lines 529–31, see *Aeneid* 4.160–1; and for the doves' flight and concealment, compare *Aeneid* 12.892–3.

the horror . . . was piling up: echoes Virgil, *Aeneid* 2.301 (the sack of Troy).

121 *insubstantial souls . . . without a body*: see note on 5.279 above.

possessing a nature far removed from our senses: see Lucretius 5.148–9 (echoed polemically by Vida here).

fits himself out with . . . wings: see note on 5.319–20 above.

fitting on . . . for his use: see Virgil, *Aeneid* 12.88.

they wrap . . . in a raging whirlwind: like the nymph Opis at Virgil, *Aeneid* 11.596.

around . . . the unaccustomed arms: echoes Priam's futile arming at Virgil, *Aeneid* 2.509–10.

taken down from . . . portal: see Virgil, *Aeneid* 5.360.

memorials of that unspeakable war: modelled on Virgil, *Aeneid* 6.26 (the Minotaur).

brandishes a beam-like spear: modelled on Statius, *Thebaid* 4.6–7.

a scabbard of ivory: echoes Virgil, *Aeneid* 9.305.

Some drive chariots: compare Virgil, *Aeneid* 12.287 (war between Latins and Trojans).

They thrive on . . . means of movement: echoes Virgil's description of Rumour (Fama) at *Aeneid* 4.175.

with saffron yellow: compare Virgil, *Eclogues* 4.44 (spontaneously colour-changing sheep).

And now . . . expanse of the air: modelled on Virgil, *Aeneid* 9.25 (advance of the Italian forces). The adjective here translated as 'winged' (*pennipotens*) is used of birds by Lucretius at 2.878.

thrice three . . . commanders: see note on 5.460 above.

that mighty warrior . . . in Apulia: St Michael, to whom an ancient shrine was dedicated on Monte Gargano. For Michael's victory over the dragon (Satan), see Revelation 12:7–10. For 'overtopping all by a whole head' (line 578), see Virgil, *Aeneid* 7.784, 9.29, and 11.683 (and 1.147 above).

122 *he made his way exultant*: like Salmoneus at Virgil, *Aeneid* 6.589.

the golden boss . . . sparkling jasper: closely modelled on Virgil, *Aeneid* 10.271 (the shield of Aeneas) and 4.261–2 (jasper sword).

an incalculable sin!: like those of sinners in the underworld at Virgil, *Aeneid* 6.624.

puffed up with vanity: echoes Virgil, *Aeneid* 11.854 (the warrior Arruns).

the handiwork of craftsmen: recalls the temple of Juno at Virgil, *Aeneid* 1.455.

There could be seen: see note on 1.609 above.

battalions here, battalions there: see Virgil, *Aeneid* 9.550.

joining battle . . . at close quarters: for the expression, compare Virgil, *Aeneid* 12.890.

like a . . . storm cloud or blustering South Winds: combines elements from Virgil, *Aeneid* 5.317 and 1.536.

with pursuing flames: echoes Virgil, *Aeneid* 8.432 (thunderbolts fashioned by the Cyclopes).

the dark dwelling of Erebus: 'the dark dwelling' recalls the cave of Cacus at Virgil, *Aeneid* 8.262, and on Erebus, see note on 2.694 above.

would have atoned for your crimes: compare Neptune's threat to the winds at Virgil, *Aeneid* 1.136.

123 *had not . . . all at once*: an almost exact quotation from Cicero's poem on his own consulship (preserved in Cicero, *De divinatione* 1.19 and 2.45) is here followed by a close adaptation of Virgil, *Aeneid* 11.225.

unruly warfare: echoes Virgil, *Aeneid* 11.305 (the war in Italy).

severe commands: see Virgil, *Aeneid* 9.804 and *Georgics* 3.41.

dare to throw . . . by their passions: once again closely echoes Neptune's reproach to the winds at Virgil, *Aeneid* 1.133–4 (see note on 5.620 above). In line 635, 'igniting such commotion' may evoke Maffeo Vegio's *Supplement* to the *Aeneid*, line 35.

123 *Let them settle down*: see Virgil, *Aeneid* 11.323.

broadcast . . . rage: modelled on Virgil, *Aeneid* 3.366 (of Celaeno's prophecy).

Hope and Faith and . . . Love: St Paul's triad Faith, Hope, and Love (or Charity: 1 Corinthians 13:13).

he produced a fearsome sound: imitation with reversal (here war is being averted) of Virgil, *Aeneid* 9.503–4.

What madness . . . against my prohibition?: echoes Jupiter's question to the gods at Virgil, *Aeneid* 10.9.

Where are you rushing?: see Virgil, *Aeneid* 12.313 and Horace, *Epodes* 7.1.

lay aside this anxiety: recalls Virgil, *Aeneid* 12.48–9 (Turnus to Latinus).

without my authorization: see note on 3.279 above.

eradicate the collective guilt of humanity: see note on 2.756 above.

I willed . . . harsh labours: echoes and reverses Virgil, *Aeneid* 8.378 (Venus to Vulcan).

spend his life . . . enduring every extremity: see Virgil, *Aeneid* 3.315.

124 *the end has been reached . . . his innocence*: combines elements from Virgil, *Aeneid* 12.803 (see note on 1.38 above) and 10.630.

he shudders at the sudden sight: see note on 4.415 above.

has snatched away his disordered wits: see Virgil, *Aeneid* 2.736.

if my intention were reversed: modelled on Virgil, *Aeneid* 10.6–7.

This was not how Babylon . . . by the thunderbolt: the biblical episode of the tower of Babel (Genesis 11:1–9) is here expressed in language evoking gigantomachy (see Virgil, *Aeneid* 6.580–4). For 'This was not how . . . experienced me', see *Aeneid* 11.396.

I could stir up all heaven: echoes Virgil, *Aeneid* 4.122 (Juno).

the three-pointed spear: i.e. the thunderbolt.

a time will come . . . at a high price: modelled on Virgil, *Aeneid* 10.503–4 (Turnus will come to regret killing Pallas). For the Roman sack of Jerusalem, see note on 5.151 above.

shaking . . . with a terrifying thunderclap: a close adaptation of Lucretius 6.388.

attended him with . . . prayers: compare Virgil, *Aeneid* 9.310.

on the empty ground of a field: echoes Virgil, *Aeneid* 12.710 (single combat of Aeneas and Turnus).

125 *his loyal friends . . . their enthusiasm*: combines elements from Virgil, *Aeneid* 5.450 and 5.468 (both from the boxing match in Book 5).

A copious stream . . . the trunk: recalls Virgil, *Aeneid* 3.43 (Polydorus).

the echo . . . reverberated: compare Virgil, *Georgics* 4.50 (echo).

a range of different characters: Hebrew, Greek, and Latin, according to John 19:19–20.

more abominable . . . in his misdeeds: closely modelled on Virgil, *Aeneid* 1.347 (Dido's brother Pygmalion).

He it was . . . far off: for these episodes in the history of the Jewish people, see notes on 2.282, 4.374, and 4.711–12 above. This series of reproaches recalls the Improperia, a set of responses which form part of the liturgy for Good Friday.

He it was . . . set far behind: echoes Virgil, *Aeneid* 1.15–16 (Juno's preference for Carthage).

126 *what . . . confidence remained in the one defeated*: recalls Virgil, *Aeneid* 2.75 (the captive Sinon).

his teeth . . . with bleeding: echoes Virgil, *Aeneid* 5.470 (the beaten boxer Dares).

Just like Lucifer . . . in the deep-blue wave: modelled on the simile at Virgil, *Aeneid* 8.589.

The house echoed with . . . lamentation: modelled on Virgil, *Aeneid* 12.607 (death of Amata).

as she . . . groaned bitterly: see Ovid, *Heroides* 8.107.

grasping . . . with her ears: like the helmsman Palinurus at Virgil, *Aeneid* 3.514.

she roams . . . the whole wood: recalls the deer simile at Virgil, *Aeneid* 4.72.

127 *with her cloven hooves*: for the expression, see Ovid, *Metamorphoses* 7.113.

she rushed past . . . in her way: like Anna on hearing of her sister Dido's death at Virgil, *Aeneid* 4.674.

pitying her from afar as she went: like Aeneas pitying Dido in the underworld at Virgil, *Aeneid* 6.476.

despite . . . of swift horses: echoes Virgil, *Aeneid* 12.533–4.

the ailing wife of Cleophas: Mary, the wife of Cleophas (or Clopas), is mentioned at John 19:25. Martha's sister is Mary Magdalene traditionally in Western Christianity.

beating her worthy breast . . . with her hand: closely echoes Virgil, *Aeneid* 12.155 (Juturna).

that massive frame, that strange contraption: the description may be intended to evoke the Trojan horse—see Virgil, *Aeneid* 2.150–1 (and 2.46, 2.237).

I know . . . surrounds us: modelled on Virgil, *Aeneid* 10.904–5 (hostility to Mezentius).

the sign . . . in the house: for this feature of the Passover, see Exodus 12:3–13.

And now . . . grew clearer and clearer: echoes Virgil, *Aeneid* 2.299–301 (fall of Troy).

was now . . . clutches of death: echoes Virgil, *Aeneid* 2.533 (Priam).

127 *his bedraggled beard . . . spoiled with blood*: recalls the ghost of Hector at Virgil, *Aeneid* 2.277.

128 *pitied . . . boundless grief*: echoes Juno's pity for Dido at Virgil, *Aeneid* 4.693.

returned her sweet love: like Sychaeus returning Dido's love in the underworld at Virgil, *Aeneid* 6.473–4.

dispelling . . . with his words: echoes Virgil, *Aeneid* 4.394 (Aeneas and Dido).

But let so great a grief . . . in your affliction: closely modelled on Virgil, *Aeneid* 12.801 (Jupiter to Juno).

It is not without . . . will: see Virgil, *Aeneid* 5.56.

This woman will be . . . mother: see Virgil, *Aeneid* 9.297 (Iulus takes responsibility for Euryalus' mother).

preserve the love of our shared mother: clearly recalls Creusa's charge to Aeneas at Virgil, *Aeneid* 2.789.

as she wept uncontrollably: like Evander bidding his son farewell at Virgil, *Aeneid* 8.559.

What sort of a return . . . my son: recalls the lament of Euryalus' mother at Virgil, *Aeneid* 9.491–2.

Did the thought of my love: modelled on Virgil, *Aeneid* 4.307 (Dido to Aeneas).

what sight of you meets my eyes, my son: another echo of the lament of Euryalus' mother (see note on 5.850–1 above), this time at *Aeneid* 9.481.

depraved madness: echoes Virgil, *Aeneid* 7.461 (Turnus, possessed by Allecto).

how changed . . . from that son of mine: clearly evokes Aeneas' description of the ghost of Hector at Virgil, *Aeneid* 2.274.

through the jubilant city: the slight echo of the jubilation in Troy at Virgil, *Aeneid* 2.249 insinuates a comparable ironic contrast between the joy of the moment, now viewed with hindsight, and the impending disaster.

129 *these were not the promises*: modelled on Aeneas' regrets over the death of Pallas at Virgil, *Aeneid* 11.45–6.

Is this how . . . proceed as queen of heaven: ironically echoes Gabriel's salutation from 3.331–3 above (see also 4.483), as well as Juno at Virgil, *Aeneid* 1.46.

this my . . . honour: see Venus at *Aeneid* 1.253.

if that was the fate . . . dragging out my life: compare Virgil, *Aeneid* 11.165–6 and 2.92.

the old man bade me expect: Simeon, at 3.722–3 above.

now the wound has been driven in deep: quotes Virgil, *Aeneid* 10.850 (Mezentius' lament for his son Lausus).

cast your eyes . . . greater than mine: an elaboration of Lamentations 1:12, incorporated in the liturgy for Holy Saturday and often set to music as *O vos omnes*.

if you have any consideration . . . nail me to the tree: yet another clear echo of Euryalus' mother (see notes on 5.850–1 and 5.855 above), at *Aeneid* 9.493.

come to the aid of a mournful mother: echoes Ovid, *Fasti* 6.517.

that fashioner of falsehoods: applied to Ulysses at Virgil, *Aeneid* 9.602.

Go on, then . . . divinity: echoes Dido (sarcastically) to Aeneas at Virgil, *Aeneid* 4.381, and Helenus (unsarcastically) to Aeneas at *Aeneid* 3.437.

130 *break all his bonds*: compare Virgil, *Aeneid* 12.30 (Latinus, metaphorically).

More mercifully than was strictly fair: echoes Lucretius 3.313 (human faults).

ignorant . . . and blinded by frenzy: see notes on 4.110, 4.75, and 5.30 above.

built by men's hard toil: modelled on Lucretius 1.728 (on Sicily).

Unhappy man . . . on your mind?: echoes Virgil, *Aeneid* 5.465 (the defeated boxer Dares).

paying the penalty for our sins: compare Virgil, *Aeneid* 10.32.

be with me: for similar prayers, see Virgil, *Aeneid* 4.578–9 and 8.78.

You will have . . . along with me: closely modelled on a line from Book 3 of Lucilius' *Satires* (Loeb edn., fr. 94), preserved by the grammarian Nonius.

All over his body ran . . . sweat: compare Virgil, *Aeneid* 2.173–4, 3.175, 7.459, and 9.812.

his eyes . . . weighed down by death: echoes Ovid, *Metamorphoses* 4.145 (death of Pyramus).

131 *a cup of . . . wine*: echoes Virgil, *Aeneid* 3.354, but here perverted into a travesty of normal epic practices.

steeped in . . . poison: see Virgil, *Aeneid* 2.221 (Laocoon).

he took just the merest sip of it: recalls Virgil, *Aeneid* 1.737 (Dido).

the tunic . . . woven for her son: echoes Virgil, *Aeneid* 10.818 (death of Lausus).

it was loot they were after: see Virgil, *Aeneid* 2.646 (Greeks plundering Troy).

the holy prophets . . . would happen: see Psalms 22:18.

night . . . brooded over the whole earth: perhaps suggested by Virgil, *Aeneid* 1.89.

stealing sight from . . . eyes: quotes Virgil, *Aeneid* 8.254 (Cacus' blinding smoke).

he did give out signs . . . in sympathy: clearly recalls Virgil, *Aeneid* 4.167 (ill-omened union of Dido and Aeneas).

rumblings rolled through the . . . heaven: echoes Lucretius 5.1221/6.287–8, and the Lucretian tone is maintained in the following line with 'the walls of the . . . universe' (see Lucretius 1.73, etc.).

The cause lay hidden: quotes Virgil, *Aeneid* 5.5 (flames from Carthage).

seeing the sky shrouded in shadow: modelled on Virgil, *Aeneid* 12.407–8.

panic . . . laid low the trembling wits: echoes Virgil, *Georgics* 1.330–1 (thunderbolts), also suggested by 'low-lying peoples' in line 975 above.

131 *On all sides shouting rose to heaven*: see Virgil, *Aeneid* 9.566–7, 11.745, and 12.462.

matrons . . . all together: combines elements from Virgil, *Aeneid* 2.766, 5.553, and 2.238/6.307 (see also 1.452 above).

at all the altars they prayed for peace: see Virgil, *Aeneid* 4.56–7.

132 *altars smoked with . . . offerings*: see Lucretius 4.1237.

was rent in two: the language recalls Virgil, *Aeneid* 6.540 (route through the underworld), perhaps implying a crucial juncture in the posthumous fate of humanity.

and laying down . . . his final breath: for a detailed analysis of this line, see Introduction.

BOOK SIX

133 *unburied and unlamented on that white hill*: for the expression, compare Virgil, *Aeneid* 11.372. The description of the hill once again recalls the meaning of the name Golgotha: see note on 5.477 above (and in fact the word translated here as 'hill' can also mean 'head').

of outstanding spirit . . . wealthy in land: combines elements from Virgil, *Aeneid* 11.417, 9.201, and 1.343/10.563.

scattered . . . in ignominious terror: echoes Virgil, *Aeneid* 2.399–401 (cowardly behaviour of Greeks at Troy).

in the confidence of youth: like the boxer Dares at Virgil, *Aeneid* 5.430.

sons of Romulus: see note on 2.246 above.

went . . . with all your might: recalls Aeneas and Turnus in battle at Virgil, *Aeneid* 12.528.

by treacherous betrayal: like Palamedes (according to Sinon) at Virgil, *Aeneid* 2.83.

allow . . . to be placed in earth: echoes Virgil, *Aeneid* 11.102–3 (burial of the dead).

How I'd now prefer . . . to you alive!: recalls Virgil, *Aeneid* 11.111 (Aeneas grants a truce for burial).

powers conscious of the truth: see Virgil, *Aeneid* 2.141.

We too revere . . . our household gods: modelled on Columella, *De re rustica* 10.279.

Go, then . . . with the final offerings: clearly evokes Virgil, *Aeneid* 11.24–6 (Aeneas orders last rites for the dead).

greatly stricken . . . his dear friend: echoes Virgil, *Aeneid* 5.869 (Aeneas' reaction to the loss of Palinurus).

planting their footsteps . . . from the hill: closely modelled on Virgil, *Aeneid* 6.159 and 8.604–5.

134 *with armed soldiery*: compare Virgil, *Aeneid* 2.20 and 11.516.

they were longing . . . with tearful cries: line 45 is an almost exact repetition of 3.692 above (see also 5.56). For 'were filling . . . with tearful cries' (line 46), see Virgil, *Aeneid* 11.274.

deposited them in . . . earth: echoes Virgil, *Aeneid* 11.204–5 (burial of the Latin dead).

that his frame . . . pale even then: combines elements from Virgil, *Aeneid* 4.391 (see also 9.708) and 10.822, *Georgics* 1.477, and Lucretius 1.123.

Some people . . . regions of the air: the motif is a frequent one in depictions of the Crucifixion in medieval art.

struck . . . fir-wood shaft: echoes Virgil, *Aeneid* 11.667 (see also 2.16).

the spear drank up the holy blood: compare Virgil, *Aeneid* 11.803–4 (death of Camilla).

Into their midst . . . made his way: Vida has altered the biblical chronology, which placed the events on Golgotha before Joseph's request to Pilate.

covering it with a robe: echoes Virgil, *Aeneid* 9.488 (non-funeral of Euryalus).

hasten your steps: recalls the invocation to rural deities at Virgil, *Georgics* 1.11.

Scatter . . . hyacinths: 'pale violet' and 'full baskets' echo Virgil, *Eclogues* 2.45–7. For 'narcissus tresses', compare Columella, *De re rustica* 10.98, and for the sentiment of the passage as a whole, compare Virgil, *Aeneid* 6.883–4 (mourning for Marcellus).

135 *His mother . . . the living rock*: Vida's treatment of the *Pietà* theme in lines 80–6 recalls sculptural and other artistic depictions of the subject, especially Michelangelo's *Pietà*, created in the closing years of the fifteenth century. The comparison of Mary to stone ('barely distinguishable from the cold rock', line 86) is therefore significant, as is her location: the Latin most obviously indicates that she is sitting on a rock, but it could also yield the sense 'she sits, [formed] with/of living rock', recalling the conventional description of sculpted images as being alive. There may also be a suggestion here of the myth of Niobe, turned to stone while grieving for her children.

sick at heart, her hair dishevelled: modelled on a fragment of Ennius, *Annales* Book 10 (Loeb edn., fr. 343–4), preserved by Nonius.

the gaping wound in his breast: see Virgil, *Aeneid* 11.40.

barely distinguishable from . . . rock: see note on 6.80 above. The expression is taken from Ovid, *Metamorphoses* 13.540.

beating . . . with their hands: modelled on Virgil, *Aeneid* 1.481.

Some washed . . . woven fabrics: combines elements from Virgil, *Aeneid* 6.218–19 and 3.485.

their own faces . . . big tears as well: like the mourning warhorse at Virgil, *Aeneid* 11.90.

they buried . . . tomb: echoes Virgil, *Aeneid* 2.542 (body of Hector).

135 *night and day*: see note on 1.107 above.

breathing . . . from heaven: combines elements from Virgil, *Aeneid* 1.387–8 and 1.546/3.339.

Come, breath: i.e. the Holy Spirit, invoked here as in the opening lines of the poem.

the pleasure of those on high: compare the address to Venus as 'pleasure of humans and gods' in Lucretius 1.1.

flooding my frame with . . . peace: may recall Venus' sedation of Ascanius/Iulus at Virgil, *Aeneid* 1.691–2.

in a broad torrent joy overflows: in the Latin, the word 'joy' literally overflows on to the next line.

136 *Now the god*: the episode of Christ's Harrowing of Hell which begins here and ends at line 293 ('reddening glow of the sky') does not appear in any of the gospels, but had long been enshrined in Christian theology, art, and literature by Vida's time.

out of the darkness . . . to Olympus: see 1.5–7 and 3.515 above.

inaccessible to the sun's rays: like the infernal cave of Cacus at Virgil, *Aeneid* 8.195.

had their stalls: recalls the hellish haunts of Virgil, *Aeneid* 6.286.

a terrible evil: see note on 5.594 above.

so great a longing for kingship: see Virgil, *Georgics* 1.37.

the pit . . . there is no return: combines language from Virgil, *Aeneid* 6.425 and 8.245.

while they still lived: see Virgil, *Aeneid* 5.724, 6.608, 6.661.

an enormous furnace: see Virgil, *Aeneid* 8.446 (the forge of Vulcan).

billowing murky smoke: echoes Virgil, *Aeneid* 2.609 (ruins of Troy).

The abode of the guiltless . . . in a wide circle: for this and the following description, compare Virgil, *Aeneid* 8.666–70 (the underworld on Aeneas' shield).

the fatal crime: see Virgil, *Aeneid* 6.511.

our first parent: Adam, a reference to the doctrine of original sin (see note on 1.48 above).

devout prophets: like the prophet-poets in Virgil's Blessed Groves at *Aeneid* 6.662.

divine institutions: echoes Lucretius 6.7 (of Epicurus' teachings).

137 *mothers and men . . . threshold of life*: combines elements from Virgil, *Aeneid* 6.306 (see note on 4.354 above) and 6.427–8, both on souls in the underworld.

a keen desire: see Virgil, *Aeneid* 5.138.

were enumerating: the verb recalls Anchises in the underworld at Virgil, *Aeneid* 6.682.

they exchanged . . . in conversation: see note on 2.142 above.

that day that was due . . . the vault of heaven: compare Virgil, *Aeneid* 9.7 and 4.451.

Now, now . . . offspring of God: see note on 4.190–1 above; for 'undoubted offspring of God', see 3.705, 4.510, and 5.221 above.

one for many: see note on 2.249 above.

that lion . . . mighty Judah: for Christ as the Lion of Judah, see Revelation 5:5.

the mountains . . . skip about: see Psalms 114:4–6 (and Isaiah 55:12).

streams wandering everywhere: compare Horace, *Odes* 1.34.9, and Propertius 2.19.30 and 3.11.51. In combination with milk, nectar, and honey, see Ovid, *Metamorphoses* 1.111–12 (the Golden Age).

Such was . . . their speech: see note on 4.1042–3 above.

batters against the walls: echoes Virgil, *Aeneid* 11.890.

lift their spirits . . . to the stars: see especially Virgil, *Aeneid* 9.637 (also evoked by 'murmured . . . with . . . joy' in lines 190–1).

the mightiest avenger was at hand: the first in a series of clear evocations of Hercules' conquest of Cacus in Book 8 of Virgil's *Aeneid* (see Introduction), here 8.201–3.

138 *A vast portal . . . hard iron*: modelled on the gate of Tartarus at Virgil, *Aeneid* 6.552–4.

the earth . . . shadowy caverns: clearly recalls Virgil, *Aeneid* 3.673–4 (Mount Etna). See also *Aeneid* 8.239.

in a hideous outpouring they appeared: like the monstrous Harpies at Virgil, *Aeneid* 3.225–6.

they let out . . . pitch-black smoke: closely echoes Virgil, *Aeneid* 8.248 and 8.252–3 (both of Cacus: see note on 6.198–9 above).

At once the gates . . . on every side: the passage is modelled on Virgil, *Aeneid* 2.480–5, with lines 214–15 in particular recalling *Aeneid* 2.483.

as when a jewel . . . glowing radiance: compare the simile at Virgil, *Aeneid* 10.134–5, and the description of Elysium at *Aeneid* 6.640–1 (also Lucretius 2.148).

when . . . the innermost recesses: echoes Virgil, *Aeneid* 2.507–8 (storming of Priam's palace).

recognized his hated face: see Virgil, *Aeneid* 9.734.

they were terrified . . . with their tongues: see Virgil, *Aeneid* 11.699–700 (where the person terrified is described as the son of an inhabitant of the Apennines, which may have suggested the simile of Alp-dwellers that follows), 10.656–7 (simulacrum of Aeneas), and 3.428/11.812–13 (Scylla/retreating wolf).

poking . . . out of their caves: like Scylla at Virgil, *Aeneid* 3.424–5.

138 *thundering with . . . joy*: see note on 6.197 above.

could not satisfy . . . with gazing: a clear reminiscence of Virgil, *Aeneid* 8.265–6 (the carcass of Cacus: see notes on 6.198–9 and 6.210–11 above).

139 *hailed . . . with a joyous cry*: echoes Virgil, *Aeneid* 3.524 (first sight of Italy).

how gladly . . . so long desired: recalls Aeneas' words to the ghost of Hector at Virgil, *Aeneid* 2.283–5.

we have not been cheated: compare Virgil, *Aeneid* 6.691 (Anchises awaiting Aeneas in the underworld).

to the stars of heaven: echoes Virgil, *Aeneid* 1.259 (Aeneas' assumption into heaven).

like the lamp of heaven: echoes Virgil, *Aeneid* 3.637 (eye of the Cyclops).

Who has defiled . . . a wound?: compare Aeneas' questions to the ghost of Hector at Virgil, *Aeneid* 2.285–6 (see note on 6.241–2 above).

what delays . . . held you back: modelled on Virgil, *Aeneid* 2.282 (Aeneas to Hector's ghost, again).

barriers kept you hidden away: see Lucan 10.445.

surest offspring of heaven's king: see note on 5.99 above.

Were our travails . . . those on high?: see Virgil, *Aeneid* 8.74, and 6.111 above (with note).

with joy they went out all together: modelled on Virgil, *Aeneid* 2.260 (the Greeks emerge from the wooden horse).

O happy souls: I have altered the punctuation in Hankins's/Gardner's text, punctuating after *aevum* in line 269. For the expression of line 270, see Virgil, *Aeneid* 6.669 and 6.83.

the father of the human race himself: Adam.

their temples . . . snow-white bands: modelled on Virgil, *Aeneid* 6.665 (blessed souls).

swallowed into its abyss: like the whirlpool Charybdis at Virgil, *Aeneid* 3.422.

140 *singing of their king . . . shut fast*: combines elements from Virgil, *Aeneid* 7.698, 3.495/7.598, and Ovid, *Metamorphoses* 1.662. For 'happy souls', see note on 6.270 above.

the winds fell . . . from the sky: modelled on Virgil, *Aeneid* 5.820–1.

the morning song of the winged beings: echoes Virgil, *Aeneid* 8.456, where 'winged beings' are birds, but here may be angels (a deliberate ambiguity?).

was going on . . . the void: echoes Lucretius 3.27.

a flame . . . lies low: modelled on Lucretius 4.926 (immanence of the spirit).

should revive it . . . round about: echoes Virgil, *Aeneid* 1.175–6 (lighting a fire).

that one-off bird: the phoenix, a traditional symbol of Christ. Compare Ovid, *Amores* 2.6.54 and *Metamorphoses* 15.391–407; Pliny, *Natural History* 10.2.

new, and gleaming with youth: clearly recalls the renewed snake of Virgil, *Georgics* 3.437 and *Aeneid* 2.473.

ointments of Cilicia's harvest: saffron—see Propertius 4.6.74.

they talked . . . on a variety of subjects: see note on 2.142 above.

Poor us . . . to death!: modelled on Virgil, *Aeneid* 5.623–4.

141 *at least . . . our empty service*: clearly echoes Anchises' lament for Marcellus at Virgil, *Aeneid* 6.885–6.

Tearing . . . with her wailing: echoes Ariadne's grief at Catullus 64.350, and Creusa's complaint at Virgil, *Aeneid* 2.679.

curb . . . in your minds: a clear reminiscence of Aeneas' consolation of his companions at Virgil, *Aeneid* 1.202–3.

one for all: compare 2.657 above.

draws sustenance . . . air of heaven: see note on 6.109 above.

freed from . . . subject to death: see Ovid, *Metamorphoses* 14.600–1 (immortalization of Aeneas).

he vanished into a dark cloud: see note on 2.112 above.

which (behold!) suddenly met her eyes: see note on 3.319 above.

the handiwork of its craftsmen: see note on 5.600 above.

An ugly, black monster it was: recalls Virgil, *Aeneid* 3.658 and 4.181.

a brute of the . . . sea: see Ovid, *Metamorphoses* 5.18.

the prophet: Jonah, whose story was seen as a prefiguration of Christ's burial and resurrection.

was emerging . . . restored to the air of the world above: compare Virgil, *Georgics* 4.486 (Eurydice returning from the underworld).

I recognize . . . full of true prophecy: see 6.274 above, and Virgil, *Aeneid* 4.23.

142 *that gargantuan gulf*: compare Virgil, *Aeneid* 6.296, 7.569–70, 9.104–5, 10.114 (all infernal: see note on 6.358 above).

much lamented . . . on earth above: see Virgil, *Aeneid* 6.481.

enclosed in the hollow rock: echoes Virgil, *Aeneid* 8.248 (the cave of Cacus, another infernal context).

could not get enough of gazing: see note on 6.239 above.

should clothe the fields in glowing light: echoes Virgil's description of Elysium at *Aeneid* 6.640–1.

In her love . . . face to face: combines elements from Virgil, *Aeneid* 4.101 (Dido) and 1.409 (Aeneas and Venus).

at a loss . . . mortal sight: modelled on Virgil, *Aeneid* 4.284 (Aeneas to Dido) and 4.277 (Mercury leaves Aeneas).

the burgeoning talk of the people: echoes Virgil, *Aeneid* 4.189 (Rumour/Fama).

there was no way . . . the truth: modelled on Virgil, *Aeneid* 7.591–2 (Latinus confronted with chaos in Latium).

142 *whose bones . . . long ago*: may evoke Lucretius 1.135 (dreams of the dead).

143 *light had been . . . taken*: echoes Catullus 68.93 (mourning his dead brother), and in a different context Virgil, *Aeneid* 3.358.

could . . . gaze on that face: imitation with reversal of Anchises' words to Aeneas at Virgil, *Aeneid* 6.688–9.

his sweet name . . . in the ears: quotes Lucretius 4.1062 (the lover's infatuation).

Just as when . . . the coming winter: compare bee similes at Virgil, *Aeneid* 12.587–92, and Claudian, *In Rufinum* 2.460–5. For 'come crowding together' (line 421), see Virgil, *Georgics* 4.79.

the women, still dazed: recalls Virgil, *Aeneid* 7.580.

hastened to get . . . at a rapid sprint: modelled on Virgil, *Aeneid* 1.157–8.

at first, as they wavered: echoes Virgil, *Aeneid* 5.654.

just as often . . . no longer alive: compare especially Lucretius 4.31–7 (apparitions of the dead) and Virgil, *Aeneid* 12.908–12 (dreams).

he declared himself a god: like the epiphany of Venus at Virgil, *Aeneid* 2.591.

called Didymus: i.e. the Twin.

144 *the . . . mansion of a wealthy master*: echoes Virgil, *Aeneid* 12.473 (swallow simile).

their hearts settle down . . . long afterwards: echoes Virgil, *Aeneid* 6.407 and 409 (Charon's reaction to the Golden Bough).

was stunned by the sight . . . asked the reason: combines elements from Virgil, *Aeneid* 5.90 and 6.710–11.

this light . . . breath: closely modelled on Virgil, *Aeneid* 3.600.

We lay hidden inside in fear: modelled on Virgil, *Aeneid* 2.685 (omen of Ascanius/Iulus).

in the inmost part of the house . . . there unexpectedly: see Virgil, *Aeneid* 2.508 (storming of Priam's palace) and 9.49 (Turnus' unexpected arrival; see also 1.563, 2.259, and 2.578 above, and 6.473 and 6.566 below).

the whole house . . . at his light: recalls the portent of Lavinia at Virgil, *Aeneid* 7.73–4.

we shuddered . . . apparition: see note on 4.410 above.

the five wounds . . . on his glorious body: echoes Virgil, *Aeneid* 2.278–9 (ghost of Hector).

spoke . . . in his usual manner: may be modelled on Virgil, *Aeneid* 7.357.

145 *I saw him . . . myself*: compare 6.466 above (Peter's narrative).

with these very ears I heard . . . voice: clearly evokes the apparition of Mercury as reported by Aeneas at Virgil, *Aeneid* 4.359.

the sloping mountains begin to rise up: modelled on Virgil, *Eclogues* 9.7–8.

in unfamiliar costume: see Virgil, *Aeneid* 7.167.

enquired into the reason: echoes Virgil, *Aeneid* 2.105 (curiosity of the Trojans).

at whose passing . . . perished too: a clear reminiscence of Catullus 68.23 and 68.95 (death of Catullus' brother: see note on 6.409 above).

let us . . . down by his death: recalls Virgil, *Aeneid* 4.17 (death of Dido's husband).

one for many: see note on 2.249 (and 6.174) above.

And indeed I remember: see note on 4.598 above.

planted his vines . . . in a row: echoes Virgil, *Eclogues* 1.72–3.

of men and beasts: see Virgil, *Georgics* 3.242.

146 *after so many cruel deaths*: may recall Virgil, *Aeneid* 2.283–4 (Aeneas to Hector's ghost).

driven by overwhelming frenzy: see 6.283 above ('driven by boundless frenzy'). The action of the Jews is by implication satanic.

not with impunity, though: echoes Virgil, *Aeneid* 3.628.

will be there: see note on 4.190–1 above.

he charmed our senses: like Aeneas with Dido at Virgil, *Aeneid* 4.22.

the hardness . . . the early sun: closely modelled on Lucretius 1.492–3.

entered the little city: echoes Virgil, *Aeneid* 3.276.

For although he made out: Vida's lines on Christ's appearance on the road to Emmaus beginning here and ending at line 559 ('shunned our senses') are quoted in a sixteenth-century fresco of this biblical episode by Bernardo Buontalenti in the monastery of San Miniato al Monte in Florence.

to enter . . . as a guest: evokes Virgil, *Aeneid* 8.123 and 8.365 (humble hospitality of Evander).

humbly worshipped his . . . divinity: may echo Virgil, *Aeneid* 1.48–9 (worship of Juno).

like smoke into the . . . breezes: quotes Virgil, *Aeneid* 5.740 (apparition of Anchises).

look!—the god . . . to his disciples: see notes on 4.190–1 and 6.470–1 above. For 'returning to his disciples', see Virgil, *Aeneid* 6.899 and 8.546.

147 *casting its . . . beams into the dark corners of the house*: modelled on Lucretius 2.114–15.

saw him . . . by name: see note on 3.520 above.

filled with self-reproach: see Virgil, *Aeneid* 12.612.

were again breathing . . . breath: see note on 6.460 above.

vanished from my . . . heart: echoes Virgil, *Aeneid* 1.26.

a perverse spirit: recalls Virgil, *Aeneid* 2.54 (the Trojans deceived by the wooden horse). See also *Eclogues* 1.16, and note on 3.400 above. Thomas's reference to Christ's raising of 'others' (lines 584–5) alludes to Lazarus, among others: see 1.236–99 above.

147 *without your divine will*: see note on 3.279 above.

maybe one day: see Virgil, *Aeneid* 1.203 (Aeneas to his companions).

were skimming through the salt sea: see note on 4.259 above.

they did not recognize . . . divine figure: echoes and reverses Virgil, *Aeneid* 9.659.

148 *was the first to speak: 'Hey[']*: modelled on Virgil, *Aeneid* 1.321 (the disguised Venus).

a god . . . , that teacher: see Virgil, *Aeneid* 5.391.

made their way to dry ground in their . . . vessel: echoes Virgil, *Aeneid* 10.301.

to restore their strength . . . bread: combines elements from Virgil, *Aeneid* 1.214 (the recently landed Trojans, picked up in line 627 with 'they got ready to roast': see *Aeneid* 1.179) and 8.180–1 (Evander's banquet).

revealing his divine nature: see note on 6.439 above.

praise peace: echoes Virgil, *Aeneid* 11.460, but without the sarcasm of that line.

Hail forever . . . forever farewell: recalls Catullus 101.10 (farewell to dead brother).

I am summoned by . . . Olympus: echoes Virgil, *Aeneid* 8.533 (Aeneas).

the majesty . . . proud sceptres: closely modelled on Lucretius 5.1137.

the right moment . . . the correct manner: echoes Virgil, *Aeneid* 4.293–4 (Aeneas and Dido). See also Valerius Flaccus, *Argonautica* 5.388.

kings and the powerful: quotes Lucretius 3.1027.

149 *mothers and men*: see note on 4.354 above.

sitting as assessor . . . the peoples: like Minos in the underworld at Virgil, *Aeneid* 6.432–3.

With this particular distinction I mark you out: Vida here emphasizes Peter's position at the head of the Apostles, as an implied justification for papal supremacy over the Church. This is reinforced by the specifically Roman connotations of the poet's model in the lines that follow.

do you remember . . . those who have rebelled: echoes and reworks the statement of the mission of Rome put by Virgil into the mouth of Aeneas' father Anchises at *Aeneid* 6.851–3. '[T]hose who have rebelled' may denote heretics in general, or Protestants in particular, or both.

mortal sin: see note on 6.146 above.

the shallows, sandbanks, and . . . Sirens: partly modelled on Virgil, *Aeneid* 1.111.

150 *renewed their dances*: like Apollo at Virgil, *Aeneid* 4.145.

darkening the sky: echoes Virgil, *Aeneid* 12.578 (weapons).

the double pipe . . . supplied their song: modelled on Virgil, *Aeneid* 9.618. The sound effects of these and the following lines also recall Catullus 64.263–4.

And when . . . the height of heaven: the angels' manoeuvres in these lines echo the funeral ceremonies at Virgil, *Aeneid* 11.188–90.

Remus: twin brother of Rome's founder Romulus.

Rome, supreme in her beauty: see note on 1.913 above.

gave laws to the peoples: see Virgil, *Aeneid* 7.246–7.

the victorious consul . . . went up on to the lofty Capitol: see *Aeneid* 6.836–7. The Tarpeian Rock (line 704) was part of the Roman Capitol.

the true offspring of God: see note on 1.237 above.

the tokens of his monstrous execution: the Instruments of the Passion are a common subject in Christian art. Vida's addition of the insignia of the Roman Senate serves to strengthen the parallels between this procession and the triumph of a successful Roman general (see 6.701–7 above).

Don't be afraid: echoes Virgil, *Aeneid* 9.114 (voice from heaven).

151 *join with us in . . . song*: the language recalls ritual pronouncements such as Horace, *Odes* 3.1.2 and Ovid, *Fasti* 1.71. See also 2.886 above.

the mute swimmers: see note on 4.265 above. The line as a whole has a strongly Lucretian flavour, as does much of the language of the disciples' hymn.

the sea . . . its endless windings: modelled on Lucretius 1.718, though in Vida's Latin the words 'endless' and 'windings' literally encircle the word meaning 'lands'.

he created . . . without elements or seed: a direct rejection of Lucretius 1.196–8.

stippled the lap of earth: for the expression, see Lucretius 2.375.

the boundless sky: echoes Lucretius 5.473 and Virgil, *Aeneid* 8.239.

in an eternal compact: see Virgil, *Aeneid* 11.356 (but the language of the line is again Lucretian).

does irrevocable time flee: imitates and reverses Virgil, *Georgics* 3.284.

brought their course to a . . . standstill: modelled on Virgil, *Eclogues* 8.4.

152 *the youths . . . to the stars*: see note on 3.422 above.

You divide . . . unharmed: see note on 2.282 above. For 'the ship-bearing sea', see Lucretius 1.3.

You bring forth . . . by touching them: see note on 4.711–12 above.

The very earth . . . to the stars: echoes Virgil, *Aeneid* 7.722, and *Eclogues* 1.82–3. Mount Sinai smokes at Exodus 19:18.

a place fertile with fear: modelled on Virgil, *Aeneid* 1.51. For Erebus, see note on 2.694 above.

The ruler of the domain of darkness: see note on 1.121 above.

152 *hid himself . . . in the deepest caverns*: echoes Lucan 5.84.

the rolling passage of the sun: quotes Lucretius 5.931.

Hail, creator . . . upon us: for 'creator of all things', see note on 4.63 above, and for 'look . . . upon us', see Virgil, *Aeneid* 2.690.

they sang . . . youthful throng: combines elements from Virgil, *Eclogues* 1.56, and *Aeneid* 7.812.

Just as when . . . moaning: the first part of Vida's simile recalls the hawk/dove simile at Virgil, *Aeneid* 11.721–4. For 'a . . . medley of moaning' (line 809), see *Aeneid* 4.210.

153 *the promised day was at hand*: Pentecost; a clear echo of Virgil, *Aeneid* 9.107.

in the cloudless expanse of heaven: modelled on Virgil, *Aeneid* 8.528.

with glowing brightness: see note on 6.383 above.

addressed him with . . . love: like Aeneas to Dido at Virgil, *Aeneid* 6.455.

it is . . . time to bring aid: see Virgil, *Aeneid* 10.512.

born . . . of mortal body: echoes Lucretius 5.6 (and 2.906).

But you promised . . . waver: Vida's lines here recall the exchange between Venus and Jupiter in Book 1 of Virgil's *Aeneid*, on which the scene as a whole is modelled. With these lines, compare especially *Aeneid* 1.231–7. For 'our indestructible name', see Ovid, *Metamorphoses* 15.876, and for 'acts of unparalleled daring', see 3.345 above.

relying on your faithfulness: echoes Virgil, *Aeneid* 11.787.

feet, pierced . . . a sacrificial victim: evokes Virgil, *Aeneid* 2.273 (the ghost of Hector), 11.40 (the dead Pallas), and 2.156 (Sinon as victim).

The Father . . . the following answer: clear echoes of Virgil, *Aeneid* 11.797 (prayer granted) and 8.394 (Vulcan bound in love). For 'lightly kissing him', see note on 1.956 above.

What you desire will be given to you: modelled on Virgil, *Aeneid* 7.260.

not fear . . . wild beasts: repeated almost exactly at 6.963 below.

shrink in dread from . . . the breeze: recalls Aeneas' terror at Virgil, *Aeneid* 2.728.

154 *the devastating star . . . parched fields*: the Dog Star, Sirius—see Virgil, *Georgics* 2.353.

Ganges . . . Bactra . . . Ismara . . . Thrace . . . Chinese . . . Cadiz . . . Britons dyed in their warpaint: the first two of these locations (both eastern from a European perspective) are mentioned at Virgil, *Georgics* 2.137–8. Ismarus/Ismara was a city and mountain in Thrace. For 'Britons dyed in their war-paint', see Ovid, *Amores* 2.16.39.

making all things new . . . throughout the world: I have punctuated after *novantes* in line 863, rather than after *templa* in line 864. Line 864 closely recalls Virgil, *Aeneid* 2.294–5 (Hector's commission to Aeneas).

nations . . . the whole world: a clear echo of Virgil, *Eclogues* 1.66 (the Britons). For the Golden Age language of the following line, see *Eclogues* 4.12 and *Aeneid* 6.792–3.

the fatal fault of their first father: see note on 6.146 above.

whose transgressions: echoes Virgil, *Aeneid* 6.569 (judgement in the underworld).

three hundred spans of five years: looks forward to the publication of Vida's epic in 1535, approximately 1,500 years after Christ's crucifixion.

true poets . . . among the peoples: as the following references to Cremona and the rivers of northern Italy make clear, Vida is here (like Petrarch in his *Africa*, 9.216–41) foretelling his own poem. '[I]n altered song' refers to Vida's Christianization of classical epic poetry, correcting 'the falsehoods of the Greeks'.

the king . . . swirling course: combines elements from Virgil, *Georgics* 1.482, and *Aeneid* 11.742. For the Po, see 1.25–31 and 5.178–82 above.

There . . . on the soft grass: the lines contain clear echoes of Virgil, *Aeneid* 7.699 (swans), and Lucretius 5.1392 (soft grass). For 'boys and unmarried girls', see note on 1.452 above.

155 *These . . . fixed for you*: see note on 1.88–9 above.

and sacred senate: echoes Virgil, *Aeneid* 1.426.

Oh if only, if only . . . from heaven: recalls Virgil, *Aeneid* 6.187–9 (Aeneas prays for the Golden Bough).

they exchanged . . . each other: see note on 2.142 above.

all at once . . . looked up: clearly echoes a number of portentous passages from Virgil's *Aeneid*, especially the thunderclap confirming Aeneas' destiny at 8.524–9 (see note on 5.292 above, and Introduction), the portent of Ascanius/Iulus at 2.692–3 (see note on 4.215 above, and Introduction), and the earthquake on Delos at 3.90.

a new radiance shone in their eyes: see note on 3.319 above.

Then a harmless fire . . . all of them: recalls the omen of Ascanius/Iulus at Virgil, *Aeneid* 2.681–4 (see Introduction, and note on 6.914–16 above).

just as . . . with curved tongs: the Chalybes were a people on the coast of the Black Sea, famed in antiquity for their metalworking. The simile echoes very clearly the descriptions of the activities of the Cyclopes at their forge in Virgil, *Georgics* 4.170–5 (also a simile) and *Aeneid* 8.449–53.

'It's God . . . Look—it's God!': see note on 4.190–1 above.

the breath . . . presence of divinity: echoes Virgil, *Aeneid* 6.50–1 (the divinely inspired Sibyl).

There was no delay, no breathing space: see note on 2.140 above.

156 *with its . . . winged air*: see Virgil, *Aeneid* 8.430–1, and 3.905 above (with note). For 'Engulfed . . . in the whirlwind', see Lucretius 6.395 (and *Aeneid* 1.45).

The feelings . . . their minds: quotes Lucretius 3.16 (Epicurus' teachings).

156 *which . . . for the feast*: the 'first rites' are Passover. For the expression of these lines, see Virgil, *Aeneid* 8.102 (Evander) and 4.602.

Parthians . . . Scythians . . . Phrygians . . . Garamantes: various peoples known to the Romans. The Parthian empire centred on ancient Iran and fought repeatedly against Rome; the Scythians occupied the Pontic Steppe and were known for their harsh lifestyle in an inhospitable climate; the Phrygians inhabited ancient Anatolia in Asia Minor. For the Libyan Garamantes, see Virgil, *Aeneid* 6.794.

For as though . . . the angels: for 'mortal limbs', see notes on 4.31 and 4.913 above. 'ranged with their minds' recalls (polemically) Epicurus' mental peregrinations at Lucretius 1.74; and for 'enjoyed the talk', see Virgil, *Aeneid* 8.468.

that cloud . . . human minds: closely modelled on Virgil, *Aeneid* 2.604–6 (Venus removes the cloud from Aeneas' mortal vision).

with base dread: see Virgil, *Aeneid* 2.400 (Greeks at Troy).

They did not fear . . . wild beasts: the fulfilment of the prophecy in 6.851 above is signalled by the near-exact repetition of that line here (compare Virgil, *Aeneid* 4.124–5/165–6).

carried off by a death he had not deserved: see Virgil, *Aeneid* 6.163 (Misenus).

just as when the earth . . . regains its true splendour: the simile perhaps alludes to the story of Gideon's fleece—see note on 3.460 above. Line 969, 'when every field is parched', quotes Rutilius Namatianus, *De reditu suo* 1.480; for other models, see note on 5.49 above (line 968), and Virgil, *Aeneid* 3.194/5.10 (line 970).

157 *as the prophets . . . come to pass*: see note on 1.409 above. The reference here is specifically to David: see Psalms 19:4–5, quoted at Romans 10:18.

They heard it . . . furthest edge: modelled on Virgil, *Aeneid* 7.225–7. The expression of line 978 clearly echoes *Aeneid* 3.383. There may be an allusion in line 979 to the spread of Christianity to the Americas in Vida's own lifetime.

an established system of holy rites: see note on 1.952 above.

the ingrained wickedness . . . was washed away: a clear echo of Virgil, *Aeneid* 6.742 (purification in the underworld). These and the remaining lines of the poem signal the fulfilment of the prophecy in 4.197–8 (see note on these lines above).

they called . . . after the name of Christ: recalls Virgil, *Aeneid* 1.277 (Romans to be named after Romulus). The word used here for 'Christians' transforms the usual Latin term into an epic patronymic.

the golden race arose . . . came into being: the poem ends with a final echo of Virgil's fourth Eclogue (*Eclogues* 4.5, 4.9), with its proclamation of a new Golden Age.

[in prose] *the awakening and revival . . . altogether snuffed out*: an explicit claim for the occurrence of the Renaissance in the time of Vida's patrons.

A SELECTION OF **OXFORD WORLD'S CLASSICS**

Homer	The Iliad
	The Odyssey
Horace	The Complete Odes and Epodes
Juvenal	The Satires
Livy	The Dawn of the Roman Empire
	Hannibal's War
	The Rise of Rome
Marcus Aurelius	Meditations
Ovid	The Love Poems
	Metamorphoses
Petronius	The Satyricon
Plato	Defence of Socrates, Euthyphro, and Crito
	Gorgias
	Meno and Other Dialogues
	Phaedo
	Republic
	Symposium
Plautus	Four Comedies
Plutarch	Greek Lives
	Roman Lives
Propertius	The Poems
Sophocles	Antigone, Oedipus the King, and Electra
Suetonius	Lives of the Caesars
Tacitus	The Annals
	The Histories
Thucydides	The Peloponnesian War
Virgil	The Aeneid
	The Eclogues and Georgics
Xenophon	The Expedition of Cyrus

A SELECTION OF **OXFORD WORLD'S CLASSICS**

	An Anthology of Elizabethan Prose Fiction
	Early Modern Women's Writing
	Restoration Literature: An Anthology
	Three Early Modern Utopias (Utopia; New Atlantis; The Isle of Pines)
FRANCIS BACON	**The Major Works**
APHRA BEHN	**Oroonoko and Other Writings** **The Rover and Other Plays**
JOHN BUNYAN	**Grace Abounding** **The Pilgrim's Progress**
JOHN DONNE	**The Major Works** **Selected Poetry**
JOHN FOXE	**Book of Martyrs**
BEN JONSON	**The Alchemist and Other Plays** **Five Plays**
JOHN MILTON	**The Major Works** **Paradise Lost**
EARL OF ROCHESTER	**Selected Poems**
SIR PHILIP SIDNEY	**The Old Arcadia** **The Major Works**
SIR PHILIP and MARY SIDNEY	**The Sidney Psalter**
IZAAK WALTON	**The Compleat Angler**

A SELECTION OF **OXFORD WORLD'S CLASSICS**

	Travel Writing 1700–1830
Frances Burney	Cecilia Evelina
Robert Burns	Selected Poems and Songs
John Cleland	Memoirs of a Woman of Pleasure
Daniel Defoe	A Journal of the Plague Year Moll Flanders Robinson Crusoe
Henry Fielding	Jonathan Wild Joseph Andrews and Shamela Tom Jones
William Godwin	Caleb Williams
Oliver Goldsmith	The Vicar of Wakefield
Samuel Johnson	The History of Rasselas
Ann Radcliffe	The Italian The Mysteries of Udolpho
Samuel Richardson	Pamela
Tobias Smollett	The Adventures of Roderick Random The Expedition of Humphry Clinker
Laurence Sterne	The Life and Opinions of Tristram Shandy, Gentleman A Sentimental Journey
Jonathan Swift	Gulliver's Travels A Tale of a Tub and Other Works
Horace Walpole	The Castle of Otranto
Mary Wollstonecraft	Mary and The Wrongs of Woman